Traveling Through Adventure

- 2ND PRINTING -

Stephen Burnett

ISBN 978-0-9938380-0-2

Copyright © Stephen Burnett 2014
Printed by Allan Graphics Ltd.
Kingston, Ontario

FOREWORD

After several drafts and initial massaging by my charming Canadian editor Maureen Garvey and the enthusiastic and critical eye of my Scottish editor Ian Furman, I completed the first edition of *Traveling Through Adventure* - an incomplete version of my career as a human gun dog in the tourism industry and general observer of life. With the extraordinary fine eye of my wife Hélène who's first language is French and not English, I have now completed the second edition. And what a luxury it has been (and still is), to quietly observe the world going about its business, while wandering through the bazaar of life, which is sadly now more dangerous and less welcoming than when I started my journey. Being a creature of habit I love returning to former locations and experiencing what made the past such a rollicking adventure, but nowadays in some countries that would probably get my head lopped off and spoil an otherwise interesting life. Despite the current sad state of international affairs, I have to confess that I am brimming with optimism for the future and still (perhaps naively) believe that with a tad less politics and a tad less bureaucratic intervention, we might just make a better go of things. Writing four books at the same time was an absurd idea and now that TTA is completed I am looking forward to focusing on my other three tales; the building of The Kingston Jaguar historic race car, a children's book about trolls and a "how-to book" about operating a recreational trawler. Thanks for the pleasure of your company and I hope you enjoy these adventures as much as I did.

Reminiscences, Experiences
An opening rant

Reminiscing is an odd feeling

Describing my experiences in print has been cathartic and troubling and occasionally a blending of both emotions. While a degree of discretion and protection for some of my sources makes it impossible for me to name all of the characters and to place exact dates on all of the experiences – they are as real today as when they were current. All too easily faces come flooding into my minds-eye, accents rattle around in my head and the smells and tastes are as sharp today as when I was in Mali, Rio Dulce, Srinagar or Kettlewell in the Yorkshire Dales. On reflection - the view in my rear view mirror often resembles several lifetimes crushed together, where experiences tend to converge, often merging into a curious mixture of angst and pleasure.

There is nothing unique in claiming that people have been the central point of my experiences - invariably shaping my views of life and this still holds true despite the magnificence scenery, the superb built heritage and the countless vibrant cultures - which in no way diminishing their importance. On my journeys I have met and been influenced by a considerable number of people and not all of them pleasant - in fact some of them were disgusting excuses for human beings and a disgrace to humanity - where inflicting pain and suffering and disadvantaging their neighbours was an acceptable part of daily life. Happily the vast majority were the opposite of this, being inspirational, charitable, concerned for their fellow inhabitants and worthy of a place inside the pearly gates.

TA-101

I have been blessed with continuous employment from the time I left school and most, but not all of my work has been associated with the tourism industry. In the early days there were no tourism schools or hospitality colleges or degree granting universities that offered a structured curriculum and I remember taking a conscious decision that I had better structure my career around a self-administered program - that nowadays one might call "Tourism Autodidact 101" or TA101. Growing up in Leeds many of my buddies were in university pursuing a variety of disciplines which would take them into the professions and it was pure racer's luck that my close friend John Gorney, knowingly or purely by coincidence nudged me towards TA 101.

From the moment I realized there was an actual industry that embraced what we now call "tourism", I realized that much of this took place overseas and if I was to make a success of my life I might be residing outside the UK - which is exactly what happened. As opportunities opened up, more work became available and the more varied the work the closer I inched towards fulfilling my TA101. At this point it is important to confess that not all of my work was done within the envelope of the tourism industry – principally because other "industries" became aware of my ability to ferret out information in foreign lands and were willing to pay for my access to locations, virtually anywhere on earth. Being able to verify the story behind the story and personally auditing it's provenance before handing over the goods became a valuable asset and as the old saying goes "never were boots on the ground as valuable as they are now". It was at this point that my career became overly complex and I have to admit that while gathering information for high-value clients was more lucrative than my core career – it was nowhere near as satisfying, with a couple of exceptions.

My 180 degree pivot

I find it curious how my view of human behavior has altered over the years, undoubtedly shaped by what I have observed and experienced in my travels - to the point where I have made a complete 180 in how I view some aspects of life. Growing up in what I like to call "articulate Yorkshire" – a region which possesses a curious mixture of culture and coarseness, I became obsessed with liberalism and became an advocate for the laissez faire attitude which was popular at the time. Where slinging out accepted practices for the sake of renewal was acceptable and where rules were to be broken - boundaries tested – and where national discipline was branded a fascist sport practiced by others.

I remember joining the voices that reviled that British political outcast Enoch Powell as he railed against potentially unbridled, out-of-control immigration and the mayhem and instability it would bring to the UK. At that time we thought Enoch was a racist rather than a rationalist and I am humbled by his amazing ability to peer into the Cloudy Ball of immigration and predict with laser clear vision what would and has gone wrong. Over the years I was often mistaken in my headlong rush to embrace the seductiveness of liberalism and looking through the rear view mirror of life I was accompanied by quite a few others. I wonder if they now share my view of these altered viewscapes - probably not.

Sustainability, compassion, acceptance and boundaries

For any diverse society to be sustainable while remaining true to democratic principles it has to abide by a complex code of acceptable behavior - whereby boundaries are codified and with consequences for those who threaten it. I arrived at this conclusion after traveling the globe and witnessing how some societies - often with few natural assets, were able to mature with spectacular success while others were abject failures. If we take what I call "the helicopter view" of life and look down from aloft it is not difficult to understand why this occurred. I believe societies which adhere to acceptable social boundaries and a high degree of personal and national discipline have been able to mature and prosper and are able to withstand the impact of mass immigration and economic woes, while maintaining their core values and culture. Sadly it is all too easy to identify those countries, some with self serving dictatorships where the approach to personal and national discipline is missing. To add fuel to this toxic mix, we have recently witnessed the terrifying effects of rampant out of control sovereign indebtedness, where some nations simply cannot pay their bills and guess what? Once more it's the disciplined and codified societies that are equipped to weather this particular storm.

A shining best example of how immigration should work was when entire communities of Jews were fleeing from Russia's Pogroms and Hitler's advance through Europe - to take up residence and sanctuary in the UK. Along with these poor immigrants came decades of cultural and religious practices, strong family traditions, a love of music and story telling, with a built-in passion for higher education, discipline, loyalty and philanthropy. Years later - looking down from our helicopter, what we see is a 21st century Jewish community which is staunchly and proudly British, fully integrated into society and embracing all of the wonderful traditions of their new country. The same can be said for those Jews who settled in Australia, The United States and Canada, who never for one moment thought about altering the core culture of their new country and never once did rejected the social and behavioral framework of the nations which accepted them. Contrast this with some of the entitled and aggressive attitude of more recent immigrant communities - where altering the core culture of the host country to suit their transparent agenda is just as important as accepting their monthly welfare payments.

School board cowards dilute Christmas

Recently I was offended to hear of Canadian district school boards that are denying the tradition of Christmas by cancelling Carol singing, Nativity plays and Christmas decorations - lest they offend minority immigrants who might not celebrate this magical Canadian tradition. In their haste to be politically correct and pander to our non Christian immigrants they are actually discriminating against the core culture of this country and denying children their Christmas celebrations at school. Of course we need to respect the variety of ethnic traditions that are making their way to Canada and embrace them as they become part of our emerging culture, but diluting Christmas is reversed discrimination and a dash for the basement where these spineless board workers will no doubt hide until the New Year comes around.

I was recently visiting my in-laws summer home beside a lovely tranquil Quebec Lake, with one eye watching the loons glide by and the other watching the evening news. Once more we were viewing the images of rabid Islamic militants destroying the temples, shrines and built heritage of a historic outpost in Timbuktu Mali – just as the Taliban did when they blew up the historic Buddha's in Afghanistan. In this book you will stumble upon a description of my extraordinary visit to Timbuktu and the amazing happenings which could have resulted in mayhem and violence - but thanks to the goodwill of the Taureg tribesmen, this ended in a light-hearted chuckle. Now those same buildings are being destroyed before our eyes by these out-of-control philistines. These actions are an extreme example of what we have to defend our society against - and one way we can do this is by strengthening the disciplined and cultural boundaries that have allowed us to enjoy the freedom we have. This in no way speaks against sensible, well filtered and absorbable immigration, rather this is a cautionary warning to those who would open the flood-gates without a reality check. A late thanks goes to Enoch.

Travel along with me through these experiences and using your imagination and a bit of logic, hopefully you will be able to fill in the gaps - which I have purposefully left open.

I am dedicating this book to my motoring mother May Burnett, daughter Nicole Sinclair, Son Daniel Burnett and my lovely wife Hélène Lavoie.

Stephen Burnett
Kingston July 2014

TABLE OF CONTENTS

Chapter
1. On the Starting Grid 1
2. The Balkans, Greece, Turkey and Israel 11
3. The UK-Switzerland-Tunisia 21
4. New York- Crossing the Atlantic-Oriental Asia-Africa 35
5. Emigration to Canada-Caribbean-Texas-Pacific-
   Self employed 45
6. In the Footsteps of the Lost Franklin Expedition 55
7. Expedition Cruise Planning-Cuban Mig Fighter Pilot-
   Penal Colony 75
8. Belize and Guatemala: one of the best cruises I have
   ever taken 95
9. Not Kidnapped in Timbuktu 113
10. Polar Bear Tracking on Hudson Bay 129
11. Exploring Canada on My 650 143
12. The Goodwood Revival 159
13. Journey to the Uttermost Part of the Earth 169
14. Rescuing Jean Marc and Suzanne 183
15. Sniper Takes Over 205
16. Racing Toward My Seventieth Year 219
17. Delivery Cruse of the Trawler *Caper* 231
18. Multiple Passages to Manhattan on Trawlers *Caper*
    and *The Full Monty* 245
19. History of Tourism - Last Supper on the Last Cruise 273
20. The Battle for Barriefield 283

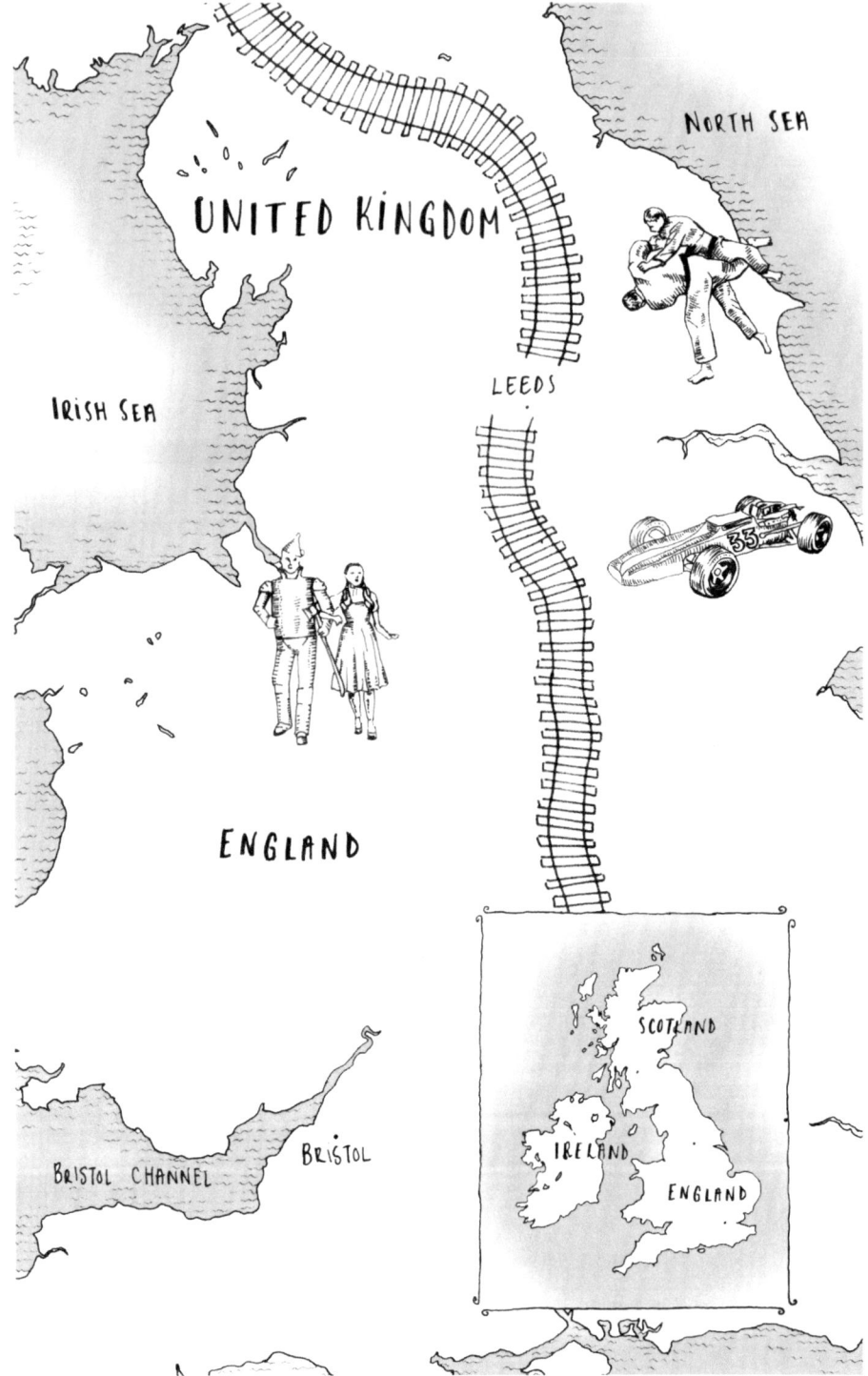

CHAPTER 1

On the Starting Grid

Coming face to face with a massive polar bear on the western shoreline of Hudson Bay would be a life-defining moment at any time, but sitting astride my idling All Terrain Vehicle while Nanuk let loose a deep primeval growl thirty paces from my nostrils brought this sharply into perspective. Encounters such as these are incubators of natural stimulants that squeeze forty years of adventuring through one's consciousness in the space of several moments–bringing each of them into sharp focus for the briefest of nano-seconds–before they exit stage left, allowing another adventure to occupy the slide-screen in my mind. In that compressed instant I thought of dinner in seductive Havana with the Cuban fighter pilot who maneuvered his high performance MIG against outdated Mirage fighters which the South Africans sent aloft to challenge him, of my stranding in Mali close to where our diplomat Robert Fowler was kidnapped by an affiliate of Al Qaida, of my privileged role in the rescue of Jean Marc Abbot, a fellow Canadian sailor from his tormentors in Columbia, and landing my Cessna at the extreme end of the Markham Ontario airstrip when I flew solo for the first time. And then after these truncated nanoseconds, I was back to reality face to face with Nanuk who was becoming more agitated by the second. What really brought me back to reality was the distinctive "clack-clack" of a round being chambered in case Nanuk decided to attack.

Looking back over life from my perch in comfy Kingston, slightly out of mainstream Canada, hidden beside the 1000 Islands and Lake Ontario, I can hardly believe how I have jammed so much excitement into such a short period of time. Reflecting about this has been enormously interesting for me, but at times disturbing and I freely admit that sharing it with others has been intimidating. Therefore, to place this in some context it might be useful to know something about the path I took along the Yellow Brick Road to the destination of creative self employment, which in my youthful dreams I could never have imagined being as meaningful, stimulating and lucrative as it turned out to be. I freely admit that the path itself was not always my choice and looking back I was frequently a passenger rather than the driver, and while I am fully aware there are some gaps between the chapters, these tales would not have been possible without taking the Yellow Brick Road.

Looking through my seventy two year old cracked and clouded rear view mirror, I am grateful for the privileged of being born into the "Middle-Kingdom" of the UK, not that I was born into the lap of luxury because this was most definitely not the case. I emerged towards the end of WW II when life in the UK was challenging for many people and particularly with respect to decent employment. The war had virtually bankrupted the country and the bombed and damaged infrastructure required massive capital to rebuild and chart the future, but what sustained so many after fighting a costly war which consumed most of our national treasure and the loss of family members, was the potential for life to improve–and with that in one's back pocket the rest was sheer grunt work. Growing up in Leeds was a very comfortable experience for me and as they say in "Upstairs Downstairs," my family was "in trade"–the ladies underwear trade to be specific and although we offered no competition to Victoria's Secrets, our "long-combs"[1] were popular with ladies in the north.

Running a successful business was not easy and our parents worked long hard hours to provide the comforts of home along with a few frills when affordable. The Leeds Jewish community in which I grew up was divided into four main segments; those working in the professions, those who were in businesses, those working in education and we trades people–which in many respects mirrored mainstream society. Leeds had long since gone through the industrial age and was thriving on the garment industry before the jobs were exported elsewhere. The current angst in North America about manufacturing being exported to Asia and South America is reminiscent of what Manchester went through in Gandhi's days, when the cotton trade was failing, partially because of a boycott in India. I suspect I inherited an interest in mobility from my upbringing because in those days families typically migrated from neighborhood to neighborhood while still remaining within the town's borders and our family like Lemmings diligently followed this migratory pattern and ended up at the edge of town. This also mirrored general society in the UK, which continually migrated to more affluent neighborhoods and eventually into the country. In London residents may have started in Clapham and ended in Chipping Norton and in Leeds this paired Chapeltown with Allwoodly and Lovell Road with Roundhay.

Looking back, any time I become concerned about the stock market or the potential for Greece to leave the Euro and how this might impact my retirement savings, I reflect on how tough it was in those days and my circumstances glow by comparison. Turn on the news and see millions of young people without meaningful work, wandering from city to city looking for a future, while the Syrian dissenters are living a nightmare being massacred by their own "leaders." I suspect a similar toxic mix of poverty, hunger and civil strife has always been happening, but thanks to our instant media we learn about the troubles much sooner. On that note I recently traded my fully functioning mobile phone for a so-called smart phone which is an odd thing to contemplate, because I always thought a basic mobile phone was an incredibly smart device, so I felt downright wasteful parking my LG in exchange for a Samsung Galaxy S II 4G Android GT 1910OM (and now an iPhone). Turn on this miniature computer almost anywhere in the world and news; good, bad, horrible and often dreadful, comes flooding onto the screen like never before–which for a newshound like me is a double-edged sword.

Shadow of the 2nd World War

I grew up in the long shadow of the 2nd World War where Leeds was an important manufacturing center for munitions, battle-tanks and urgently needed wartime devices of destruction. As a schoolboy I imagined myself as the epicenter of The Fuehrer's plan to destroy the Jews and one of my few regrets was being born too late to go up against Hitler's youth and show them what damage we could really do. That might seem a ridiculous, even foolhardy notion to those of you who are removed from this conflict, but I am deadly serious. Others eventually gave their lives doing that on my behalf and for that I am so humbly grateful.

First class education

Education in Leeds was first class from excellent primary schooling through to one of the world's finest universities; in fact the UK offered every opportunity for a superb higher education which for a time was free–the government believing that investing in an educated population would make a more successful nation. In contemporary times, urban studies theorist Dr Richard Florida advocates this passionately, emphasizing that competition between nations will ultimately not be for oil, or water or Manganese, or Chromite, valuable as those may be. Real competition will be for the best brains that nations can develop or attract, reasoning that brains will develop innovative economic processes and through their application will wealth be built. Dr. Florida directs the Toronto based Prosperity Institute and The Rottman School of management.[2]

The Jewish community has always considered education a high priority just as Asian communities in Canada do nowadays and in those tough times education was recognized as the key to success, therefore my family wholeheartedly supported hitting the books. My mother's brother, Walter Stanton was a prominent Oxford-trained educator who received The Order of The British Empire from The Queen, and our many cousins, close relatives and friends were to graduate from those disciplined UK universities. Sadly when my opportunity came this was just not going to happen and for some reason, formal education was something I was unable to handle which was odd because my friends were at university, my social circle had a substantial university component and I loved hanging around the campus, meeting buddies coming from their lectures. No point in beating this to death, for some reason that was not the right time for me. With the advantage of hindsight I can't help wondering if the UK and other disciplined societies could have taken a slightly different approach to encouraging a tyke like me to stay within the system. But after much thought on this topic I blame no one but myself for failing to grasp the opportunity that so many today are yearning for. Mea Culpa dear world and an opportunity lost.

Traveling with Dorothy and Tin Man

Earning a decent living without a degree was something of a challenge and although the family business was an option, my two pals Dorothy and Tin Man reported something intriguing over the mountain which I wanted to see for myself. However figuring out how to scale it was another matter entirely so to incubate my thinking I wandered in and out of various jobs, even laboring in a steel mill as a recording clerk for several months, learning that it sometimes takes boring work to teach you what you don't want to do for the rest of your life. I am surprised that a course on handling failure is not built into the educational system because failure can be a marvelous way to re-tool your thinking and I freely admit that boring work was galvanizing me in a way I had never before experienced. None of these jobs were at all distasteful, they all paid me on Friday and most of the firms employed ladies who were interesting enough to make life enjoyable–but this easy work shrouded the view over the mountain where Dorothy and Tin Man were heading, so in desperation I folded my spotted handkerchief, slung it on a pole and wandered off to see for myself. However I soon discovered that Dorothy and her pal were only partially right when they talked about the Yellow Brick Road, because where I was looking at was definitely not yellow and the only bricks I could see were grey and glistening on the wet quay in Calais as I caught the night train into Paris.

The following years were often a blur as I wandered around Europe poking my nose into the corners of various republics and looking into the shop windows of entirely different cultures. Europe has always held an allure for me and coming from homogenous Britain it was fascinating to see how national boundaries became vague on the Continent, with relatives living on each side of the customs shed. At that time the Yugoslav federation of ethnic enclaves was held together by the brutally iron hand of Marshal Tito, while Milosevic and his nasty mob of racist gangsters were dreaming up dreadful ways to murder their neighbours. I first experienced Greece along the confines of the slender Corinth Canal on a small ferry, until we emerged the other side to see the heavenly islands long before Bridgette wrote her diary and Thompson Holidays discovered them. For an Anglophone there was something seductive about this part of Europe and I was unsure if it was the relaxed pace of life or the proximity to warm, lustrous water or both. From Cyprus I was able to hitch a ride to Haifa and begin my life-long love affair with Israel.

Track and Field–Racing with Dennis Jenkinson–a lifelong passion

From an early age I became infected with a highly competitive urge that started with Track and Field, which the Brits quaintly called "Athletics." Leeds was a marvelous center for competitive sports with excellent coaching at all levels, from primary school through to University–augmented by a broad selection of sporting clubs to incubate local talent. I was infused with an irrepressible urge to compete (and win) and found an early niche for myself in this milieu, which opened a few doors that had previously jammed closed, also broadening my circle of friends, many of whom survive to this day. About the same time that I was looking down a 110 meter cinder hurdles track, the world of Motor Sport burst into my life in the days when Formula One Cars were painted in national livery with the Brits using green, the Belgians yellow, the French blue and the Germans sporting their cars in silver or burnished aluminium. The competitive atmosphere for motor race fans in the fifties, sixties and seventies was comparable to today's world cup soccer with national honor at stake and great scorn poured over a British driver who deserted British Racing Green cars (BRG), for the red of Ferrari, the blue of Matra or heaven forbid the silver of Mercedes. It has to be said that this nationalistic fervor was tempered with a modicum of pride when great drivers like Stirling Moss were offered factory seats in cars of "enemy" manufacturers. To this day the UK remains a hotbed of competitive motor sport, but sadly the tradition of national racing colors have surrendered to sponsors logos and slogans which are plastered over the cars.

The racing print media made a significant impact on me and for someone (originally) not too fond of reading the opportunity to become truly knowledgeable was only possible if I was able to "study form" and become informed. To this day I read, and have continually done so since I was thirteen, that fabulous British racing magazine simply called "Motor Sport" which faithfully follows the same business principal of excellent writing, factual reporting and the fearless pursuit of the truth. Dennis Jenkinson, known to his readers simply as "Jenks" was the heart and soul of this monthly green striped sheet and like many of his readers I hung on every word their "foreign correspondent" wrote. Jenks blasted from race to race, along deserted continental roads in his early E-Type Jaguar or Porsche 911, reporting on the performance of these road-rockets in the real world of serious long distance fast driving with few cops hanging around as spoilers. Jenks' writing did a great deal for me and I once had the opportunity to repay his monthly tutorial, when he announced that he was making a trip to Montreal and driving down to Watkins Glen to report on the Grands Prix.

Dear Dennis
I have been reading your monthly dispatches since I was twelve years old, living in Yorkshire and I am now writing from Canada, which is my new home. Last month you indicated that you were planning to visit Montreal and Watkins Glen and I would be happy to offer you accommodation and advice on making your trip more enjoyable. I am connected to a large circle of Motor Race enthusiasts, many of us racing our own cars in North America and it would be a pleasure for us to meet you in person and hear about your experiences.
Yours truly
Stephen Burnett

Dennis soon wrote back with typical warm expressions of thanks, indicating that unfortunately he was pressed for time and due back one day after the American Grand Prix. This motoring scribe remains something of a legend and initially became famous for navigating Stirling Moss on the Mille Miglia race in which Moss drove one of those amazing Mercedes 300SEL's–which was a thinly disguised

Grand-Prix car in drag! One can only imagine how challenging this was for a navigator, looking down at his innovative roll of toilet paper on which his route notes were written, yelling out instructions, occasionally glancing up as Moss hurled this 160 MPH projectile between corners. Jenks' legacy at Motor Sport Magazine lives on to this day and their ability to offer excellent writing, factual reporting and the fearless pursuit of the truth makes it the world's most enduring authority on the sport.

The Gentle Way and the quiet ruffian

One morning my father introduced me to a quiet green grocer whose alter ego was the ruffian who served with him in Iceland during The Second World War. What impressed me most about him was the understated intenseness and the way he angled his body when he talked about his exploits. Apparently his wartime employment was as a surgical demolition expert, which he described as being fairly simple–once he arrived at his chosen target, and instead of what we might call "big-bang" destruction, his speciality was destroying high value machinery by damaging their vital components. It was however the way in which he got to his targets by midget Submarine, Lysander short-field landing aircraft and parachuting onto a mountain with skis strapped to his back that was fascinating. It was this veteran who suggested that I start practicing something which translates from Japanese into "The gentle way," which practitioners of the sporting-art will know as Judo. I was always a keen athlete and applying my sports-honed fitness to this Japanese cultural discipline was an interesting opportunity and subsequently, when heading out to Japan to work, had a few side benefits for me, one of which was the opportunity to train in a Japanese Dojo alongside the masters and experience the full cultural impact of this discipline.[3]

My formative years were quite varied–not always under my control and at times the glide path went against my inclination and caused unintended consequences. I have purposely left out some of the… let's call them "bridging moments," as these assignments were not part of my tourism career and marginal to this tale. This bridging work benefited from my training as a quiet observer and my uncanny ability to access most countries and while this work was intellectually challenging and often highly stressful–it was far from lucrative.

Blame John Gorney

But my life was about to be turned upside down with the perplexing news that my friend John Gorney had joined Aer Lingus, as Irish Airlines was called at that time – not an environment where a free spirit like John could possibly be happy – until stories filtered out about free flights, lots of fraternizing and exotic foreign travel which was seemingly part of the job. Was it possible that my own foreign travel knowledge could be of use to a similar firm and would someone employ me for similar reasons? That was an amazing notion to contemplate although not quite so easy to realize, but John had unwittingly become the catalyst that moved me in a direction which would dominate my life and before long, I too became part of the extraordinary tourism industry. Conventional wisdom of the time suggested that you lived where you worked and worked close to where you were born and reflecting back on that curiously structured thinking I am amazed I was able to break out of the mold and slow-waltz along the Yellow Brick road in the footsteps of John Gorney, Dorothy and her Tin Man pal.

---

[1] "Long combs" refers to and is northern England short-speak for 1960's ladies "long combinations" – or warm bloomers (underwear)

[2] His books *The Rise of the Creative Class* and the *Flight of the Creative Class* are required reading for any global think tank

[3] One of the narratives in Judo is that neither size nor strength matters. Which on the surface seems correct. Many Judo "throws" are more achievable by shorter persons, because their center of gravity is lower than taller Judoka and they find it easier to pivot beneath them. Therefore shoulder throws such as Tsuri-Comme-Ashi and hip throws such as Uchi-Mata are much easier for smaller practitioners – often with devastating effect. On the other hand there is an entire series of leg and ankle throws which taller Judoka such as me find more practical and I was particularly fond of a devastating combination, using Diashi-Harai (a leg throw) for the initial attack, immediately followed by Ouchi-Mata (a hip throw). The strategy was to go for the first throw and if that failed, you have now destabilized your opponent, setting them up for the hip throw.

CHAPTER 2

The Balkans, Greece, Turkey and Israel

While I was digesting the impact that John Gorney was having on my life, I decided to take some time off for another look at the Mediterranean and I recall that on my first visit to the Balkans I found the former Yugoslavia to be authoritarian, drab, poverty stricken, and the poor inhabitants of this failed Communist state to be more depressed than any I saw in Europe. In total contrast next door, I then experienced joyous free-spending Greece where in those days it was possible to exchange my UK pounds and pay for two weeks in a pension on the slopes of Mount Lycabettus for less than a good meal for two would cost nowadays. The Greeks were a marvelous collection of colourful characters, many with families living in the UK, North America and Australia and I instantly loved them.

I had also met some Turkish students who were studying in the UK and their tales of Constantinople and the mysterious Grand Bazaar made me determined to visit modern Istanbul. So after a wandering about the Greek mainland for some time, checking out the extraordinary mountain communities close by Meteora and failing to find either Zorba or Melina Mercouri, I reserved a series of amazingly efficient Greek island ferry rides–one connecting seamlessly with the next and in no time, I was looking up at the Topkapi Palace as our boat slid into Istanbul harbour. Similar to the Greeks I met in the Islands, the Turks were warm, welcoming and approachable, many also with family in the UK, working in restaurants and hotels. Istanbul was a real eye-opener for a young Brit, and the cliché that the city straddles East and West was simply the truth. At that time the Turkish economy was not as advanced as that of Greece and they struggled with widespread poverty, although in retrospect the Turks may have been more prudent about international borrowing, which is now such a boat-anchor for the Greeks.

Years later in Turkey I experienced an extraordinary episode as a young planning manager with Wrights Holidays, a creative British holiday firm which was pioneering Turkey as an alternative to Spain. The boss took the research lead in the firm and after an exhaustive series of field trips, I was handed this new and as yet untested Turkish holiday series to operate. As readers from the tourism industry will instantly know a holiday program no matter how creative and dramatic, will live and die on the ability of the firm to offer a smooth seamless experience–something we call "Operations" and I remember being nervous. The program was simple and consisted of a weekly flight using an eighty five seat twin-engine Jet called a BAC 1-11, coupled with a solitary hotel in a modest resort on the Bosphorous, close by Istanbul. The boss had set this up over ten months earlier and made what looked to be an articulate written contract with the owner, a certain Murat Guler whose claim to fame was secured in 1954 when he became the first Turk to swim the English Channel (taking sixteen hours and fifty minutes from the UK to France. His friend told me this was the 1,623rd fastest crossing out of 1,903 solo swims!)

The new holiday program which I was to operate could be described in modern marketing terms as "cutting edge" or "edgy and creative" and by some professionals as downright foolish–but the boss was a brilliant planner and having seen his successes in Tunisia, I had every reason to focus on the operation and learn as much as possible. The first clue that something was adrift was shortly after the first charter landed in Istanbul and calls started coming in from irate and in some cases screaming vacationers, who were ranting on about sheep, goats, knives and smelly men with glass eyes–hardly a recipe for a badly needed semi-rural holiday in the Eastern Mediterranean. As the operations lead in the firm I took all of the client calls, listening as carefully as I could between screams and client obscenities, gradually building a picture of what sounded like utter mayhem at the other end. And yes, I was able to hear sheep bleating, goats goating and an extensive amount of un-holiday-like noises, which did not bode well for the firm.

Luckily I was able to learn a great deal from our resort rep who arranged to speak with me as soon as he was free to locate a quiet corner where he was able to calmly and succinctly bring me into the picture. My boss had definitely negotiated a careful, practical contract and typical of the man, I admired the way in which he conceded a livable room tariff to the hotel owner–which was the key to building a relationship of trust and mutual respect. The room blocks were synchronized with the eighty five seats on the 1-11 and the meal plan featured sufficient local food to market the holiday as "exotic," with some English specialities at breakfast as appropriate. Sadly, one element missing from all of this paperwork were a series of interim visits between when the deal was signed and yesterday at mid-day when the first group of clients disembarked and were escorted to the hotel. Meanwhile the planet on which this family-owned hotel resided had tilted–and we were no longer dealing with the affable Guler family.

I have learned a great deal traveling the world working in this industry, and one principle I adopted fairly early in my career is–"the only element that remains constant in life is change," and what we were dealing in Turkey was a huge amount of change that was impacting our ability to deliver the holiday dream. I called Turkish Airlines and managed to secure a seat on a flight next morning to Istanbul airport, where I was met by our resort rep who traveled out with the first group–which were now calling itself the "Guinea Pigs"–and most of what I gleaned over the phone was seemingly true. Forty five minutes later as our taxi drove into the compound, our driver was obliged to slalom around sheep and goats and quite a few rough looking characters–but thankfully no smelly men with glass eyes–at least not yet. Cut down to manageable proportions, the short story was that the hotel had been "lost" in an epic gambling match and the winners of this bizarre happening had taken possession of their prize–literally inhabiting the place, along with herds of livestock and their guardians. Not only that, the new owners were new to the existence of the holiday business, coming from a rural environment on the Black Sea coast, where sheep and goats were the prime measure of one's wealth. You can imagine why they were totally perplexed when hordes of angry British vacationers descended upon them demanding heavens knows what?

Word rapidly spread amongst the guests as well as the new owners that someone from management was onsite, and before long I was meeting with irate guests who were beside themselves with anger– and then later with the new owners who were beside themselves with curiosity about this incoming Brit. Considering their predicament, the guests were entirely justified for being as angry as they were and I rapidly depleted the stash of cash I was carrying by renting clean hotel rooms in Istanbul to accommodate these displaced persons. At this precise moment I knew the firm was relying on me to rescue their reputation and thankfully I had sufficient funds to draw from, which enabled me to provide excellent accommodation, equally excellent food and an extensive series of daily excursions–which delivered far more than they had paid for–but given the circumstances was entirely justifiable. Now I had three major issues to resolve, the first was rescuing the current batch of travelers–and we were well on the way to buying ourselves out of a nasty predicament, which given today's legislation and social media might have sunk the firm there and then. My next issue was resolving the state of the hotel and the third issue was dealing with the new and inexperienced owners.

I distinctly remember my first meeting with the "Black Sea Shepherds" as the firm now called them and for reasons that became clear much later, they were as curious about me as I was about them. This livestock family consisting of several brothers and extended male relatives were waiting for me in the lounge, arranged in a semi-circle around the perimeter of the room–so once I was inside, they surrounded me on three sides, which became our physical negotiating positions as they closed the French doors behind me. To complicate matters we spoke not one word of each other's language and relied on a translator we had hired to work with our resort rep. I have to confess the Black Sea Shepherds were a truly rough looking bunch and taking my time to scope them out, I actually spotted the fellow with the glass eye, but in no sense was he smelly–in fact the only smelly one in the room was me as I had flown in that morning wearing a business suit and was now sweating like a sheep from their Black Sea flock needing a short back and sides.

We soon got down to business and it was apparent that despite their roughness, these were canny business people who were more interested in resolving the issues and making money out of their new acquisition than putting up any type of false defense–which was a relief for me. Through the translator they told me that at first they were distressed by the irate attitude of the guests in their hotel, taking it quite personally because their experience with accommodation was far removed from what we were demanding. However, after several hours of intricate painstaking discussion, I felt I was making progress as we started to rewrite the contract and identify some of the basic elements that in other circumstances might not have been necessary. This went on for ever and after three days of intense discussions (these were hardly negotiations) we had the framework agreed–with one major achievement which was to jointly hire a new General Manager, a kitchen manager-Chef, Front Desk Manager and House-keeping Manager so we could justifiably bring in guests and be assured of decent service. My boss agreed to place the program on hold for three weeks while we ramped up the operation, during which I slept, ate and worked in the hotel until we felt it was ready to rejoin the 20th century.

The Black Sea Shepherds were descended from Turks that had repulsed the British invaders in 1915 as they stormed the Dardanelles–led by a certain young officer called Winston Churchill, and the sheep herders were intensely curious to meet the first Brit in their lives–who surely must be related to those grimly determined and amazingly disciplined British soldiers who embarked on what the Turkish defenders knew to be a certain suicide mission. The Gallipoli Campaign was a disaster for the British and damaged the early career of Churchill as he experimented with the use of naval power in this blockade. Once I got to know these characters better they asked if I was descended from any of these soldiers, but I decided not to tell them about my Russian ancestry which I felt might have been even more difficult to explain.

Despite the extraordinary impact that Istanbul makes on its visitors, what impressed me most in Turkey are the excavations at Ephesus and the way in which history in this corner of the Mediterranean is laid bare. Ephesus was originally a Greek city close by the coastal Turkish town of Izmir and during its Roman period, around the 1st century BC, it housed over 250 thousand inhabitants, making it the largest settlement along the Mediterranean coast. Its prominent temple, which was dedicated to Artemis, predates 500 BC and it is said that the gospel of St. John may have been written there. At the time of my first visit I was totally unprepared for the scale of this site and clearly remember standing in one spot looking through 360 degrees for an entire hour. I had done some amateur excavating at Carthage in Tunis, but the sheer scale of this Christian enclave and the amount of restoration work before me was staggering. Since that first visit to Ephesus I have returned many times to this extraordinary outpost of St. John and each time I make a pilgrimage there, I seem to connect in a different way with the past. For a young male Anglophone, there was something very seductive about the Mediterranean and I was unsure if it was the relaxed pace of life or the proximity to the water or a combination of both. From Istanbul it was a short ride across to Cyprus, where I was able to hitch a ride to Haifa and continued my life-long love affair with Israel.

Israel

Arriving in Israel was at first blush anti-climatic, because after successive conflicts with its neighbours and mindless Arab terrorism, I imagined an uptight atmosphere with nervous people on edge everywhere–but sitting in a Haifa sidewalk café observing busy people as they strolled by en-route to work revealed another reality. In fact this place was not too different from other Mediterranean countries– whereby a relaxed community enjoying blessed weather was simply getting on with life. Of course it is impossible to ignore that tiny Israel, not much larger than Wales, is surrounded by countries committed to the destruction of their tiny state and being amongst 4.2 million Israelis who are surrounded by eighty five million belligerents is to understand an inescapable reality that Israel would ignore at its peril. My first day was even more revealing as I met up with friends and motored down for a look at the biblical desert, passing columns of armour heading towards maneuvers in Sinai.

My connections with Israel over several visits during the Sixties and Seventies became quite varied, embracing many facets of this extraordinary land. My local buddies Bert and his best pal Ernie (Muppets anyone?) were curious to show me the Kibbutz system of collective community farming and how that compared with the slightly less communal system called a Moshav which seemed to offer semi-private ownership of the enterprise. Bert and Ernie were Sabras[1] and these characters knew an awful lot about their socially engineered systems of food production which he explained were products of necessity–when the state was barely surviving and the ability to feed one's family was as important as the ability to defend them. Pooling resources is a remarkable way to incubate a society when assets are scarce and particularly when the enemy is banging at the door–and Bert maintained that Israel society has benefited greatly from these innovative and successful land movements. My personal experience was with Kibbutz Dorot, a large and successful collective farm on the edge of the desert, which was home to some amazing characters, but what impressed me most was the diversity of their members' backgrounds. For many people idealism was high on their life-agenda and the engineers, medical professionals, pilots and scientists who chose to live the life of a simple Kibbutznik was impressive.

I have a great interest in the capability of the Israeli armed forces as well as their ability to innovate and out-think their foes. Again Bert pointed out that while a number of standard doctrines cover the prosecution of mainstream conflict–given the overwhelming scale of the surrounding antagonists, Israel badly needed to rewrite the narrative of how the chess-board conflict was approached–even debating if the chess board was appropriate. They possessed few weapons to defend themselves when their independent state was declared in 1948, when the United Nations was welcoming Israel into the family of nations. Surrounded by the five Arab armies of Egypt, Jordan, Syria, Lebanon and Iraq, comprising no less than sixty million inhabitants, this tiny nation of four million Holocaust survivors, idealists, writers, historians, futurists, musicians and intellectuals, were tasked with defending their families while tending their olive groves next to the field of battle. If Bert was an example of their thoughtfulness, part of their success in defending the state has come from the unshakable reality, that if Israel loses one single war, there is absolutely no fallback position and no cliché ever written would allow them to regroup and "fight another day." I am currently reflecting on the slaughter in Syria where Assad is murdering his citizens alongside the atrocities caused by the so called "rebels"–which makes me wonder how is it possible to reason or negotiate with these types of people?

Over the years I have come to believe that Israel's ability to defend itself will increasingly be dependent on two types of Intelligence, one being ultra-high level intelligence that is technologically driven–better described as the "Battle of the Algorithms," and low level boots-on-the-ground intelligence which is people-driven and utterly irreplaceable. Armed with this intellectual capability the hardware necessary to do the job will need to be sophisticated, blunt, and innovative, because the enemy is also innovating in its quest to destroy this tiny democratic state. I have made many visits to Israel and my respect for this amazing resilient country has deepened with each visit. What was apparent in those early days was that innovation, daring and fearlessness would go a long way towards securing their future survival and ultimately their prosperity. Today Israel is known as the "Start up Nation" and a book of this name had recently been published.

---

[1] Native born Israelis are named after the "Sabra Plant" which reputedly is a tad prickly on the outside and rather soft and sweet inside. Having never tested the fruit variety I don't feel qualified to comment further.

Corinth Canal transit – Greece

Monastery in Meteora – Greece

Author in Quebec City

Author in Monte Carlo

CHAPTER 3

The UK–Switzerland–Tunisia

Returning to a secure job within my field in the UK was a strange experience, because when I left home to explore the Yellow Brick Road I had no idea where I was heading and truthfully had no field to call my own. Now after glimpsing some of the amazing opportunities that resided over the mountain I had some idea what Dorothy was discussing with Tin Man as they waltzed hand in hand, complicitly planning their escapades.

My employer at Heaps Travel in Leeds was a small firm with a few older style coffee and cream, green-striped vintage coaches, but the owners knew enough to realize that domestic travel would not last forever and holidays in Europe might just bring prosperity to the family enterprise. This was a time when the UK holiday industry was starting to flourish and the world's most creative tourism innovators were pushing the boundaries and heading up those firms. One of the techniques which these Brits pioneered, was facilitated by the arrogance, stupidity, and lack of vision within Britain's national airlines and their European counterparts. BOAC, as it was then called, along with BEA dominated the flight scene in Britain and as a consequence of their state monopoly, air fares were high and accessible only by the privileged few. Not for long however, because the UK tour operators reasoned that by chartering and guaranteeing payment with a non brand-name airline, they could significantly lower the cost of an airline seat–and thus emerged the charter flight phenomenon which became the backbone of an expanded holiday business. I arrived in the UK just as this revolution was taking place and the joys of long distance travel would soon be affordable by many and no longer the purview of the few.

"How would you like to visit Biarritz?" my boss Nancy asked, as I opened my lunch bag on the very first day I joined the firm. Frankly I was puzzled and my inclination was to enjoy a visit to visit Biarritz, but I needed to work for about ten weeks to assemble the cost of the round trip airline seat, let alone pay for my hotel, food, and entertainment. Something in Nancy's face encouraged me to bite my tongue which turned out to be an excellent decision–because she was about to introduce me to one of the amazing hidden benefits of working in tourism–something which we then called "The Educational." What Nancy had just dropped in my lap was what my friend John Gorney tried to explain when he first joined Air Lingus. And yes, the trip was free–and yes, the firm would continue to pay my salary while I was being educated–and yes, it included the flights, accommodation, food and entertainment–and yes, it was being offered to me on my first day on the job. What happened next was like an adventure, because as the firm expanded, I expanded with it and before long I was being offered several Educationals each year, visiting many of the same places that Dorothy and Tin Man had shown me on my previous travels in Europe.

Dinner at Maison Gorney

I had fallen in love with John's sister Carolyn who was a wonderfully talented theatrical , possessing a curious blend of her parents' talents and the exotic look of a Hungarian gypsy. Carolyn eventually left that seductive and tough profession to become active in social work in the British capital. Along with my friendship with Carolyn came the extraordinary Gorney tribe of Manfred, Thea, John…and Carolyn. Manfred and Thea were Jewish refugees who had fled the Nazis prior to the outbreak of the war and were now fully established on the British social scene as importers of fine European perfume, where they were loved and respected by everyone they came into contact with. Manfred was a classical music and opera fanatic and Thea was just as passionate about music, art, theatre, and food. Dinner at the Gorneys' was always a grand occasion for debating current affairs, discussing the peculiarities of their adopted country which they loved so much, and laughter–always peals of laughter as Manfred cracked one of his (purposely) corny jokes in his charming accented and perfectly correct English. One never quite knew what to expect visiting the Gorney household or for that matter who might be there. One evening I bounced in for dinner to be shushed by Thea who was pointing a finger silently upwards towards the guest bedroom. Driven by his passion for music Manfred had befriended the famous conductor of the Manchester based Halle Orchestra, the diminutive and mercurial Sir John Barbirolli who was resting his conductor's arm above our head before his evening concert at the Leeds Town Hall. In no small measure this amazing family became the stimulus for me to take stock of my life, and the Gorneys became the "fork in the road" in my headlong pursuit down The Yellow Brick pathway. Thea was incredibly attractive both physically and intellectually and she had a charming and disarming way of approaching even seemingly intractable issues, occasionally sitting alongside me at dinner rubbing shoulders gently while talking quietly about the family past and my future. In retrospect this family was a well-integrated unit, acting independently when tactically advantageous but always with their eye on the ball and never deviating from the overall strategy. Thanks to their son John, my experience working for Heaps in Leeds was an excellent first window into the greater tourism industry, because they represented all of the well known British tour operators in addition to running their own fleet of buses. They were a superb family business, always kind to their employees and seemingly happy when one of them succeeded and moved along. It did not take long for me to realize that just over the horizon was a fascinating career with plenty of opportunities on a global scope.

Based in Switzerland

My breakout from the UK in the mid 1960s was aided by an offer in *The Times* of London. A Swiss American tour operator was seeking a selection of low-level clerks and for reasons that still remain a mystery I passed all three interviews and found myself working in the picturesque Swiss lake town of Lugano–described as "Pretty like a box of Werthers candies."

My journey from Leeds to Lugano was made in a menacing black 1954 Citroen Grand Quinze–the same model which the French detective Maigret drove across British television screens each week, which I owned jointly with John Gorney and which for obvious reasons we called Maigret. John and I had sufficient funds between us to buy only one car, which we decided we could share. The problem was that neither of us thought particularly far ahead, and when I got the job in Lugano, the last thing on my mind was how to share the big black Citroen. However my new job paid a basic outbound travel allowance from the UK to Lugano and when I calculated the gas consumption I was amazed to discover that if I took the Grand Quinze on the channel ferry and motored to Southern Switzerland, I might realize a modest profit. The car was therefore loaded to the roof with all of my portable possessions and I proudly left Leeds en-route for the channel ports and booked the night sailing between Dover and Calais.

This trip was a 1960s classic European motoring holiday as I slept in the car, picnicked through France, rumbled up several mountain passes and slithered carefully down the far side. The Grand Quinze had some interesting performance characteristics that included a typically tall (French) top gear allowing me to cruise the Autobahn at a reasonable clip. Sadly its ability to climb the passes was restricted to grinding up in first gear and coming down safely on the far side depended on how long the tiny Popsicle brake pads would survive. My downhill strategy on precipitous mountain passes was to hug the side of the road in case the brakes faded, which in theory would provide sufficient maneuvering room for me to slide the car sideways if I lost it and come to a rest straddling the road. As the passes in those days were rather narrow and as I was not about to drive like our prim Miss Daisy, this was an exhilarating ride.

The Grand Quinze caused quite a stir when it arrived in The Federation and I had forgotten that I had absolutely nowhere to park it. Moreover I had to re-register the car with the Swiss authorities and buy new locally issued plates sporting a bright red stripe identifying us as "strangers" (read "police targets"). However this car had instant curb appeal and for all the right and wrong reasons it was a great hit with everyone I knew. Sadly my agreement with John was for alternating six months ownership with The Grand Quinze, so after my time was up John appeared in Lugano and motored Maigret back to Leeds.

My clerking position in Lugano could best be described as being one of several trainee seals who were being drilled in "follow my leader," working under the watchful eye of another trained seal. In real terms I was a trainee planner in the well-known Globus tourism enterprise where their exceptional business model emphasized discipline, organization, a high degree of accuracy and for us peons…absolutely no innovation. It soon became obvious that our employer was visibly perplexed with most of their non-Swiss staffers, mainly because we were a high-spirited bunch, disdainful of authority, continually rambunctious and not quite fitting into the Federation mold. There was a studied complicity of convenience amongst the foreign workers in Globus, which created a rare and welcome coalition of British, German, Israeli and Dutch interests. In those days the Swiss regarded all foreigners with suspicion and we diligently watched each other's back, often providing alibis when one of us went AWOL. As you know the Swiss jealously guard their vaunted neutrality, which was formulated after decades of infighting between states–whose boundaries bore some resemblance to today's Cantons. At one time the Swiss were a fearsome community of traders who guarded their mountain passes and accessible valleys with fierce determination, defending them against their aggressive neighbours who surround them–360 degrees! The Swiss are a product of their historical detachment from the rest of Europe and I suspect their inbred suspicious nature was manifesting itself in how we were treated.

These were wonderful exciting years for me and even though we lived hand to mouth, we made the most of our magnificent surroundings. Lugano is a wealthy, understated and opulent town with magnificent villas in the surrounding hills and costly apartments surrounding the lake, so during the summer the Piazza was covered with sidewalk cafes where people-watching and Ferrari-counting were favourite pastimes. On many weekends we left town, travelling in my tough (small oval window) Judson Supercharged VW Beetle, walking for hours in Venice, Milan, Locarno, or Ascona. Other times we blasted up the passes to the nearby ski resorts of St Moritz and Silvaplana, terrorizing the local sports-car drivers, then sitting all day in a sidewalk cafe nursing a cappuccino pretending we knew Omar Sharif. My best weekends were spent at the Italian race circuit at Monza, and the Union Jack you saw madly waving on television was me cheering our British drivers in front of the perplexed Italian Tifosi.

One weekend my department of trained seals decided to splurge and spend an evening across the lake in the Italian gambling enclave of Campione. Twenty of us rented tuxedos and lavish gowns, caught the evening ferry to Campione, and sat down to a pre-reserved dinner before dancing the night away in the local disco. Predictably we missed the last ferry home and the sight of twenty revelers stranded high and dry and somewhat tipsy on the quayside, gazing at the lights of Lugano across the lake, was a pathetic scene and un-nerving to the local police. Next morning we bleary eyed semi aquatics were able to catch the first ferry back to Lugano, but arriving too late to change into business attire, we strolled in unison straight into the office–after which our Federation bosses were stunned to see the entire department dressed in tuxedos and ball gowns dutifully working away at their desks.

Victoria, our office administrator, was a leggy fellow Brit who spoke fluent Italian, German, and French and that uncanny mastery of four languages made her an absolute oddity, because in those days Brits were expected to be unilingual. She was willowy, often whimsical and had a distracting old world charm about her which was similar to Lady Mary in Downton Abbey and which I found quite appealing– but she mysteriously vanished somewhere each weekend and then reappeared on Mondays like magic. Only when she knew me better did she tell me her tale. On one of her weekend train sorties, Victoria had sat in a carriage next to Father Marcello, a Dominican monk who was an administrator in his order's Swiss abbey. On arrival he gave her directions to her hotel near Piazza San Marco, and when she climbed down from the train she stumbled and her weekender fell open. Father Marcelo gallantly helped retrieve Victoria's Secrets and carried them to a nearby Vaporetto or water taxi. By way of thanking him, Victoria gave the Dominican a lift by canal to his modest lodging and bid him a good weekend. Three days later Father Marcello was on the same train travelling back to the Federation whereupon they spent four happy hours laughingly comparing their work. Marcello invited Victoria to a reception on nearby Monte Bre, and Victoria reciprocated with an invitation to an art show in Campione d'Italia. Three years later Marcelo the Dominican was no longer Victoria's Secret or for that matter a Dominican and the couple are now happily married and living in the UK.

Globus were good employers, and we gave them fair value in exchange for their Federation Francs, but after two years I knew it was time to move along, so I applied for a curious sounding job in Tunisia where I could use my newly acquired Swiss-trained brain, and practice my repressed need for innovation.

Moving to Tunisia

My arrival in Tunisia during the late 1960s was the result of an opportunity offered by a small specialist British firm pioneering North Africa as an alternative winter resort to Spain. This turned out to be an absolute culture confrontation, where I learned a great deal about an Islamic country making an inspired effort to bring itself into the twentieth century. Just about everything I saw and did was different from my previous life and it was a unique opportunity to learn about this exotic national blend of Islam, Christianity, and Berber culture, with layers of colonization acting as the glue between.

Tunisia was once an outpost of the Roman Empire, the crossroads between Africa and Europe and because of its dry climate, much of its built heritage is intact, magnificent and standing proud. Its signature archaeological attraction is the ancient city of Carthage, closely followed by the magnificent coliseum at El Djem. Tunisians are either worldly city people with the good looks and sophistication of southern Europeans, or rural country folks–with Berber blood in their veins. Many older Brits will recall the desert theatre this country provided during the Second World War, with Erwin Rommel the brilliant German commander up against the diminutive, ruthless

British General Bernard Montgomery, or "Monty," as he was known. To digress for a moment, visualize a typical wartime desert morning, the dew still glistening on the palm trees, the sun just peeping over the sand hills. British tank crews inside their Lager are quietly servicing their armour, loading heavy ammunition and meticulously cleaning their guns for the day's battle with Erwin's formidable Panzers. Over their shoulder at a small card table eating breakfast sits Monty–not the well-pressed ruthless general with the narrow eyes and trademark black beret, but a stark-naked slim elder gent happily tucking into his bacon and eggs. Before long, word got around that "the Full Monty" was now on display–which is how the term originated.

My role in Tunisia was managing the destination and administrating several resort representatives who were living in various hotels. I was also tasked with administrating our flights through Tunis airport, for which the aviation authority conveniently issued me with an airside pass–allowing me to keep an eye on the sharp end of the business. Tunisia is an exceptionally interesting country with traces of former civilizations everywhere you drive, and I spent quite some time with guests on the spice Island of Djerba, although my favourite location was the troglodyte community of Matmata. The firm I was working for kindly provided me with a more modern Citroen than the Maigret we had in Lugano. This Citroen was a DS19 which I called Émile (after Zola), and she came with Hydrolastic suspension allowing her to rise and fall gently, accommodating the lengthy undulations in the roman laid roads. Tunisia was once administrated by the Romans and the French, both of whom built superb arrow-straight roads down which the DS19 with its tall top gear sped like a hare. These amazing roads, with an absence of traffic save for the odd camel or mule enabled me to move around the country quite rapidly and it was pure good motoring fortune that my hard driving put Émile in the workshop, so when I decided to visit Matmata, the firm lent me a Panzer-like Peugeot 404, which I immediately named Rommel. The 404 proved to be a tough-as-nails superb Third-World desert car, and while it may not have saved my life, it definitely made life easier towards the end of my journey.

Reversing into a strange village called Matmata

Matmata is one of the strangest places I have ever visited, yet it functions superbly despite its overwhelmingly odd location. I would wager most people have seen a great deal of Matmata, although to be fair it was called by a different name in the now quite famous series of movies. It is located in the foothills of the Tunisian desert on the slopes of the Atlas Mountains and what makes it so odd is that everyone lives in caves to escape the oppressive heat.

The approach to Matmata was along a reasonably well paved road, but as I was in a mood to go exploring and accompanied by Eric Bull who worked for "Wings" another UK firm, so we decided to take a shortcut and pursue sand-tracks that with time became steeper and progressively less packed. There is a skill to desert sand driving and contrary to popular belief it's possible to make quite good progress with skinny tyres if they are softly inflated. The car needs to be well balanced fore and aft–and to encourage traction you have to use low revs and as high a gear as possible, which is what we did for about two hours until we reached a plateau where the surface actually improved. However the downside of this exposed location was the constant wind, which had obliterated all signs of the track, changing most landmarks into small hills topped with beards and sideburns of tufted grass. Now the issue was not so much traction over the sand, but which direction we needed to take and with no recognizable track to follow it came down to marine-style dead reckoning, using the sun, a local road map and an orienteering compass that would at least give us a direction to aim for.

In the desert the sun goes down at a regular clip, but when it dips below the horizon, the light fades fast, so before long we knew we would be driving by the glint of our own lights and the reflection of a half moon on the sand. Then just as we started to sort out the route, Rommel gently dropped two wheels into a long shallow trench, and in movie-style slow motion the 404 drifted sideways until all four wheels were mired in sand, which resembled fine talcum powder. Now the challenge was not so much sorting out where we were heading, as to how we might get out of this mess, but once more our trusty angel

Dorothy and her tin mate were hovering close by and had conveniently placed 150 feet of rope in the trunk–which we were delivering to the Matmata Troglodyte hotel to be used as an external handrail between rooms. Not only that–we had just motored past a huge pointed boulder (bit like a Scottish road cairn), which was now thirty feet behind us and I started to connect the dots realizing that the cairn, the rope, Rommel, and we desert rats were somehow connected. The challenge was to figure out exactly how that connection would work to expedite a quick extraction from that bath of clinging talc.

We would have loved a winch. In fact we would have loved an LR3 Land Rover kitted out with sand tires and a high lift jack, but making a reality check, we realized that if we used some imagination and improvised we had the tools to make an extraction device for Rommel– providing we were able to manhandle the pieces and make them work as an improvised winch. The first move was to take out the spare wheel and dismount the tire and inner tube which was easier said than done because we had neither tire irons nor anything resembling a tool chest. However once more Dorothy lent her inspiration and taking our coconut machete we slit open the spare tire and dissected a perfectly good Michelin. By this time the light was fading which actually turned out to be an advantage because as the sun went down the outlying lights of Matmata appeared in the middle distance, encouraging us that if we extracted the car, we might not have to sleep so rough that night. We quickly jacked up poor Rommel, took off his right rear wheel and replaced it with the naked wheel rim, which we bolted firmly in place. We then wound the rope around the naked wheel rim and secured it so it would not slip off. We managed that by hacking off one of the wheel bolts, inserting the rope through the hole, and triple knotting it on the inside of the rim. The trick was to wrap as much as we needed to secure the rope around the rim and run the balance of the line back to the cairn, ensuring it was securely fastened. You may have figured out that we were improvising a winch by using Rommel's reverse gear and by turning the naked spare wheel rim into a winch drum. But the danger remained that while we winched him in reverse, Rommel might capsize and fall onto his side to become well and truly stuck in the talc. So to forestall this we unloaded and re-packed every available item into the opposite diagonal corner from the winch-wheel, filling coolers and every available space with sand in an effort to re-ballast Rommel. Reverse gear in most cars is a really powerful force, so ever so slowly we engaged the gear, let out the clutch and started to pull Rommel backwards out of the sand towards the cairn. I was fully prepared for the worst, but our biggest challenge turned out to be occasionally halting the process, unraveling the rope from the wheel rim and then retying it to the cairn, so we could inch our way back to a firm surface. Given the remoteness of the location and our considerable fatigue this was quite a relief, but on reflection I was far more interested in the success of my improvised winch than enjoying our restored liberty.

Matmata very late that night was a welcome sight as we motored up to the door of the Hotel Sidi Driss–which you may remember from Episode 4 of Star Wars as the home of Luke Skywalker and his Aunt Beru and Uncle Owen Lars.

My work in Tunisia was an opportunity to put into practice the wonderful disciplined business process which the anal Swiss had drilled into my head and that the British system could not, and living in Tunisia also taught me a great deal about how the hospitality side of the tourism industry functioned. It demonstrated the absolute necessity of understanding what we call "Operations" and innovating on the fly, which had been forbidden in the Federation.

Drums of War

At that time in 1967 the Arab world was rallying its troops for yet another war against Israel. Tunisia, a more enlightened Arab state located alongside Morocco, Algeria, and Libya, was also encouraged into joining this historical and hysterical madness. I had been travelling throughout the entire Arab world with my tourism and bridging work, so I knew most of these Arab states intimately and therefore this idiocy was not news to me, I had seen it coming.

What disgusted me about the behaviour of these states was that instead of putting their energies where they were badly needed–to elevate their societies from poverty, they were spending scarce resources on militancy, hatred, and war. These states desperately needed to move their dictatorships towards some form of representative democracy, to focus on poverty reduction, build strong education systems, institute health-care reform and build their scientific and cultural institutions. They needed to join the Common Market, twin with European cities, encourage technical exchanges with European universities, the list goes on ad infinitum. However, instead of engaging in worthwhile nation-building, these zealots were once more roaming the streets brandishing their Kalashnikovs in the curved arm of revolution and heading for the Jewish state.

For some time I had been working at ad-hoc assignments (bridging work) alongside my work in tourism and to deliver the information that my employers needed, it was easier if I melted into the background, sipping coffee and reading my book in a corner café. On reflection it was amazing to discover how much this first-hand knowledge was valued and how scenes and documents that I saw with my own eyes and heard with my own ears were so important for others to have. So while these dictatorial Arab nations beat their drums of war, I was moved from one country to the next, sampling the coffee, while reading my novel and being paid to observe on behalf of my part-time employer. Looking at the current Arab Spring revolution of 2011-12, it was inevitable that these energetic, intelligent and misdirected people would one day awaken from their nightmare and realize their leaders had been leading them into a cul de sac. Each day they wasted on hatred and each day they wasted blaming others for their misfortunes, the gap between their societies and the developing world increased and instead of pursuing their blind, anti-Semitic madness their energies could have been spent developing their own societies and putting their own houses in order. I hold the same view of Communism and what the Red Party imposed on millions of Russians and Chinese along with their satellites–with similarly pathetic results. Our democratic system is badly flawed, but it has delivered more to ordinary people than totalitarianism ever did. Einstein's definition of madness can be readily applied to these totalitarianisms, which were "repeating the same process time and again and expecting a different answer."

Soviet-Built Migs Head for Israel

It was 1967 and the commute from my home to my work in Tunis was now strewn with glass. Tunisian Jewish businesses were burning in the streets courtesy of Arab looters and a great deal of Jewish property was desecrated. I diverted along alternative roads to reach Tunis Airport, determined to keep the firm in business and luckily Émile the Citroen was wearing local plates, so I was able to film the looting and destruction, smiling and waving two fingers at the looters while chuckling to myself at the same time.

As an aside to you motoring enthusiasts, I need to emphasize how tough these early Citroens (and Peugeots) were and how capable they performed in a third world environment.

The airport was in turmoil and my telex was clattering with twenty questions from the firm. What was happening out there–could they have an immediate "sit report". Meanwhile, on the airstrip, Algerian Air Force Migs were gliding in for a landing en-route to the fight against Israel–so I wandered over to search for "lost luggage" and these elegant Migs also became part of my Tunisian film travelogue. It was apparent that a war was about to break out, so I commandeered the telex and effectively closed down the operation, asking HQ to fly out Britannia repatriation charters and bring our tourists home. The Swiss might have been perplexed with my improvisation. The firm was impressed with my analysis of the situation. The Tunisians just kept looting.

CHAPTER 4

New York– Crossing the Atlantic– Oriental Asia–Africa

I met many exceptional people while I was working in Tunisia, and the Vanderveld family of Americans who were living in Britain and on holiday in Hammamet was some of the best. Hans and Greta were to become bosom friends as well as my mentors and were guilty of encouraging me to cross the Atlantic. Hans was an engineer responsible for building a new hotel chain in Europe and the Middle East and Greta was a talented antique collector, gourmet cook and a marvelous doe-eyed raconteur. After the Six Day War I was unfortunately unemployed and looking for work, so Greta fixed me with her baby blue eyes and softly said "it's about time you went stateside and I have just the way to make it pay."

Hans and Greta had been collecting antiques for the past five years and needed to transport their huge consignment to sell in New Jersey. Their stateside distributor had just moved to the West Coast, so they proposed that I handle the sales and stand in as their agent on-site. Moving from tourism to antiques had not been in my career plan, but as I was used to trading this was a fascinating opportunity with excellent side benefits, so I set sail from Southampton, antiques nestled in their container acting as ballast below.

The ship hit horrendous weather and we rocked and rolled like Mick Jagger staggering stage left to stage right. We had encountered a multi-directional North Atlantic storm with waves hitting us square on the beam and on the bow, rendering us like washing inside a Maytag. Three lifeboats were wrenched from their davits before our eyes which was not an encouraging omen and what aggravated our concern was the total absence of seafarers to at least help out. We and several hundred stinky voyagers eventually limped into Manhattan more or less in one piece, thankful to see the back of that excuse for a trans-Atlantic steamer. Emerging into the city streets of Manhattan was quite an eye opener and my first impression was the stark contrast between incredible wealth and just two blocks over–extreme poverty. I had read a great deal about U.S. political affairs so this odd distribution of wealth was not new to me–just incongruous. Overall I was truly surprised by what I was seeing and reflected that with this split in wealth the US society seemed to going backwards towards Edwardian Britain.

The world of antiquities was new to me, but commerce is similar the world over and I found it pleasurable to slip into the temporary role of Antiquarian Man and started bartering. I enjoyed the rough and tumble nature of business in Manhattan, and it was the wonderful people who made the biggest impression on me. The place seemed to be full of larger than life egotistical, sharply defined characters and not only in the antique business. In those days Bleecker Street was the epicenter of my sales job and my recent visits to Manhattan with daughter Nicole and her family are strolls down memory lane.

Before long we had buyers lined up for Greta's treasures, and when the last brass scale left the storage, I thought it might be an interesting place to drop roots and as I was really enjoying this huge metropolis I started looking for work. At that time a tour operator called Sign Posts was a reputable firm with excellent long-distance escorted tours in Asia, Africa, and the South Pacific. They were something of a legend in the industry having been founded two generations earlier by the grandfather of the current owners. I risked a cold call to their odd-ball Hungarian immigrant senior manager who granted me the briefest of interviews, asking in a heavily Eastern European accent "are you called shtefan, shteven or Etienne"? After reflecting on my resume for a nanosecond, I'm convinced all he saw was the phrase "Swiss Trained" and I was instantly hired. And why not? Tourism-focused education at that time was non-existent in the USA so most tourism firms trained staff on the fly as best they could. My Swiss and British employers on the other hand took a formal approach to employee relations and offered me excellent training in some of the basic tourism systems. Having developed my career as a tourism researcher, a critical observer, a negotiator and a planner, this opened an opportunity which was formerly unavailable. Luck was with me in Manhattan, and as I didn't have a parrot on my shoulder, a black patch on my eye or a wooden leg, and Dorothy and Tin Man were out of sight in the lobby–I got the job.

My new position as a planner was three rungs up from my former work as a Swiss trained seal. The boss generously allowed me to refine the work schedule, to alter how we analyzed the issues, and to ramp up communications overseas. We even discussed how best to innovate, and soon I was moving to another position as manager-planner for Asia and Africa. Six months later I was flying to Asia, reviewing hotels, talking with suppliers, examining routes, and reviewing pricing. It was an extraordinary opportunity and someone was paying me to indulge my passion. John Gorney would have been proud of his protégé and his words "These goons are paying me to do this work" resonated in my ears.

Oriental Asia

The firm was not in great shape and I was tasked with redesigning many of their routes in order to make them more exciting and therefore more salable. My time in Asia was a similar cultural-confrontation to that of the Middle East–each day seemingly on another planet. My new beat was "Asia"…but I never really understood the description, because looking around this was definitely "the Orient" and I was constantly moving between Cambodia, Thailand, Singapore, Taiwan, Hong Kong and points between. I discovered that I was looking at the Orient through several prisms. For work it was through the expectation prism of an American visitor, so I needed to refine and improve the holiday experience. Looking through my personal prism was entirely different because my interests lay well beyond main street and I was beginning to develop a passion for what we now call geopolitics whereby geography and politics converge–and particularly how political muscle was shaping countries and their economies. The cold war temperature was still below zero and the Soviet Union, with its dreadful failed social experiment, was spreading its Communist disease via costly client states in a bid for world dominance. And facing the Soviets was the U.S. team - with much the same end game, only a different way of operating on the field. Meanwhile the swimming pool of my Bangkok hotel was filled with thoughtful U.S Aviators and their local lovelies, enjoying R&R from their bombing runs in Vietnam. One evening we accompanied these air-jockeys to see M.A.S.H. which at the time was deemed too "subversive" for screening on the U.S Mainland. As we strolled back to our hotel I would glean from these brave fellows that the war was not going well.

My proximity to this conflict offered a unique opportunity for a closer look at Asia and with a pocket full of semi-legitimate excuses I headed for the Cambodian border. My Thai contacts were not too impressed with my interest in their historical rivals, but that became moot as I wandered through the fabulous ruins of Angkor Wat peering at extraordinary stone carvings and attending evening performances inside the walls. In Cambodia the atmosphere was tense and locals knew that Viet Cong agents were in the country, scoping out the land and assessing the mood of the community. I loved the atmosphere in Siem Reap which in retrospect, reminds me of Saigon based "The Quiet American," starring Michael Cain. In Siem Reap the mood swung from somber to festive and back again as bad-news-good-news filtered in from the front lines while the presence of U.S. "advisors" lent a surreal atmosphere to the bars. While in Cambodia we rented a jeep and bounced our way though to Batambang which was a relic from when the French ruled Indo-China. But the prize was the temples of Ankgor and especially at night when the stars were aligned and the breeze was both scented and warm. The firm kept calling me but disingenuously I was unable to hear what they were saying. Actually I was hearing quite well, but for a young traveler in the Orient, life was interesting and educational and I was not too keen to return. Also, the scope of my behind the scenes part time bridging work was expanding, but remembering what it was like to be unemployed I packed my bags and headed east.

Africa

Apparently my dispatches from the Orient were of some use to the firm, because on arrival in New York an envelope was waiting with a short letter, an extensive briefing and a cheque. Next day I met with my boss and learned about grumblings from the firm's clients, who were becoming resistant to the Apartheid regime in South Africa but the firm needed sufficient research to justify an alternate destination. There was a long list of countries to investigate but I needed to develop a situation analysis in several African states and to do that I needed to get behind the scenes. There were issues with bribery that needed cleaning up and I needed to root out the management rot in the field and replace them with fresh troops. Most gratifyingly, I had an actual money advance from the firm and I remember sitting in "Chock full of Nuts" on 5th Avenue, sipping a Cappuccino repeating to myself, "not only are these folks paying me to travel–they are now paying me in advance." When my head cleared I could visualize a complex agenda of eight African countries, several concurrent weeks of intensive investigative work, and scores of negotiations–a university course without the walls.

It is easy to like Africa. The air has a taste all of its own, the landscape is always engaging, sometimes dramatic and the people often surprising. For some reason the colors and shades of African landscapes are different from anywhere else, with the possible exception of Australia. It had a softness that was definitely more pastel than Crayola and the sounds and smells of Africa tends to work its way into your mind. The worker-bee people are a curious combination of naïve, super street-smart, open, warm and always–absolutely always generous. However the politics in Africa has also been and still is disturbing–the political influence from abroad has not always been positive and the divine influence from other cultures often at odds with their traditional beliefs. The next few years were fascinating and the more time I spent on the continent the more I became attuned to its culture and I learned a great deal.

RSA

The Republic of South Africa is a powerful country with a unique tribal mix, a complex colonial past, a troubled present and if they handle themselves well…an amazing future. Apartheid, then in existence was an abhorrent and artificially structured form of racial engineering, whereby the white community subjugated the black community with the use of many odious techniques. Complete physical separation was impossible because of the sheer numbers involved, but the indigenous community was marginalized in every way you care to imagine, including health care, education, economic development, political voice, security, accommodation and nourishment. For the white Africana to survive, they believed that Apartheid could be sustainable, but to an outsider with the advantage of a different perspective, Apartheid could not possibly be sustained. How long could a minority of whites subjugate a vast majority of blacks? The real question was when would the bubble burst?

Visiting the RSA was an education in localized, regional and international geopolitics, with the west grudgingly lined up against the Apartheid regime (trade was still a priority) and the Soviets financing liberation movements in neighboring countries. "Grudgingly opposing Apartheid" is probably the right description because although western states were nominally aligned against the RSA, many of their citizens were not and cracks were beginning to appear in those countries, while around the world there were anti-Apartheid demonstrations, trade boycotts and debates at the UN. Opposing this were those who quietly supported separate development of the races and this was by no means a comfortable debate. As the old political adage (courtesy of Winston Churchill) goes, "Countries do not have friends–they only have interests" and nowhere was this clearer than in the RSA.

The country is truly magnificent in so many ways. The physical scenery is as grand and varied and dramatic as anywhere on earth, while the rugged coastline is a significant component of its Cape heritage and equally as grand as the interior. The wildlife is what most people come to see and wildlife tourism was well managed in a series of game parks with names like Kruger, Llluwie and Umfolozi. While most urban centers had developed rich enclaves for the white population, the poor black residents lived in ghettos similar to the famous Soweto and while the Apartheid regime was stumbling towards its appointment with destiny, the native population was marshalling their opposition–with Nelson Mandela or Madeba as he was called, as their leader. Home-grown protest and border terrorism was suppressed by the Apartheid regime using a combination of brutal power and bribery, whereby tribes were pitted against each other in the classic colonial technique of divide and conquer. South Africa's tribal affiliations were clearly defined and nowhere as apparent as the extraordinary mine dances where several hundred Ndebele, Xhosa, Zulu and Swazi, demonstrated this peculiarly awesome display of athleticism, rhythm and power. Mining still is a core industry in the RSA and low cost native labour facilitated competitiveness in the extraction of gold and diamonds. Farming was yet another core industry with huge enterprises grown partially by low cost labour, which facilitated the atmosphere of artificial competitiveness. While destiny was approaching on its own unshakable schedule, the Soviets were facilitating liberation movements in neighboring Angola and Mozambique. This pitted their proxies against the RSA and it was against this deteriorating climate that we contemplated a move to East Africa.

East Africa

After my lengthy time in the largely white controlled RSA my visits to East Africa seemed peculiar. In the RSA, the native population was carefully restricted to service sector roles, with the more prominent client-contact roles reserved for the white population. But in East Africa the reverse was seemingly true as Kenya, Tanzania and Uganda emerged into self-governing independent states. But let's be perfectly clear–these East African states were a far cry from the egalitarian fair minded democratic states which western idealist-led protest movements envisaged and had lobbied for down south. Similar to most African states, their leadership tended to form along tribal lines with privilege, wealth and power migrating towards those affiliated with the controlling tribal party, leaving the dregs for the rest. This is how most of Africa has emerged since we introduced the concept of democracy.

In East Africa the imprint of a colonial past was still part of the business and social landscape, but there was no doubt about who was in charge as each of these states lurched towards confused nationhood. Tourism was flourishing here and as a tourism enterprise we didn't need rocket science to make the necessary adjustments. The former British administrators had left the twin legacies of education and an administrative framework, which worked well for the transition–until the inevitable tribal-based power struggle eroded public confidence. At that time these were safe and welcoming countries where crime against visitors was unheard of and the game parks were well tended and our service delivery, which included drivers, guides, managers and administrators was by local natives–once again organized along tribal lines.

During these trips I made several memorable visits to "Treetops Hotel " in Kenya and each time met someone of interest. I spent one evening with a professor from Japan who spoke zero English, but soon discovered that we shared a third language which was French–which considerably enlivened the evening. Another evening was even more memorable when my 10 year old son Daniel descended from the tree and ended up wrestling a half wild warthog. Famously, this was where Princess Elizabeth climbed up into this unique hotel and next day descended as Queen Elizabeth II when news of her father's death reached her.

As we grew our business in East Africa and developed relationships with local tourism agencies, one or two characters from the colonial past were still running enterprises and one of these was the jovial and benign Peter Mikelson an expatriate Dane who wandered into Kenya, somewhat like The Von Blixen family from "Out of Africa." Peter was an interesting fellow and a skilled raconteur with a fund of first person hilarious stories from his life in Kenya and he was also a shrewd businessman with a flair for negotiations. He was a larger than life fellow with a foot in two cultures. When they were nippers we took Nicole and Daniel for an extensive safari through Kenya and Tanzania and had several dinners with Kenya-Grandpa-Peter as we passed through Nairobi. Two years later he was dead. To cut a very complex story down to manageable proportions, the long arm of the resistance located Peter Mikelsen and he was executed for the collaborator he was and for what he did during World War II.

Uganda and Idi–Heavenly protector of the People

My ties with East Africa were becoming deeper and soon we were extending our range into Uganda which was an enchanting country with ochre red soil, massive twelve feet high road-side anthills, charming humorous people and the River Nile. The fabulous Nile emerged near Chobe National Park, cascaded through the Uganda gorges and foothills to start its multicultural journey to the sea. It is here the fabled Nile crocodile are to be found in massive herds resembling logs floating down to the sawmill. These were not the puny North American Alligators which we see in Florida nor the slender Caiman of Central America, these were huge prehistoric monsters, straight out of Jurassic Park, which frequently hunted inland as well as in the Nile. These Nile crocs were predatory animals. They are cunning, relentless hunters with merely one natural enemy with whom they shared their Nile. This was the massive hippopotamus, which paddled the river alongside these carnivores and uneasily co-existed in the fast flowing river and on its grassy banks. A mature hippo could snap one of the crocs in two using the unbelievable power of its massive jaws–which mostly happened when hippos were breeding and their babies became fair game for the ever hungry gluttonous Jurassic crocs.

There was no doubt that our guests would be interested in this exceptional area if we could provide access in small boats–with sufficient freeboard for safety. Chobe National Park was home to the Nile and this amazing wildlife and where Stanley uttered that presumptuous phrase when meeting Dr. Livingstone. Nearby are the mountains of the Ruwenzori in the Congo, home to a tribe of nomadic Pygmies and nowadays the same hills give refuge to the genocidal rebel movement called "The Lord's Resistance Army." Towards the end of our product development period in Uganda the Obote administration was toppled by a portly army officer by the name of Major Amin–soon to be self promoted to Field Marshal Amin, "Heavenly protector of the people." I was in Chobe National Park making adjustments to our safari program when the military coup happened and we knew that because the BBC World Service was offering a different story from Radio Uganda. Given the antics of this Field Marshal and his alcohol and drug fueled soldiers we decided to immediately evacuate all staff personnel and more importantly our guests.

Chobe is a good six hours drive from Entebbe Airport so we stocked up with supplies, gassed up our Land Rover, filled all the VW Safari buses with guests and in convoy started the five hour trek to the airport. Entebbe Airport is on the lovely shoreline of Lake Victoria and we always strained our necks for a better view as we flew in. Now we strained our eyes to identify potential problems as we passed villages with concerned people crowded around radios, peering into burned out smoldering police posts. Twice we passed through army checkpoints answering twenty questions from under-age soldiers but as yet no red eyes. Our third checkpoint was more like a roadblock with jeeps recessed into the bush and heavy weapons trained down the road and another twenty questions once more, this time with plenty of red eyes and the stink of stale beer. We were about 30 minutes from Entebbe, approaching our fourth roadblock, but this time red eyes in uniform made a passport face-check and mentioned money. Entebbe Airport was too far down the road for me to see even the control tower, but an East African Airways F27 was hovering above us on approach, so we knew we were close. I decided to take control of the money issue, surmising I might provide the perfect excuse which Red Eye in uniform was looking for–but unable to articulate. I asked "Was this the new toll road to the airport and how much was the toll"? This fortunately gave Red Eye in uniform an excuse to nod in the affirmative and for me to "purchase" the last few kilometres to safety.

The airport was not a happy place, but we were the happiest people there and eventually made contact with the airline which was frantically working to facilitate flights to Nairobi. Under extreme pressure and I can only surmise misgivings about their upcoming life under Field marshal Amin, these wonderful people performed like pros. Later that night we saw Lake Victoria once more, as the lake water receded under the wing and we headed for Kenya. Years later Entebbe Airport was the scene of a far more extraordinary incident when an Air France jet was hijacked by Arab terrorists with a large number of Israeli citizens onboard. It was mainly because Israel had been a principal aid donor to pre-Amin Uganda that they had detailed knowledge of the airport layout and was able to plan that audacious successful night raid and rescue their people.

CHAPTER 5

Emigration to Canada–Caribbean–Texas–Pacific–Self employed

After working around the globe and despite my excellent business connections in New York, I started to get an uncomfortable feeling that establishing permanent roots in the U.S. would be an unwise move. I had many excellent friends and dozens of interesting acquaintances and I was attracted by the exceptional dynamism and commercial success of the United States–while at the same time being uneasy about how it conducted itself domestically and how it took to the global playing field. Alexis-Charles de Tocqueville, the great French political thinker known for his Democracy in America may have become uneasy seeing how the U.S. wielded its power and might have been motivated to publish a supplementary volume entitled American democracy gone-wrong. Decades earlier imperial Britain had wielded its dominant firepower for self interest across a vast empire of emerging economies and it appears that the egalitarian U.S. was trying to do the same–while large segments of U.S. domestic society resembled the class divisions in Edwardian Britain. Looking back and in light of the so called Wikileaks and the Edward Snowdon affair, what worries me most is not what nations do covertly–but the appalling lack of internal oversight that monitors the excesses of governments which ultimately safeguards those who are governed. My uneasiness about settling in the U.S. may or may not have been prescient, but I was detecting an odour and it was not pleasant.

Given what I had experienced chasing Dorothy and the Tin Man around the globe it was time to evaluate my circumstances, take stock of my assets and make some basic life-decisions about where to drop roots and call home, when a quick trip into Canada made a great impression on me. Canada had a relatively familiar parliamentary system which appealed to me more than the U.S. system of governance. The Canadian economic approach to business life was quite similar to the U.S. with some welcome differences on the banking and finance greed-sectors. I liked the fact that Canadian society was equally concerned with the welfare of others and not so focused on what was only good for "me" so embracing these qualities I took formal steps to "drink the maple syrup" and was duly admitted to the country as a worker-bee-freshman. Looking forward in time I am impressed with Marina Gorbis who maintains "we are all immigrants to the future"– which means that we are moving through an age when the social contract is changing and we are all immigrants in whatever the new future will bring.

Looking for work in Canada was a different experience from New York, largely because it was a much smaller market but I was now able to offer more substantive experience to a prospective employer. My work now covered a vast geographic and political area and luck once more played a part–with an offer from a Canadian firm with the oddball name of Intervoyage-CTAL run by a charismatic character from the old country. I could understand why my planning and research capabilities were quite marketable, but what really helped was my growing black book of contacts which allowed me to access valuable information from a broad variety of sources.

My new home in Toronto was partially defined by the north shore of Lake Ontario which is one of the five Great Lakes and I knew that schoolboy geographic tidbit before I emigrated–but while descending on the glide path into Pearson Airport for some odd reason I was surprised to see this massive expanse of water alongside my new home. I am shamed to say that for a passionate geographer it took a good deal of head shaking before I remembered my geography and realized this was Lake Ontario! The Great Lakes of North America are still an under-appreciated natural asset, but in those days I regarded much of it as remote territory full of excitement, exploration and promise.

In a curious turn of events soon after arriving in Toronto, I was able to make a flying visit to Canada's Arctic region which in those days included the Yukon and the North West Territories. My new boss had a vague idea that tourism might just explode in the Canadian far-north and after an uncharacteristically rapid fact-finding visit I had to agree with him. Canada's Arctic region has the measure of any exotic location on earth and with time it will claim its place in that category–but more about this in a later chapter.

Planning in the Caribbean

Soon after returning from the cool (in both senses of the word) Arctic, the owner of my new firm who was a charismatic Irish Immigrant from Enniskillen in Northern Ireland, hustled me off to the sweltering Bahamas to research the potential of those fabulous tiny specks of land which were then called the "Out Islands" and are now branded as the "The Family Islands."

At the Nassau airport private aviation hanger I was met by the pilot of a small twin-engine aircraft, known locally as Eddie the Eagle. Not the British ski jumper–this Eddie was so named because he flew his Beech Baron like an eagle with eyes to match, sadly without a silk scarf and leather flying helmet which would have been oppressive, yet impressive in the Caribbean heat. Eddie's speciality was dropping his buzz-bomb down to deck height whenever he spotted a yacht with a lady on the foredeck. Typically we would be cruising at 150 Knots at an altitude of 1500 feet, when he spotted a new target and within seconds we were skimming 50 feet off the water, heading between the masts. This was an odd and novel experience but in no sense intimidating because Eddie piloted the Beech with considerable skill and made every move with delicate care and precision. What did concern me was his attitude towards the islands, especially if there was a small coastal hill with a gap in the center. This represented a bulls eye target for Eddie and we zoomed through a few of these dimples, flying parallel with the coconut palms with our pilot grinning fiendishly from ear to ear. "Lean out and grab one" he would say, snatching a sideways glance to see if I was listening and I was not sure if he meant a coconut or the clothing hanging from the washing line.

I fell in love with the Caribbean and was soon spending quality time working through every nook and cranny of this blessed area. However, despite the appearance of decadent laid-back opulence many indigenous locals were unable get a piece of the tourism pie–existing on the fringes of the service industry, living hand to mouth on modest means. Haiti was the most graphic example of this poverty gap and was always a conundrum for us–which despite massive injections of capital and technical know-how hardly seems to improve. In Canada with its energy-sapping winter temperatures this subsistence living would be a life ending challenge, but with Caribbean weather the necessities of life such as a four season wardrobe, insulated homes, two sets of car tyres, and a high calorie food intake were unnecessary in order to survive.

Planning in the South Pacific

Years later Australia provided a different type of challenge when the firm sent me down-under to make routing adjustments to our South Pacific program. It was actually selling quite well and our guests loved the urban centers of Sydney and Melbourne, as well as Tropical Cairns and Ayers Rock, which Australians call "The Center" and aboriginals call "Uluru," but we needed to augment the routing with Adelaide. Happily, this program was already commercially mature and stable when the entire Australian Airline industry shut down because of an industrial dispute. We could still reach Australia, because the international carriers were still flying to Oz, but our highly mobile domestic touring which was done by internal flying was now rendered impossible.

I had other excellent reasons to visit the lower segment of the earth. Australia was a preferred destination for Brits emigrating abroad, and my friends Malcolm and Angela Ellenport had left for Melbourne in 1965 and I wanted to meet their growing family. This planning trip would also be a fantastic opportunity to indulge my life-long passion for motor racing and meet up with friends and fellow Buckler racers Dawn and Graham Brayshaw in New Zealand. I met Graham through our ownership of the same obscure make of British race car and as with other specialist hobbyists we kept in contact. At that time Graham and Dawn operated an automotive business located in the former Bruce McLaren Garage in Auckland which is hallowed ground for motor race enthusiasts.

Sitting in Canada during mid-winter with a huge amount of revenue tied up in our strike-threatened South Pacific tours required a creative solution and for three days solid I ensconced myself in the Australian consul general's office in Ottawa, the Australian Yellow Pages on the table, searching for owners of small private airlines we might contact. I presumed the Aussie business community had every available aircraft tied up, but remembering the high expectations of our guests pushed me onward.

Hour by hour while racking up a huge telephone bill I pieced together a small fleet of quite varied charter aircraft which could handle our tours for the entire winter season. Our first three tours used a Canadian-built Twin Otter and a restored DC3 "Combi," which was a freight and passenger aircraft. Another four tours would use a full passenger-configured DC3, and the balance used two Twin Otters, which apparently flew side by side with guests waving to each other. I remember the reaction of our guests when we broke the news that we were replacing Boeings with this eclectic wing-flapper fleet and although we didn't lose a single guest I fielded many interesting questions from rightfully inquisitive people. However it was the sight of the smiling handsome young Australian pilots in their crisp white shorts welcoming them onboard, that significantly restored their confidence. Years later I kicked myself for not buying the planes because what we spent on chartering them would have purchased at least the two DC 3's.

The crisis taken care of, I was now looking further afield to augment our core Australia and New Zealand programs and started to include the romantic island destinations of Western Samoa and Tahiti where the focus was the Robert Lewis Stevenson story and the magic of Bora Bora. In Western Samoa I soon met Aggie Grey who was the founder of the hotel of the same name–an exceptional character and a living institution on that seductive island. Aggie was borne Agnes Genevieve Swan and her father was a British Chemist who married a local Samoan beauty. She opened Aggie Grey's hotel in 1903 where her life transitioned through the pre and post colonial eras. Western Samoa was a protectorate of New Zealand and was completely different from nearby American Samoa which was overly commercialized and quite rough. Both communities shared a special human characteristic which was the ability to harmonize alongside a modest ukulele orchestra and at that time Sunday church services were staggered so one could stroll from church to church in the warm Pacific breeze, listening to hymns being competitively harmonized by these talented islanders. Aggie ran a wonderful earthy hotel at the edge of town with open sides to all the public rooms and with palm trees instead of curtains. Most Americans visited Western Samoa because of the legacy of Robert Louis Stevenson but the island was much more than the home of this adventure writer, it was a true refuge from the mainstream hustle of life and an oasis of peace and tranquility.

Planning in Texas–Meeting the Luftwaffe

During my early days in Canada I was also tasked with a research project that involved a senior planner from Air Canada because although the airline's new route to Texas was showing promise they needed to augment the oil-patch business with regular tourism. Texas is a wonderful state, which I happened to know well and I was happy to leave behind -20 degrees below zero and be toiling in +85 degrees above zero with continual sunshine for three weeks–a difference of 105 degrees and not at all unpleasant. Years later we flew charters from Winnipeg to Barbados where the departing temperature was -30 and arrival in Bridgetown an energy sapping 85 degrees–which was 115 degrees difference. Most clients opted to sit on their balconies and acclimatize for a day, but a few zealots hit the Bacardi, later collapsing on the beach with exhaustion.

My research partner from the airline was the charming Ulrich Weber, a capable bright Heidelberger who migrated to Canada after the war. Ulrich was one of those uber intelligent people who could size-up a situation in a nanosecond–which would serve our joint mission well. I am sure this helped him excel as an effective Heinkel pilot during the second World War and as a "war baby" I was curious to hear more about that. Ulrich and I met for dinner to review the Texas mission and I was happy to discover he possessed a well honed sense of humour, a disarming old world courtly manner and above all he was an amazing raconteur. On many a warm Texas evening Ulrich describe stories from his youth and before long we exchanged views about the 2nd World War. He was naturally curious about my upbringing in Leeds and I described my theory about being Hitler's bullseye, to which he listened with eyes slightly narrowed and his brow ever so slightly wrinkled. He was thoughtful for some time, trying to locate an item in the hard-drive-of-his-mind, recalling details of his bombing sorties over the UK and how they were harassed by young R.A.F. pilots flying like fiends to keep the Heinkels at bay. He knew exactly where I was during the war because the nearby tank and munitions factories were his bombing targets. Thus my new friend Ulrich was my "once upon a time" tormentor.

Ulrich was a resourceful and fascinating fellow and one of his first post-war jobs was a sales rep in the UK and when he told me this it was my turn to narrow my eyes and wrinkle my brow in surprise. Hearing this I built up an image of Ulrich the former Heinkel bomber pilot in his double breasted grey suit, with a matching trilby on his head, carrying his worn leather German briefcase, making sales calls in postwar Britain. This would be as contentious as my old pal Nori Tanaka from Kyoto making sales calls in New York after Pearl Harbour. There are very few humans I know who could pull that off and survive but not only did Ulrich do that, he was highly successful and rose to prominence in the firm. His ability as a raconteur provided endless entertainment and a weekend expedition to the village of Witney near R.A.F. Brize Norton was typical of the man. I was not there, but I surmise that he was wearing a tweed jacket with leather elbows, Viyella striped shirt, Black Watch tartan tie and I am guessing well polished brogues. He stepped into the Plough Inn & Pub and asked if anyone knew Martin Harris. The publican nodded towards the snug whereupon Ulrich positioned himself at the perimeter of the alcove waiting for the chit-chat to die down. Ulrich asked which drinker was Wing Commander Harris, whereupon he introduced himself as former Luftwaffe Captain Ulrich Weber and according to his records, Harris had shot him down over the Pas de Calais while he was returning to base. One can only imagine the scene as the drinking Brits fell totally silent and digested this well rehearsed introduction. Apparently a great many pints were consumed while Martin, Ulrich and the other fliers recounted their tales of survival. Years later Ulrich and I were heading for the Confederate Air Force Museum in Harlingen Texas. We thought it had potential as one of the city's tourism attractions so the museum kindly assigned an amusing and knowledgeable former U.S.A.F. pilot as our guide. The visit went well and as were touring the hangers in a restored Willys Jeep we discovered an un-restored Heinkel bomber which was in excellent condition. Our host kindly allowed us to climb into the aircraft and the image of me in the cockpit and Ulrich gazing up from below was a reversal of roles that was not lost on him. We smiled at each other and no words were necessary.

Independent activities–dropping out of sight

After working for several years as an employee I eventually bought a portion of the firm and after adding value to its worth with several years of hard work, it was time to sell my shares and reacquaint myself with Dorothy and the Yellow Brick Road–which held the promised of an adventure worth embracing. After working for my entire life as an employee within a structured firm and then in my own firm–and having worked for some excellent international travel organizations, the notion of selling out and becoming a one-person show was… well, strange. Would Dorothy and Tin-Man still speak with me or more importantly would they listen when I uttered a few comments of my own? In some respects I was shedding the considerable prestige that comes with a title in a well known firm and embracing the identity of a low budget sole practitioner with not much to offer those who are used to taking and not used to giving. Let me explain the dynamics of that curious transition for those of you who might be contemplating it.

In my previous enterprises as an employee and as an owner, each of the firms were research driven and produced outstanding travel experiences, and let me emphasize that those amazing programs were the product of a multi-talented team of which I was merely a component and team-leader. We depended heavily on tour escorts who possessed a critical eye in the field, on our superb accountants to keep on top of our cash-flow, on our detailed orientated operations people to attend to the daily minutae and the fearless internal critics who were never afraid to tell me that I was wrong. The result of this inclusive management style brought us considerable success, which meant that we were significant buyers of quality hotel rooms, airline seats, bus charters and vast quantities of high quality meals. We were therefore a magnet for sales reps, vice presidents of sales and occasionally the presidents of firms that badly wanted our business. That was the case until Friday at 19:00 when I sold the firm and headed off to meet Dorothy.

For all of you who might be contemplating a similar move, I would suggest that you park your ego in the bedside closet because when Monday morning arrives, the vast majority of those sales reps, vice presidents of sales and occasionally the presidents <u>will have forgotten that you ever existed.</u>

CHAPTER 6

In the Footsteps of the Lost Franklin Expedition

My immigration to Canada came in a rather more circuitous manner than most of my expatriate friends, all of whom came directly from the old country. My personal detour seems to have been influenced by my work and my curiosity for how different countries conduct themselves, and even though I was not working or domiciled in the UK at that time, the rules obliged me to return and formally emigrate from there. The vastness of the Canadian landscape and its diversity had always fascinated me, and because tourism exploration is my speciality, I gravitated towards the expeditions of the early explorers while identifying strongly with their thirst for discovery. My focus on this research trip to Bathurst Inlet was impacted by the curious period in English history during the mid-1800s when the British were trying to find a route through the Canadian Arctic as a shortcut to the orient. England was not at war for a change and peacetime exploration was one of the few options open to many naval officers hoping to enhance their standing in society and increase their stand-by pay. When Franklin came a-calling for a jaunt to the Northwest Passage, there was no shortage of takers.

John Franklin was a curious man and in some respects, not entirely suited to this type of brutal exploration. In his day he was an ambassador; nowadays we would call him a diplomat, and in former days he would have been a plenipotentiary. He began his career early, enlisting in the Royal Navy when he was 14 as a crew member on the 1801 South Pacific expedition commanded by his uncle, the now-famous Mathew Flinders. Franklin participated in the Battle of Trafalgar, the Battle of New Orleans and the downfall of Napoleon after the Battle of Waterloo. He later spent time in Australia representing the crown as Lieutenant Governor of Tasmania, then called Van Diemen's Land. Franklin's views on reforming the penal colony and other liberal (for the time) ideas were not entirely popular amongst his Australian society peers. He was a curious combination of a liberal reformer and a battle-hardened adventurer, ready for action. When the opportunity to lead the greatest expedition England had ever mounted was offered to him, John Franklin answered the call.

Nowadays, climate change has altered our perspective of this inhospitable region, and Franklin's conclusion that the Northwest Passage was an impractical sea-route now looks quite different through my 21st century eyes. Today, a number of public and private sector enterprises are active in the High Arctic, many of which are reinforcing the Arctic sovereignty of Canada; Unfortunately the United States, along with other nations considers the Northwest Passage to be an international waterway, although it lies squarely within Canadian territorial waters between two sovereign Canadian land masses. Recently the Russians planted their flag on the shelf adjacent to our territorial seabed, trigging alarm bells as to their motive. Hapag Lloyd of Germany is cruising their ice-class ships Hanseatic and Europa through the North West Passage and Quark Expeditions, Cruise North and Adventure Canada are offering High Arctic cruises each summer. However the real prize in this region is access to the exceptional richness of the land with its substantial deposits of oil, gas, gold, copper, Chromate manganese and other precious commodities. To protect these resources, the Canadian government is building a High Arctic naval base in the Northwest Passage and encouraging occupancy of this region. These modern initiatives have the benefit of superb technology and the watchful eye of government; transiting "The Passage" however, still remains an awesome challenge until someone paves it over.

Traveling Through Adventure

In my line of work I have passed through most of the accessible parts of the world and a few that were supposedly inaccessible–which has occasionally caused me some stress. For me, "passing through" has a different meaning than "staying a while," which is different again from "dropping roots" or "living in a place." I was carefully trained in my work assignments by a series of experienced mentors who encouraged me to develop into an aggressive researcher and at other times to assume the role of a seemingly passive observer. It has often been rewarding to "lean against the door of the cantina," merging into the background and taking it all in, and I have discovered that if you really don't want to be noticed, most people will forget you are there–and it's extraordinary what you observe when you are invisible. I also find it useful that Greeks think I am Hellenic, Arabs think I am Semitic, Americans think I am Australian, and the Brits think I am Irish. Having just read *The Juggler's Children* by that excellent writer Carolyn Abraham–a book about genetic research, the analysis of personal DNA and how modern genealogical research comes together, it would not be surprising if my Russian blood was mixed with more than a few drops from each of the above. Despite all of this I do not have an identity crisis.

When I first arrived in Canada, I bought a wonderful motorbike and with time off from work, travelled the length, breadth and height of this amazing country–which the CBC describes as "from sea to sea to sea," which would be Pacific, Atlantic and Arctic. However, no Harley wannabe-biker culture for me, as I much prefer oriental "rice rockets" with multiple cylinders and as many valves as possible, although I do admit to liking the "*potato potato*" sound coming from the back of a Hog. The beauty of motor-biking across Canada is the potential to sample the often traffic free open road, much as it was in the UK during the fifties, and even though Canada has many growing urban centers, there is still plenty of open road to sample.

In the tourism industry my speciality is product development, but I truly enjoyed studying what the geniuses in other industries have achieved. Consider the amazing results, which the late Steve Jobs delivered to Apple. Consider what Sergey Brin is doing for Google. What Wenger, maker of the Swiss Army brand did for the lowly pocket knife and what Chip Wilson at Lululemon did for dressy yoga apparel, before he alienated part of his customer base. Each of these characters had an original basic vision, but they needed to somehow take those ideas and develop their thinking into products which would be embraced by the consumer and make sales. It is extraordinary that each of them knew that a continuous never-ending development process was the true answer to success and they committed themselves to this unreservedly. In my tourism niche at that time we needed to discover and develop additional unique destinations, while research indicated a trend towards "experiential holidays." That concept advances a more involved insider's look at a destination and in some cases, a hands-on holiday experience. I have always believed a successful holiday includes returning home enriched by the experience, so this fits neatly within my own vision.

Which brings me to Bathurst Inlet.

In business it often makes sense to follow one's passions, mostly because that is where a great deal of creative and analytical thinking takes place, and passions carry masses of energy which is an essential ingredient for any successful business. I have several passions, which sometimes work with and against each other–occasionally with unintended consequences and three of these are–geography, history and Arctic Canada. So on my next holiday cruise I curled up with Franklin's *The Lost Franklin Expedition* and unintentionally became inspired and intensely intrigued with the story of Bathurst Inlet and the fact that the resident Inuit can trace their occupation back 5000 years.

Bathurst Inlet Lodge in Nunavut was the brainchild of Glen and Trish Warner, a visionary husband and wife team who hail from Yellowknife in the Northwest Territories, Canada. Glen's career started as a Canadian Mountie, patrolling his beat by driving dog teams across the tundra from Inuvik at the delta of the Mackenzie River to the village of Coppermine, both coastal communities located on the Beaufort Sea. His experiences form part of the fabric of Canada and his contribution to law, order and respect for the Inuit people is well known. Glen was a man who moved with the times, and after he learned to fly he was replicating his dog-team patrol route by air, soon becoming an accomplished pilot and landing his famous Piper in the most unlikely places. I flew with Glen a number of times in his restored canary-yellow Piper Super Cub, and watching his steady hand on the stick and the calmness of his gaze aimed towards the horizon was an experience to cherish. In those days the world was moving not quite as fast as it does today, but Glen was a visionary and he knew something called "tourism" was pushing closer to the Arctic coast. As he approached retirement from the Royal Canadian Mounted Police, a plan started to form in his mind.

Over the years Glen and Trish developed a warm, deep friendship with a fascinating group of Inuit people living in Bathurst Inlet called The Kingaunmiut, or "People of the Nose,"–who trace their ancestors back 5000 years. What emerged from this friendship was Bathurst Inlet Lodge, a history and nature centre located 30 miles north of the Arctic Circle and a partnership between the Warners, the Kapolak and Akoluk families who were descendents of the Kingaunmiut. It was the first of several tourism enterprises in the NWT inspired by Glen and Trish Warner and their talented offspring. In later years, Glen's family founded Air Tindi and a chain of travel agencies called Top of the World Travel. Glen was also interested in staking mineral claims, and over time he developed what might have remained a hobby into an interesting commercial sideline.

Located at the extreme southern end of an Arctic fjord lies the village of Bathurst Inlet, with homes dotted around the slopes and the steep hills (resembling people of the nose lying recumbent) as a backdrop. For many years, remote Bathurst Inlet boasted a Hudson Bay trading post and a tiny church founded by the Oblate Fathers, a religious order based in Belgium. These two institutions served the immediate region as well as the people at Bathurst Inlet, with the Hudson Bay enterprise buying furs from the hunters and the Oblates ministering to their souls. Bathurst Inlet is a relatively wide fjord that runs 45 kilometres south from the Beaufort Sea on the northern Arctic coast of mainland Canada. Close to the mouth of the inlet at the northernmost tip is the tiny community of Coppermine and to the east, west and north lies the Arctic Ocean and the Northwest Passage that John Franklin sought. Franklin passed through Bathurst Inlet on one of his expeditions and as Glen Warner was interested in history and knew about the lost Franklin expedition, as did the Kingaunmiut–a plan began to formulate that would bring together a confluence of ideas for an entirely new type of tourism.

Franklin's search for the fabled northern route to Asia remains one of the greatest endurance races the world has ever seen. Ships were commandeered from crowded and underworked English dockyards and able-bodied men hired from the Royal Navy and the Merchant marine. A considerable mix of talents would be required for such an undertaking, which ranged from highly skilled Royal Navy captains down to shipwrights, doctors, cooks, historians and coopers skilled in the maintenance of large barrels of food. Finance was raised to underwrite this risky venture, and provisions sufficient for potentially three years stranded in Arctic ice were assembled. The choice of supplies was typical of the day and included ample casks of flour, liquor, wine, chocolate, tea, canned meat, soup, vegetables, tobacco, candles and lemon juice–ascorbic acid, to ward off scurvy. As Franklin provisioned his epic expedition, there was a definite tension attached to this adventure and a significant social prize for discovering the Northwest Passage–even though no one was actually sure it existed. Commercial whalers had been hunting in the Arctic for many years and had extensive knowledge of ice conditions. Perhaps they knew where this route might be found?

Franklin was nothing if not tenacious, participating in several expeditions to the Canadian Arctic. His first seaborne attempt ended abruptly and shortly after it commenced when pack-ice in Spitsbergen blocked further progress. His second attempt was an overland trek from the south end of Hudson Bay, north towards the Coppermine River which ended in disaster with many on his party dying of starvation, with a suspected case of cannibalism. Food was so scarce that the men ate lichen scraped from rocks, eventually boiling their boots to soften the leather before they too were consumed which earned Franklin the nickname of "The man who ate his boots," lending tangible meaning to possessing a thick skin. In 1829 Franklin married the indomitable Jane Griffin, a former friend of his deceased wife and in 1836, King George IV added the prefix "Sir" to Franklin's name, making him a knight of the realm and creating Lady Jane. It was however, the epic struggle of his 1845 expedition to find the North West Passage that catapulted Sir John and Lady Jane into the public domain, capturing imaginations in both England and Canada.

The 1845 expedition was a fine and tragic example of the danger associated with structured hierarchical thinking complete with a few unintended blunders, which is not to cast negative aspersions on the brave men who led and participated in this struggle. These men were a bold cut above the rest when it came to resourcefulness and sheer drive, but it remained to be seen if their colonial attitude and their navy-based discipline and maritime techniques could beat the odds in such a harsh and terrifying environment. At that time, Britain was still dominating the waves with her wooden vessels and ship-building techniques which were unparalleled for strength, efficiency of design, and capability under any conditions and His Majesty's Navy was master of the Seven Seas, which had not been achieved by using sub-standard equipment or untrained men. However, what Franklin faced on the 1845 expedition was an enemy far more subtle and irresistible than any foe which Britain had met at Trafalgar or New Orleans or Waterloo. Franklin was now up against the awesome power of an Arctic winter, which turned oceans into crushing zones of ice and waves into towering, often collapsing mountains, while the bitter cold sapped brave men's spirits and strength as the thermometer plummeted downwards.

British exploration by sea was preceded by Christopher Columbus and Giovanni Caboto (John Cabot), although the Northwest Passage was not identified as the grand prix until sometime later. In the sixteenth and seventeenth centuries it was Henry Hudson, John Davis, Martin Frobisher, and William Baffin who pushed the northern boundaries, giving their names to many of the prominent landmarks which we see on our current maps. In the eighteenth century, the explorers' names changed…to James Cook, Alexander Mackenzie and George Vancouver, enriching the same maps with the Cook Straight, the Mackenzie River and Vancouver Island. However, contemporary reasoning in England was arguing that a Northern Passage might not even exist and scarce resources might better be invested looking for trade routes further south. It took John Barrow, a driven visionary at the Admiralty to reactivate this northern search, unleashing no less than nine capable and immensely powerful explorers on the Arctic challenge. These characters, the Who's Who of nineteenth-century exploration enriched our maps even further, included John Ross, David Buchan, William Edward Parry, Frederick William Beechy, James Clark Ross, George Back, Peter Warren Dease, Thomas Simpson and John Franklin.

On the ill-fated 1845 expedition, the 59-year-old Franklin had two exceptional captains commanding HMS *Erebus* and HMS *Terror*–ships with respective capacities of 340 and 370 tons. Franklin had insisted that their financiers underwrite a first-class list of contemporary equipment, which included several in-period innovative marine inventions. Each ship had a steam engine probably out of an early railway engine, augmenting their sails, permitting them to cruise at seven knots under engine power alone. This engine also generated a central heating system and a water purification plant (early desalination?) for the benefit of the crew. Their naval architect had designed an innovative system that withdrew the ship's vulnerable rudder into its hull when stuck in pack-ice, and the hulls were specially designed and reinforced to withstand crushing by sea ice by sliding upwards as the ice closed around them, rather than trying to withstand the irresistible pressure of deeply frozen water. Their commissary was brimming with vast quantities of canned food for (possibly) three years in the ice and to minister to the crew's intellect, they boarded a well-stocked library, writing materials, and a hand-cranked organ. Historians are grateful that Franklin carried a new piece of apparatus called a camera.

Many of the crew came from Yorkshire, the region of my birth in the north of England, with a few Scots and Irish to round out the gene pool. Making a vessel ready for departure is always a complex process, but Franklin and his two skippers, Fitzjames and Crozier, set about their tasks with efficiency honed by active service in the Royal Navy and by 19 May 1845 they were on their way. Three months later, a good distance north, on 26 July they met up with the *Prince of Wales*, an English whaling schooner and at this point in the expedition Franklin's ships were observed moored alongside an iceberg in Lancaster Sound. Amazingly, this was the very last time that Franklin's expedition was seen by Europeans - but perhaps not by the Inuit and after two years with no word from them, most people back home believed the expedition was lost.

In response to this rumor Lady Jane Franklin mobilized her considerable financial and personal assets, initiated the first of several rescue expeditions and over the following 25 years, this formidable woman along with her financial and political sponsors organized no less than six rescue sorties. What made this continual endurance race possible was the exceptional nature of Lady Franklin's character, her ability to articulate her cause, and her magnetic personality. While in Australia, as wife of the Lieutenant Governor, she had trekked on foot and horseback between Port Phillip and Sydney, calling on minor colonial settlements along the way–which was unusual for a woman at that time and hardly the behaviour of a diplomatic wife. She also possessed a keen intellect, founding several schools, proposed innovative penal reform, even corresponding with Elizabeth Fry about the plight of female convicts, and fearlessly offering her opinions to anyone who would listen. Lady Jane would have been a formidable person in any era, but in nineteenth-century England she was an irresistible force and her ability to raise capital, offering considerable rewards for news of her husband, was one way of keeping Sir John Franklin in England's consciousness. I was fascinated that her heroic organization of these rescue missions was embraced by the Canadian media of the time, and the Toronto Star which in April 1850 offered a reward of £20,000 for assistance in the search and a further £10,000 for news of Franklin. The *Globe* in 1859 commented on the tragedy and the *Illustrated London News* paraphrased their version of events in an October 1859 edition. Eventually Leopold McLintock brought home conclusive news of Franklin's death which was a terrible shock for Lady Jane. At that time she had no reason to suspect it might have been avoidable.

My research trip to Bathurst Inlet left me with many questions. Would it be possible to attract visitors to walk in the footsteps of Franklin? Was there sufficient evidence of his travels through Bathurst Inlet? Could Glen Warner and the Kingaunmiut together package this offering as a unique travel opportunity? Would people pay to travel to remote Bathurst Inlet? How would we get them there and where would they stay? These were questions I had to answer if we were to succeed.

My flight to Bathurst Inlet was not listed on the Toronto airport monitors, nor was it listed at Edmonton's international airport and not even acknowledged at the airport in Yellowknife. Bathurst Inlet may be a speck on the map, it may be where the lost Franklin Expedition passed through while looking for salvation, it may be an exotic destination in a travel brochure to which one could fly, but it did not possess an airport. As Glen's vision for a history and nature center moved closer to becoming a reality, he had to work out how to transport visitors to the lodge and typically, Glen organized that from his base in Yellowknife, originally using a fleet of Canada's legendary Twin Otter planes on floats to land a stone's throw from the village, tying up between two aluminium fishing boats. Another of what I call "Glen Warner stories" happened later in the development process of Bathurst Inlet Lodge when he flew over a lonely, seemingly abandoned bulldozer in a nearby community, and with that discovery came yet another of his brilliant ideas. If they could somehow repair the diesel engine and restore the hydraulics of this earth mover, then drive it oh-so-carefully cross-country in minus 45 degrees after winter freeze-up, across streams and rivers to Bathurst Inlet, they could plow a gravel runway adjacent to the lodge. This suited Glen's fledgling airline, because in the world of Arctic aviation many small aircraft are operated in the summer on floats or wheels and in the winter they are converted to carry large diameter skis. However, during the summer the technique was to fit the aircraft with so-called "tundra tires" which are large diameter balloon-type tyres capable of handling rough runways such as Glen was now building. Today we use a Cessna Caravan Amphibian, which has retractable wheels, making it possible to take off from a hard runway and land on water.

Twenty five people and a great many supplies were heading out to Bathurst Inlet Lodge and I flew in the Twin Otter on floats, while the tundra tire Twin Otter flew in formation alongside. The flight was quite lengthy, about 2.5 hours, so we stocked up with reading and plenty of snacks and were soon dozing as the Otters droned north to the Arctic coast. The Twin Otter is one of Canada's most successful aircraft, originally built by de Havilland Canada and now manufactured by Viking Air in British Colombia. The Twin Otters first flew in 1965 and were an immediate success because of their twin-engine, short take-off and landing (STOL) capability, their nineteen passenger payload and a reputation for being tough and durable. Nowadays the original Twin Otter is being flown in over thirty five countries with over one hundred and twenty ownership firms in every continent on earth. On my overseas research trips I have often flown this amazing little aircraft, and in marginal flying weather often in the third world, the reputation of the Twin Otter has been of great comfort to me.

The approach to Bathurst Inlet by air is dramatic, and on this visit our pilots flew across a high plateau leading to the ocean, reducing altitude after they crossed the ridge, descending to a landing below. This gave me a wonderful perspective of the Inlet and the Arctic Sea ahead of us. One minute we were flying low over the plateau, the next moment the land disappeared beneath us as we crossed the ridge with the lodge several hundred feet beneath. Arrival by air is the only current access to the lodge, although a mining firm was making noises about an all-weather road and although this has been shelved, the rising price of minerals may make it worth resurrecting one day. The land is challenging for anyone who lives here or decides to pay a visit. The harshness of the winter temperatures and the potential to be cut off from the rest of Canada can make it an exercise in arctic sustainability. While the region can be battered by snowstorms, it is the constant wind and the brutal low temperatures that make up this challenge.

After our plane landed on floats and taxied to the fishing pontoon, I wandered over to watch the tundra tire Otter land on the hard gravel runway. The pilot touched down as early as possible because the strip was relatively short and in no time he was on the ground, pedaling back to the lodge's waiting ATV. This was a dramatic moment for me, standing on the same earth where Sir John Franklin walked and I was less than our hundred feet from the same inlet where his crew members sculled their boats and explored.

Bathurst Inlet Lodge is not a lodge in the traditional sense of a main accommodation building, with dining room, lounge and bar–in fact there are no bars in Bathurst Inlet, which long ago voted to be a dry community. Sadly alcohol has been a tragic element in the life of many indigenous communities, and in voting this out of their lives the elders of Bathurst have made a courageous and sensible decision. The accommodations consist of several modest wood chalets with tiny compact rooms, and the distinctive red and white decommissioned Oblate church, which had been converted into a four-bedroom facility. The Hudson Bay trading post now serves as the dining room and lounge where everything of importance happens, from lectures and Inuit drumming to crafting demonstrations and discussions about the next day's program.

This was an Inuit host community of smiling children, working parents, and dignified elders who were looking after us during our stay in their village. The respect that guests and hosts offered each other provided an instant atmosphere of trust, friendliness and anticipation, and before long Inuit hosts and guests were chatting away discussing inevitable questions such as; what are the winters like? (brutal), where do the kids go to school? (Coppermine) and how do they feel about the rest of Canada? (belonging–but cut off from mainstream life). And there was plenty of anticipation amongst the guests, most of whom had traveled considerable distances to relive history and walk in the footsteps of the Lost Franklin Expedition. One young Scotsman was definitely the exception. His connection was not to Franklin. It was to the Hudson Bay Company (HBC), the oldest trading entity in North America, having received its charter as far back as 1670. In those days the HBC was virtually a government unto itself, owning vast tracts of land and holding trading rights on even larger tracts. Originally a fur trading enterprise, HBC at one time owned over 15 percent of the North American continent, eventually becoming the dominant land owner in "the Overseas Dominion of Canada." When fur trading declined, the HBC strategically moved into general merchant commerce, establishing Hudson Bay trading posts in the most unlikely locations, including Bathurst Inlet. As the HBC expanded, so did their requirements for educated, capable post managers, whereupon the term "Hudson Bay factor" was coined for the position of manager/trader/administrator and money handler. It was a role the Scots seemed to fulfill with considerable flourish and legendary skill.

This young Scotsman was here because his uncle had been the last HBC factor in charge of the Bathurst Inlet trading post, and his mission was to discover how his uncle disappeared thirty years before, when a powerful snowstorm hit the community, causing havoc and several deaths. One evening, he showed me the photograph taken of his uncle in front of the trading post and as I wandered off to bed, the nephew was wandering through the undergrowth holding up his grainy image against the lodge, trying to match the picture in his hand with the juxtaposition of the dining room and the background hills. Next morning I discovered that this was his third visit to the lodge. Bathurst Inlet is surrounded by hills which are covered in short grass with a peat-type surface that gives softly as you stroll across it. It is like one massive continuous meadow with bold outcrops of rocky ridges, which resemble foothills leading to the mountains. Nearby Wilberforce Falls are deeper than Niagara Falls and cascade out of a cleft in the rocks, creating a fine cooling mist of spray if the wind is in your face. Paige Burt's Husky trotted alongside us as we completed one of these day-long walks with canine sized picnic supply panniers hanging on either side of his considerable body. What I loved most about these Tundra walks were the giant Inukshuks, the herds of Musk Oxen and the occasional pack of shy lone Wolves skulking within earshot of our group.

Paige Burt was educated in the United States, currently lives in Rankin Inlet and authored *Barrenland Beauties*, a definitive catalogue of Arctic plant life found in the region around Bathurst inlet. Paige was able to bring alive the extraordinary natural history at Bathurst and we spent many happy hours together traipsing over the tundra with her fabulous husky trotting alongside. Often we elected to make ten hour hikes along the ridge behind the lodge to Wilberforce Falls and on several occasions we were trailed by ghost-like wolf packs which silently reversed down the ridge when we approached them. It was an extraordinary feeling to hike along ridges where possibly no other human foot had previously trodden, past the ancient Inukshuks where the Kingaunmiut herded muskoxen several hundred years ago.

The Inukshuks resemble giant human figures, arms outstretched sideways with palms pointed upwards exclaiming "did I not tell you how grand this land is"?–as they marched along the valleys towards the horizon. The Inuit built these giant stone statuettes to help with herding the Musk Oxen and Arctic deer along specific hunting corridors so they could pick them off in the chosen killing field. Inukshuks also performed another function, acting as Arctic signposts to assist the Inuit to navigate this challenging landscape–especially in winter when the visibility was marginal at best. Occasionally we encountered a herd of 30-40 large heavy breathing Musk Oxen that immediately and almost automatically created a defensive circle with the larger bulls facing outward, their massive horns inclined towards the sky and their cows and calves located towards the center. This land is utterly magnificent with what can best be described as a "big sky" tapering down towards the ocean. The silence is exceptional to the point where it almost becomes audible and can be mistaken for a combination of wind whistling through the short grass and the occasional gust as it accelerates down from the slopes from above. Looking up towards the clouds can bring you rapidly back into the 21st Century, gazing at the contrails of large passenger jets blasting their way across the Polar route from Europe to Asia or to the west Coast of North America.

The Warners and their Inuit partners had built a huge pontoon boat to facilitate excursions on Bathurst inlet and I was anxious to see how it handled. Over an entire season this industrious family had flown in component parts of the pontoons strapped to the floats of their Twin Otters stowing various sections of the boat into any available corner of the fuselage with some components even slung between the floats.

Eventually they had sufficient parts to build this wonderful excursion platform powered by two 100 HP outboards and it looked like a capable machine. The crowning glory was "the Blue Loo," Glen's very creative onboard toilet, complete with a cut-out harvest moon, painted in a delicate robin egg blue. Being in the Arctic our daily program was weather dependent so each evening we met in the Hudson Bay Post lounge to discuss the options. Glen had provided two specialist guides to enhance our stay at the inlet, to assist the Franklin buffs understand the complexities of his expedition and to interpret the amazing wildlife in this brief Arctic summer.

Our other resident expert was Jack Sperry, the retired Anglican Bishop of the Arctic and author of *Igloo Dwellers Were My Church*. Bishop Sperry was a Leicestershire-man who became a missionary and in 1950, started working with his own dog team, travelling 3,000 miles each year visiting his parishioners along the Arctic coast. He translated the St. James Bible into Inuktitut and his life in Canada was devoted to the well-being of the Inuit people. Jack knew a great deal about Franklin's first exploration of this area between 1819 and 1822 and it was on this epic visit that John Franklin, John Richardson and their party of twenty two men mapped the Coppermine River and Arctic coast as far as the Kent Peninsula which included Bathurst Inlet.

Our daylight excursions on the forty foot "Blue Loo" with Glen, Trish, Jack and Paige in the twenty four hours of daylight were unforgettable. Temperatures hovered generally in the 60 degrees Fahrenheit range, and on some days zoomed up towards just over 80 degrees, which was hard to imagine being forty five kilometres north of the Arctic Circle! On these sorties we packed a considerable amount of food and some building material for a temporary shelter in case of an enforced overnight stay. The plan was to replicate the journey of a European explorer along the inlet, occasionally beaching the boat, hiking ashore and making a meal as Franklin might have done in the 19th century. In fact, we encountered several campsites used by the 1819-22 expedition, keeping a reverential distance from the 19th century mechanical artifacts lying intact in the tent circles. Relics such as these do not easily deteriorate in the bone chilling cold of the Arctic winter and with no one to plunder them, they rest there to this day.

I had been lucky to obtain a copy of John Franklin's 1819-1822 expedition diaries and could easily visualize myself in the boat alongside his men, as they sculled down the inlet, not knowing what they would encounter. Franklin wrote,

Franklin:
"We were somewhat consoled for the loss of time in exploring this inlet by the success of Junius in killing a Musk-ox, the first we had seen on this coast; and afterwards by the acquisition of the flesh of a bear that was shot as we were returning up the

eastern side in the evening. The latter proved to be a female, in very excellent condition; and our Canadian Voyageurs, whose appetite for fat meat is insatiable, were delighted. On the 6th we were detained in the encampment by stormy weather until five pm (remember the twenty four hours of daylight) when we embarked and paddled along the northern shore of the inlet. The weather still continuing foggy but the wind was moderate. Observing on the beach a she bear with three young ones, we landed a party to attack them; but being approached without due caution, they took the alarm and **scaled a precipitous rocky hill with a rapidity that baffled all pursuit.**"

I hope you are as charmed as I am by the in-period description and the use of language, particularly of the bears that "scaled a precipitous rocky hill with a rapidity that baffled all pursuit."

Franklin was an excellent planner, and accompanying *Erebus* and *Terror* was a supply ship with a hold full of live oxen which were to be gradually slaughtered for fresh meat when the ships reached Greenland, at which point they bid goodbye to their English colleagues who carried letters written by crew members to family back home. Sometime later, the expedition met an English whaling ship and exchanged intelligence about ice conditions, and this was the last time the expedition was seen by European eyes. As history records, Franklin chose the wrong route, heading straight into immense walls of pack-ice that encased both *Erebus* and *Terror* for two long terrifying years. At one point, Franklin dispatched an overland party, reasoning they had a fair chance of survival if they made it to the mainland and trekked due south. Sadly, their training which was orientated toward survival at sea, their lack of Arctic knowledge and the prejudice of their superior naval experience conspired against them, and remains of their small boat and equipment are still being discovered. Roald Amundsen, the great Norwegian explorer was far more cerebral in his approach to Arctic exploration, taking an alternative, less ice-choked route, wearing clothing inspired by the Inuit and as a consequence, he was the first European to cross the Northwest Passage and survive.

That evening in Bathurst Inlet Lodge, a lively discussion focused on possible reasons for Franklin's failure to complete his mission. Was he an incompetent leader, so hidebound by British naval tradition that he was unable to innovate and cope with local conditions? Was the expedition's ice-planning based on faulty data, and were the leaders unaware that entire tribes of Inuit were easily surviving close by in the same climatic conditions? Into these twenty questions, catapulted the extraordinary 21st century research completed by forensic anthropologist and pathologist Owen Beattie and the investigative reporter John Geiger, who together solved an important element in this mystery.

It will be helpful if we reflect that England in the mid-1800s was a country in considerable transition and equally considerable contrasts. We have only to read Charles Dickens (1812-70) to get a sense of the grinding poverty of those living "downstairs," while the Bronte sisters, writing in a similar period, (1816-55) described an altogether more genteel lifestyle. At the time when Dickens, the Bronte sisters, Elizabeth Browning, Thomas Hardy, Rudyard Kipling and Robert Louis Stevenson were flexing their pens, England was also a hotbed of technical innovation. To understand how this impacted Franklin, we need to focus on Cornwall in Southern England where new tin mining technology was emerging.

In filling his ship's commissary with the best supplies that money could buy, Franklin realized the practicality of what we now call canned food and how more efficient this was compared to wooden casks filled with meat pickled in brine to keep it edible, or vegetables soaked in vinegar to keep them from rotting–both methods being efficient but rendered the food appalling. The tin mines of Cornwall produced excellent quality metal that could be thinly cast and bent into what we now know as cans. The process was perfected in 1811 and instantly adopted by the navy for use on its ships. Once formed, the cans were filled and sealed with solder which in the mid-1800s with its 90 percent lead content, was slowly poisoning Franklin's men, gradually lowering their ability to perform under stress, with *deadly* consequences.

Canadians Owen Beattie and John Geiger were to unravel several parts of this mystery through a combination of excellent science and dogged research, and as Beattie had worked on forensic cases for the Royal Canadian Mounted Police, he was the right scientist in the right place at the right time. However, before their fieldwork in the High Arctic could start, they had to navigate through layers of government bureaucracy, which at times was as impenetrable as the ice fields that Franklin faced. To make this trip, the two forensic explorers used the same Twin Otters that flew us safely to Bathurst Inlet, although their route took them much further north to the High Arctic archipelago of King William Island, Devon Island, Erebus Bay, and finally Beechy Island. Their search was for the gravesites of expedition members to exhume whatever they could find, complete a field autopsy and then let science take over.

The researchers soon discovered the forlorn graves of Franklin's men, and while colleagues stood by with loaded rifles to scare off inquisitive polar bears, the forensic team eventually and tenderly exhumed several bodies. The wonderful book *Frozen in Time* and a video by the same publisher, tells the amazing story of this pathology expedition which by pure luck indicated the stunning news that that a previous similar expedition had also been examining these crew members bodies! Once carefully exhumed and with an equally careful plan of how they would restore the gravesite to its original status, they opened the coffin containing the body of able seaman John Torrington, who died January 1st, 1846, at twenty years of age. A true defining moment for Beattie and Geiger. Months later, after exhaustive testing and much heated debate, conclusive evidence pointed directly towards the devastating effects of lead poisoning, and it seemed that contemporary technology to preserve food was inhibiting their ability to survive. For Franklin's explorers to cope with the debilitating winter climate and extreme ice conditions was challenging enough, but to battle those conditions while being poisoned by lead and rotten food was more than anyone could overcome. When the pathologists eventually took on-site X-rays and saw the body of John Torrington, it was apparent that an earlier and unrecorded expedition had performed a similar investigative sortie. Who this was, and when it took place is still an unresolved mystery.

We had traveled from many corners of the old British Empire to be part of this exceptional glimpse into the life of Sir John Franklin and Lady Jane, and to walk in the footsteps of his lost expedition. Along this personal journey we became familiar with the grass, the earth and the water where Franklin and his crew had sculled their boats and landed for an English tea break, and we had truly walked in the footsteps of these brave and condemned explorers. We had identified the location where the bears "took the alarm and scaled a precipitous rocky hill with a rapidity that baffled all pursuit." We gratefully basked in the unparalleled knowledge of Paige Burt and Bishop John Sperry. We made friends with our Inuit hosts in Bathurst Inlet, and none of this would have been possible without visionaries Glen and Trish Warner to whom I will always be grateful.

Folk song *"Lord Franklin,"* embraced by Lady Jane Franklin:

In Baffin's Bay where the whale-fish blow
The fate of Franklin no man may know
The fate of Franklin no tongue can tell
Lord Franklin along with his sailors do dwell

And now my burden it gives me pain
For my long lost Franklin I'd cross the main
Ten Thousand Pounds I would freely give
To say on earth that my Franklin lives

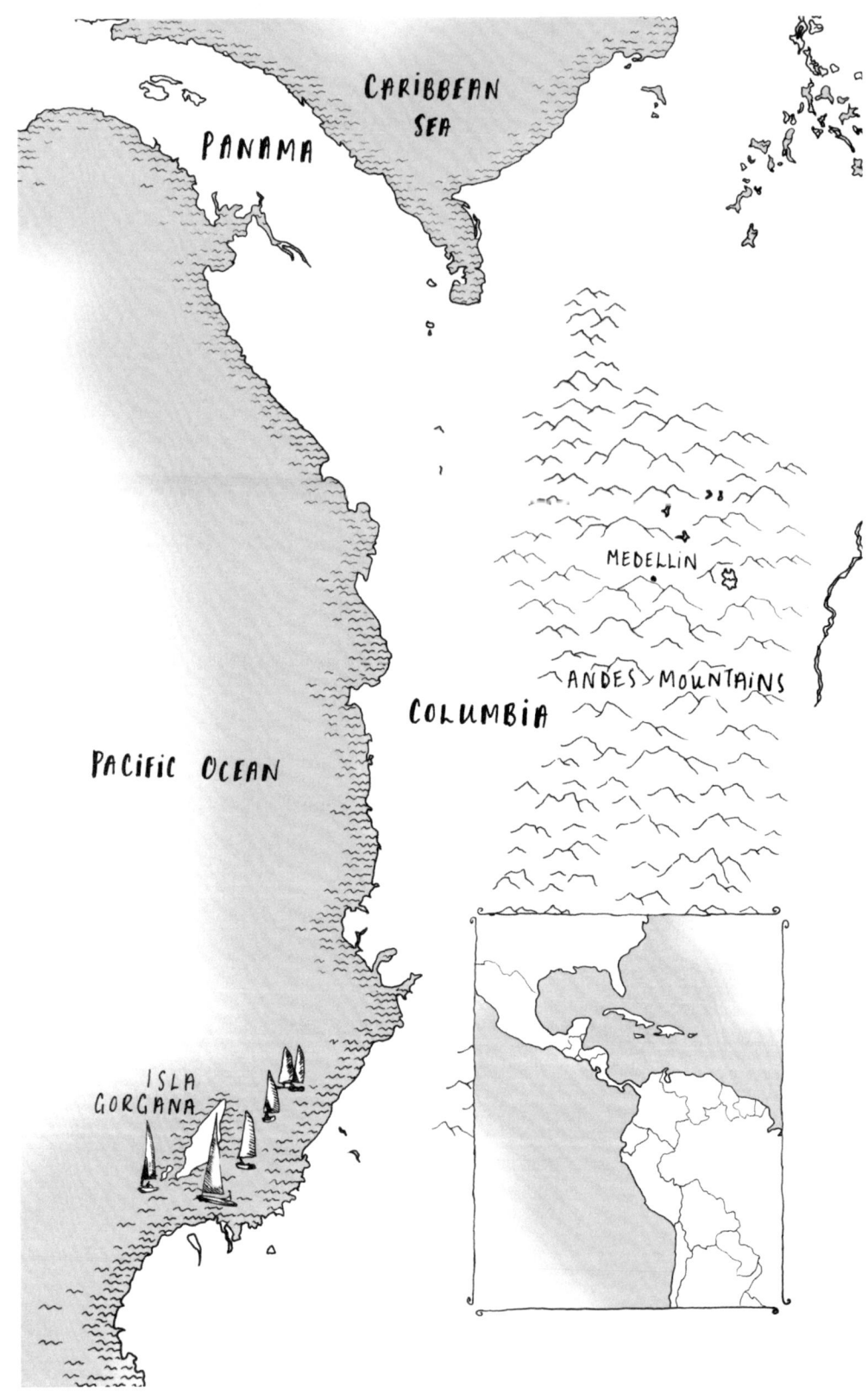

CHAPTER 7

Expedition Cruise Planning– Cuban Mig Fighter Pilot– Penal Colony

Our client with the expedition cruise ship was contemplating a circumnavigation of South America and as I had been spending considerable time developing land routes on this pear- shaped continent we were tasked with the job. In terms of market positioning, their ship was placed mid-way between mainstream cruising and expeditionary cruising, so planning with a foot in each segment was complex and at times counter-intuitive. On the one hand there was the need to plan for wealthy mature clients with limited physical mobility, and on the other hand the demand for experiential shore-visits was compelling, but these requirements did not always work well together and occasionally conflicted. Taking these polarized planning requirements into consideration I wanted to avoid a series of unintended consequences while guests were ashore in these chaotic and complex countries. The firm's initial plan was to cruise the ship across the South Atlantic to the northern tip of South America, visit some of the lesser-known Caribbean islands such as Saba, Les Saintes, Virgin Gorda and perhaps Andros, then circumnavigate Cuba and cruise through the Panama Canal and south down the Pacific coast of South America.

At first Cuba may seem like a curious addition to this cruise itinerary, but in many respects it makes perfect sense, particularly when you look closely at this huge island and what it has to offer. Supporting its natural beauty and intense culture, Cuba has no less than seven UNESCO World Heritage sites inscribed on the United Nations list, plus another two sites recognized for their natural significance. Cuba is therefore worthy of an extended visit if only to collect these cultural trophies, however the island is much more than a compressed UNESCO heritage site. It has to be said that Cuba excels in many other fields, and one wonders what this country will achieve when the repressiveness of the Castro regime is relaxed and the US embargo is lifted. I particularly love the complex Latin music which comes out of Cuba and the group "Buena Vista Social Club" is as good as it gets as the charming film of their Dutch tour amply demonstrates. Under the Castro regime these aging troubadours became destitute working at menial jobs to make ends meet–their considerable talent submerged under the cloud of an oppressive regime until American guitarist Ry Cooder invested in their genius and shared them with the world. Cuba also excels in sports, pharmaceutical production, ballet, medical sciences, and scrumptious Coppelia Ice Cream, named after the ballet which is so popular on this island. Cuba has a feel of the Fifties, and at times it just seems that the passing of time has stalled in Havana and we are inside a historical movie set.

With its natural beauty augmenting its splendid UNESCO World Heritage sites, Cuba is therefore an attractive cruise destination, and before long we were roaming the island looking for shore excursions that would work for the ship and its guests. In this situation it's not always possible to meet someone from the diplomatic corps and solicit advice, mainly because they are attending to the affairs of state with more important issues to resolve than meeting a visiting cruise planner. However, Cuba was different, and the ambassador was not only available, he was attractive, charming, and disarmingly open about local conditions. He was also much younger than my television image of what ambassadors look like, casually dressed and relaxed–a rare public servant any country could be proud of. The meeting was duly arranged, tea was the better option, and at the appointed hour we walked up to his residence and knocked on the door.

Cuba has a considerable number of magnificent buildings–indeed, the architecture of Cuba is a compelling reason to visit this island with exterior stonemasonry and woodwork that has been intricately crafted by skilled workers into a blend of disciplined Spanish colonial coupled with Caribbean informality. Most of the better known cities in Cuba have their share of architectural gems but Havana's are particularly interesting both in the center and in the suburbs. The ambassador's residence was a magnificent former tree lined suburban home, and walking through the gates I felt I was about to meet the Great Gatsby or Ernest Hemingway in person.

In fairness to the plenipotentiary I'm not free to tell you exactly what we discussed, but suffice it to say that His Excellency's views were startlingly candid and, with the benefit of hindsight they were deadly accurate. He succinctly analyzed the state of the nation, told some wonderful stories about Fidel Castro, and was helpful and practical with his commercial advice. If you have never read Graham Greene's *Our Man in Havana,* I would urge you to enjoy this short, implausible novel of a vacuum cleaner salesman sent out from the UK to assume an absurd role in Cuba. His Excellency was far more accomplished and quite unlike any of these characters in this tale, but given his generous nature I regret not pulling his leg about his place in Greene's novel. While I was in Havana the first Russian warship for many years was visiting, offering tours for local residents and the line snaked almost round the harbour with Cubans who remembered their old Soviet friends. Later that day we met several of the jolly officers in their outsize caps, out on the town for a sailor's day ashore, laughingly fortified by Cuban rum.

Animating guests' time ashore is one of the many challenges which cruise planners face and depending on the cruise line the quality and nature of the shore excursions can vary greatly, with some high-end firms including shore visits in their tariff. Mid-level lines tend to offer them as optional extras, charging a reasonable amount and expecting to make a profit while the lower-cost discount cruise lines depend on shore excursion sales (amongst other sales) to contribute badly needed revenue. One additional challenge for cruise planners is to discover something the competition has not yet stumbled upon, which is increasingly difficult, as island vendors offer the same menu to everyone. Our quest in Cuba was to be creative while staying within the bounds of affordability.

The other side of animating an enrichment cruise is to offer compelling on-board events and this firm was known for the quality of its guest speakers– but due to the restrictive nature of Cuba, discovering and facilitating an onboard guest speaker was going to be challenging. Listening in an intimate setting to someone you have always admired and having access to them afterwards for a question-and-answer session or perhaps even dining with them can be a powerful selling point for any cruise. Think about someone you would like to cruise with and perhaps encounter on deck while at sea, and you will understand how enticing this can be. But the challenge in this controlled society was locating interesting characters who would be allowed to come aboard while the ship was in port and talk about their speciality–even explain what has made them famous.

The Cuban fighter pilot was introduced to me by a mutual friend. The two had known each other since primary school and although they pursued separate careers, their friendship endured over many troubled years. To place this in perspective, let me take you back to a period between the late Sixties and the Eighties when a nasty proxy war was being waged between South Africa and Angola. On one side the Republic of South Africa, which in those days embraced the policy of apartheid; on the other the South West Africa People's party or SWAPO and its allies, which meant Cuba and Russia. Cuban involvement in this African war still has deep roots in Cuban society, and it's possible to meet a considerable number of elderly Cubans who served as combat troops in the jungles of South West Africa. By 1957 there were an astonishing twenty five thousand Cubans in this conflict, and as recently as 1988, Cubans still had "skin in the game."

I would describe this as a proxy war because Cuba was essentially backed by Soviet Russia, and the RSA was covertly backed by the West. It was also a highly complex war of multiple so-called "liberation" movements, often with competing and confusing agendas. The Russians encouraged the Cubans to join the fight, reasoning that

Castro was obligated by years of receiving above market price for Cuban sugar and he could be persuaded to take up arms. Over the many years of this commercial friendship many Cubans were educated in Moscow and were indoctrinated into the soviet way of thinking, so in 1961 when Castro embraced "the revolution" and when the Soviets came calling, Castro said yes. Russian thinking was quite shrewd on this issue reasoning that the Cubans were used to tropical weather and were (still are) a community of really tough hombres, so who better to carry this war to the South Africans? The South Africans can also be really tough hombres, and the region of South West Africa experienced some dreadful atrocities as each side lost ground and then paid back in-kind to reverse last week's losses. And as always, the indigenous population were being kicked around by both sides–for joining the opposition–for not joining the opposition–for letting the opposition pass through their villages–for not letting the opposition pass through their villages–or for just being in the path of whomever was coming through.

As the war raged on, the Cubans imported a squadron of advanced Mig 23s and in 1988 they bombed the South African Hydro Project, destroying it in a single run, killing a dozen South African troops, but shortly afterwards, one of the MIGs was brought down by a shoulder-fired missile. My new contact was one of those MIG 23 fighter pilots, and had an exceptional story to tell if we could only get him onboard for a lecture. However to gauge the veracity of his stories I first needed to know more about his aviation exploits, so we met for a quiet dinner in old Havana to chat through his life story. Like many fighter pilots, he was interested in the technology of his trade and spoke knowledgably about the obsolete and underperforming South African Air Force Mirage F1-CZs and F1-AZs, which they were flying against and their ability to out-maneuver their opponents.

I was surprised by the quality of this old Cuban attack pilot's English and by his quiet, almost delicate mannerisms as we eyed each other across the table and ordered drinks. As we chatted about tourism in Cuba, he immediately picked up on my accent and astonished me by enquiring which part of the north of England I came from? How on earth could this former Cuban Air Force pilot pick out my well-hidden regional accent when I had been away from the UK for at least forty years? The answer of course was that our mutual contact knew quite a bit about my background and had probably passed along some details of who I was, so without spoiling the game of acquired personal intelligence, I played along and acknowledged my roots. However, the surprises were not over, and when I asked what he thought about modern fighters, he launched into a critical and informed analysis of current American F16 and F18 equipment and in the process discovering that we shared considerable admiration for the amazing A-10 Thunderbolt, aptly named "The Warthog." What really impressed me was his intimate knowledge of aerial fighting tactics and the process the Brits called "Viffing."

In the Falklands War, the subsonic relatively slow flying RAF Harrier fighters were challenged by the French-built lethal Exocet Missile-equipped Étendard fighters which the Argentine Air Force was flying against them. Argentina had about 220 aircraft in its inventory, but as a result of the crippling embargo during the brutal military regime, many were non-operational. To casual observers, this slow British fighter was something of an enigma in a world of hyper performing jets, but the RAF pilots trained hard on these highly technical aircraft and were ready for the faster French machines with an unusual aerial combat technique. From start-up, the Harriers were able to take off vertically, a bit like a helicopter and when they were at a suitable height, they just altered the direction of their jet engines which then flew them forward like a conventional fighter. This technique enabled them to take off from aircraft carriers or battlefields or even football fields if necessary, but this was not what destroyed the Argentine Air Force. It was how they used their "slow-down" technique while flying at high speed that really counted.

Visualize the RAF Harrier pilot blasting across the sky, scoping out the Argentine coastline when his wingman alerts him that a faster Argentine fighter is on his tail and closing fast. The RAF jockey has to instantly calculate how close he will allow the Argentine flyer to come before he executes the evasive technique called "Viffing." He must instantly juggle a series of inputs and make a series of instant calculations–with life or death as the payout. He has to calculate the closing speed of the Argentine flyer, the exact distance between them *right now*, the point at which Argentine flyer will open fire with his conventional gun–or the point where he will place a missile up the Harrier's tail.

At his chosen instant, the RAF pilot 1) rotates the flow of his jet engines from full forward to full reverse, 2) deploys the flaps, 3) drops the landing gear, and 4) immediately pulls back on his stick. The combination of these four simultaneous deployments places a huge strain on the airframe of his aircraft, but it dramatically slows the Harrier, pitching it upwards about a hundred feet, forcing the faster Argentine fighter to pass below and ahead–whereupon the RAF pilot having a clear view of his adversary then shoots him down. Our Cuban fighter pilot viewed this technique as simple, crude, mind-blowing, typically RAF (his words) and devastatingly effective. What blew my mind was how up to date this retired Cuban pilot was, but there was a sad ending to his career. In recent years my new acquaintance was retired out of the Cuban air force and reduced to guarding a building at night to augment his modest military pension.

Digression–holiday in Cuba

I recently decided to plan what we hoped would be an interesting self-drive holiday so we rented a Spanish made Seat minivan and based our accommodation on the Cuban home-stay program, which use the newly minted system of *"Casa Particulares,"* the government-approved B&Bs located in every major centre. The driving was excellent, even if Cuban xenophobia means that around Havana, road signs are few and far between and road maps were out of scale when it comes to distance and place locations. I experienced this in the Soviet Union, when a river boat skipper showed me how publically sold marine charts and road maps had been altered to fool the potential invading force. Of course, with modern GPS-based navigation systems and aerial photography, this tactic is totally obsolete and their xenophobia slightly misplaced.

Cuba is quite large as island countries go–almost two-thirds the length of the UK, with an unusually large number of airports and rural roads, but the infrastructure is in bad shape, particularly in terms of sewage, water supply, electrical supply, public transport, roads and crumbling buildings–mostly evident in Havana. The Cuban propaganda machine is very active and blames the United States for just about anything that goes wrong–but most locals just laugh at this because those who understand what is happening know it is the failed communist system that has caused most of their problems.

Cuba is a paradox and in spite of its deplorable political system, in many sectors Cuba punches well above its weight including a first-class medical service accessible to everyone and a thriving pharmaceutical industry. The education system is well developed, and although Cuba ranks 134th in GDP, it ranks 11th in Olympic medals! Cuba offers modest freedom to its citizens and a gloomy failed economy but compared with many places on earth, Cubans have peace, security, and a roof over their heads, full stomachs, medical care and education. Hopefully freedom will follow.

Havana is gorgeous, and during the 1950s when these buildings were new it must have been stunning. Old Havana (Habana Viejo) where most of the restoration money has been deployed draws a huge number of visitors and the buildings are only one of the reasons. However, as you wander towards the perimeter of the central zone, you will see the rows of crumbling structures and realize just how widespread the infrastructure deficit really is.

I love political history and for me Cuba was a living laboratory and absolutely fascinating and after wandering around as a silent observer I came home with a great admiration for how Cubans survive under the inefficiencies and unfairness of communism. For all of Castro's original vision of overthrowing a brutal and anti-democratic dictatorship (which he did) and for all his bleating about egalitarianism and emancipation for the people (which he did not), he ended up taking the wrong fork in the road and waltzed his people down fifty years of failed governance in the shape of a communist dictatorship.

In today's Cuba, the stratification of Cuban society is already taking place even as Castro's communism rules. Many Cubans are driving their own cars (indicated by yellow plates), dressed to the nines and involved in all types of revenue-generating enterprises. The recent expanded access and selection of consumer goods have made cell phones and PCs available to the proletariat, and the licensing of three thousand *Casa Particulares* is part of a changing economy. At the time of this visit, Cubans were searching for any way possible to get hold of CUCs (tourist convertible currency) by participating in the tourist enterprises we have mentioned. But they also hustle for tips, sell their participation in your digital pictures–and sadly some even beg.

However the Cuba which emerges after the regime of the mercurial and somewhat devious Fidel Castro and his crushingly boring brother Raul might not be what we imagine. Surrounding Fidel and Raul are many elite ruling-class-Cubans who cherish their positions of privilege along with their consumer goods, their relative freedom, their travel abroad and I doubt that these members of this class will be interested in seeing much of that change. But if change is inevitable, they might just have a role in shaping what this looks like. Will a post-Castro Cuba adopt the hybrid Chinese model of governance-control with a free economy, or will it develop into its own model as a 21st century state?

Back to my research trip:

Having completed the Cuba segment of this research trip I happily engaged this accomplished Cuban aviator for a series of lectures and then flew Copa Airlines to Panama to enjoy a tax-free layover before connecting to Cartagena in Colombia. I have always loved this magnificent walled city. The standard of restoration is stunning, and the cobbled stones of the ancient streets are so clean one could almost use them as barbecue coals. We needed to meet our agent from Venezuela who had flown to Cartagena for a sensitive discussion about taking the ship up the Orinoco River, while considering the bellicose anti-western comments coming from President Hugo Chavez. At this time many business people in Venezuela were under considerable stress as Chavez moved closer towards nationalizing commerce, and our friends were increasingly concerned for their business and their children's future. More recently, Chavez has nationalized several international oil companies, so their fears were well founded and what the future will bring now that the general has died remains to be seen.

Cartagena is dominated by a large fort cleverly constructed around a complex defense architecture which incorporates several ingenious booby traps. When our guide started talking about that "international bandit Sir Francis Drake," I was stunned to hear this heresy because Sir Francis was the hero of every English schoolboy, so what was he talking about? Mind you, history is dependent on who is telling the story and as truth is the first casualty of war so while SFD might be a hero to English schoolboys, for the residents of Cartagena he was a marauding bandit–which is curious to contemplate. Developing plans to cruise down the Pacific coastline of South America for a small shallow-draft vessel was an exciting proposition because the increasingly larger cruise ships are becoming destinations unto themselves, and monster ships carrying five thousand passengers plus another two thousand crew have few ports they can enter. This leaves many interesting smaller ports free for shallow-draft vessels and makes time ashore less stressful when the ratio of visitors to locals is in harmonic balance. Few things are less enjoyable than strolling off one's cruise ship to become part of a large conga line snaking through a charming historic district.

The Pacific coastal ports of South America offer some wonderful opportunities for inland touring, but the port of Buenaventura in Colombia had become quite rough and touring was deemed to be dangerous. For many years Colombia had been plagued with violent factions that can be divided into two basic camps. These are the FARC (Revolutionary Armed Forces of Colombia) terrorist movement which operates with a violent strain of Marxist philosophy, and the drug barons' brand of violence which is particularly nasty. This is similar to Islamist terrorism, where the line between religious fervor and banditry has become blurred, as it was in Colombia where the line was also becoming blurred between Marxism and drug-related brutality. Because of this, many areas in the hinterland were now off-limits and in most urban centers government troops were on the streets, guarding prominent buildings and ensuring the safety of its citizens. Distasteful though it is, troops on the streets are the lesser of two evils and I can assure you that the cost to society of preventing a kidnapping is far less than the cost of a rescue operation.

One high profile abduction and rescue was that of Ingrid Betancourt, the French born member of the Colombian government who was kidnapped in 2002 and incarcerated until 2008. There have been multiple analyses probing the background of that remarkable rescue operation, and there is some opinion that a splinter group of the FARC allowed the Colombian forces (with help from outside intelligence) to rescue Betancourt and fourteen other hostages. I have friends in Cartagena whose colleague was kidnapped several years ago by the FARC and the unfortunate victim was missing for several years with absolutely no contact or indication that he was alive. Then one day he was spotted strolling along the ocean front in Cartagena, abruptly freed by the FARC for reasons that were never entirely clear.

We were not keen to assume any risks with the passengers, and the insurers of the ship might have objected to a port visit in Buenaventura so we now had a planning issue, which was to locate an interesting port of call on the Colombian coast to break up the cruise journey between Panama and Ecuador. I always travel with a tiny powerful GPS loaded with a set of world maps, and sitting in Panama Airport, it was evident that a solution might be open to us–if I could somehow cross the Colombian mainland and travel down to the Pacific coast to take a first hand look. As a land route to this region was marginal because of the unrest we decided to use an interesting option. Satena, a regional airline run by the Colombian Air Force had been established to service some of the under-developed regions of Colombia and not only was Satena the only game in town, it was the only safe way of traveling to Guapi, where my adventure would begin. The high-wing thirty three seat, turbo-prop Dornier 328 which Satena operate is an excellent tough short-field aircraft and the ideal transport for this region. During these troubled times in Colombia one could really appreciate the challenge of aviation security and I must compliment the Colombian Air Force for their excellent flying and for looking after me while I was in their care. Lending an aura of gravitas to this atmosphere, I watched the security personnel on the tarmac being screened by an even higher level of security before they were allowed to work around the aircraft.

On arrival there was virtually no transport from this third-world airport into the nearby town of Guapi, but as everyone seemed to be riding on the pillion of someone's motorbike that seemed like the thing to do. My suitcase was safely tucked into my hotel lockup back in Cartagena, and all that I needed was in my well worn number-3-size backpack and my newly acquired duty-free cameras. Fortunately I had the benefit of an excellent local organization and as we bounced our way into Guapi my handlers sandwiched me between two other motor bikes, but it was not clear if this was my close protection unit or just staff. The focus of this trip was to somehow visit a Colombian island known as Isla Gorgona, a curious place which my GPS chart plotter had identified while I was in Panama. The basic idea was to determine if we could safely bring in the ship for a unique visit to this overgrown tropical mountainous island, but from what little I could determine, there were no ports, no marinas, and no landing stage. However my GPS plotter did indicate deep water close to the shoreline, which lent confidence that our plan might work.

Guapi is a fascinating place but definitely not on the tourist beat and definitely not the place for gentle travelers. The town looks like a rough frontier movie set, with about sixteen thousand inhabitants who seem to be constantly on the move. Located on the steep banks of the Guapi river four miles from the Pacific ocean, it serves as the mercantile center for a huge region of dense jungle and countless almost inaccessible villages. The river is tidal with the intertidal zone measuring about thirty feet, so the river-front market borders a long set of stone steps which vaguely resemble the terraces of an Incan pyramid–enabling small boats to tie up no matter the height of the water.

Guapi had apparently contracted lottery fever, and every other storefront seemed to be a lottery outlet cum-money transfer business– which is not a bad combination if you think about it. What I had not seen before was the sale of "fractional" lottery tickets, enabling even poor people to purchase a fraction of a single ticket and perhaps their key to freedom. Walking the streets of Guapi, looking slightly out of place, but indulging my interest in photography took me into many nooks and crannies. As this was rural jungle Colombia, security was top of mind for me, and even though the police had a significant presence on main street I would not have given them much chance in a straight fight against members of the ruthless FARC.

Because there was no regular service my plan was to get a decent night's sleep and early next morning walk the waterfront to rent a boat for the trip out to Isla Gorgona. To do this I had to somehow acquire a boat, stuff it full of fuel and food, and set off for the island. Strolling along the waterfront, I watched villagers emerging from the jungle on the opposite bank, paddling their dugout canoes into the main channel. The market was in full swing, and the faces of the punters varied from pure African to blond Russians who were working in the nearby gold-mine. I finally arrived at a factory that was turning out really tough looking fiberglass open boats. The builder had glassed in several six-inch ribs, and the gunwales and bows were curved outward with quite high freeboard, which might be useful in a Pacific swell. The transom was extra thick, so if I could rent a large outboard motor the bolts holding it to the boat would have a good chunk of Fiberglass to bite through.

After several false starts I located a suitable twenty two footer, and while I would have preferred my own boat, *The Full Monty*[1] for this Pacific journey, waterfront beggars such as I had little choice. In no time flat we closed the deal, but renting the boat and an older 140hp Yamaha outboard was only the first step. We needed a hundred gallons of gas, five liters of oil, two spare tanks, and a substantial supply of food, as we really didn't know long the round-trip journey would take. My GPS chart plotter indicated a distance of forty five nautical miles one way, virtually due west with a forecasted beam sea running from north to south and a constantly changing sea-state, so we needed to budget for a slow, steady passage rather than fast and direct. This was fun though, and reminded me of the many years boating in the Great Lakes, along the Rideau Canal from Kingston to Ottawa and along the Erie Canal down to New York. I began boating as a sailor and then migrated to "stink pots," as my diesel cruisers are referred to by the sailing community. In this little Colombian twenty two footer, we'd be replicating what I have done over many seasons of happy boating in Canada. The only difference was that we were heading out into the Pacific, looking for a miniscule island in a tiny open boat–something I would never contemplate on Lake Ontario.

Bearing in mind that Colombia, along with its neighbours, has a long history in the illegal drug trade, I was thinking carefully about how to cope with a chance encounter even though our little ship despite its load of supplies moved along quite smartly with the 140hp Yamaha mounted on the transom. The local drug runners generally use 20hp outboards on their supply boats (which service their offshore freighters) and these we could easily outrun, but I was more concerned about their fast boats, which typically use engine combinations totaling 500hp. And there might be an issue if we had to put into a village for repairs. Our handlers were aware of these problems, so after dinner we decided to rent a brace of shotguns along with one hundred rounds of ammunition which openly demonstrated that we were fully armed and prepared to use them. We eventually carried three shotguns down to the boat, stashing them in waterproof bags for the run down to the coast.

Early next morning, we set off from Guapi's waterfront and motored west down the estuary towards the Pacific Ocean. The jungle on each side was incredibly lush, with many dugouts sliding out from tiny feeder streams which presumably led to several inland villages. We paused for a few minutes, loaded some shells in the shotguns, and fired off a few practice shots. We didn't actually need the practice, but needed to let any of the minor drug runners know that we were armed and to keep their distance. Once around the bend from Guapi, there was a complete lack of habitation and I marveled at the magnificent tropical landscape and how verdant this part of Colombia is. My traveling companions from the ship's agency were in a cheerful mood. We had just eaten a country breakfast and quaffed several cups of excellent Colombian coffee, so the company was relaxed and the speed of the boat cooled the air as we headed due west looking for Isla Gorgona.

Many tropical islands have a halo of cloud above their peaks, caused by evaporating moisture from the vegetation below and I hoped Isla Gorgona might be the same, because I thought it might serve as a navigation aid, indicating we were on the right track. I knew the island's central peak was about eleven hundred feet above sea level, and considering our speed on the GPS, I calculated that we should see the peak in about an hour. We sped westward in the long Pacific swells, the Yamaha roaring over the transom and occasionally showing its age by developing an intermittent miss that instantly cleared. The weather was superb, with no sign of the north-south swells the coast guard had predicted, and it felt good to be alive on the Pacific Ocean, a well-founded boat under our soles, with plenty of supplies, and a warm breeze in our faces.

Confounding its well-founded appearance, the Yamaha coughed and then cleared, but then it repeated the cough and misfired several times and we swayed gently forward in harmonic unison as the boat slowed and the Yamaha spluttered to a halt–leaving us dead in the water. This was not the most hospitable section of ocean in which to lose power and the GPS told me that we had covered 33 percent over the ground, meaning Isla Gorgona was still thirty nautical miles ahead, but as I have repaired many outboards over the years, and as we packed a repair kit and some tools, this seemed like an interesting diversion. After all, given the way the Yamaha spluttered, the issue was likely fuel related which turned out to be the case. Once I had the carburetor dismantled and gave it a good cleaning, using the same gasket to reassemble it, the thought crossed my mind that our fuel might be contaminated and we might be in for a series of breakdowns between here and the island. If only I had Full Monty's fuel filter with me–but who packs a monster like that in their luggage? However once I had restarted the engine, we motored flat out in dead calm water and right on cue the cloud-halo of Isla Gorgona came up due west of our position and soon after, the dark high peak that dominates the village appeared and we knew that were there.

The remote and virtually unknown Isla Gorgona is nine kilometers long and about two and a half kilometers wide. There are several disconnected cays to the north of the island and an extraordinary large mid-ocean rock formation to the south resembling a lady's high-heeled shoe (Cuban heel?). Isla Gorgona sees few visitors, and in the habitual silence of this region, visitors are always announced by the roar of an outboard engine as they approach the island. There is no indigenous human population on Gorgona but temporary residents crowded the waterfront and fifteen pairs of hands lifted us and our boat clean out of the Pacific and onto the steep pebble beach.

When I first saw Isla Gorgona on my GPS chart plotter back in Panama, something rang a bell in the hard drive of my mind. It might be a remote Pacific island, but the name was more reminiscent of Greek mythology and I recollected Gorgon who was a terrifying figure with a horrific face and a head full of snakes. What on earth was I coming to? But Isla Gorgona looked beautiful and in some respects stereotypical of Pacific Islands depicted in movies and travel brochures. Lush jungles climbing a steep mountainside, blue water crashing on all sides of the island and the climate was warm, heavy and tropical. But something was missing; there are no beaches anywhere on the island. Instead it is ringed with steep pebbled slopes and sharp rocks that would tear the sturdiest ship apart. However, the two thousand feet bay fronting the modest village was gently curved, and just two hundred feet offshore we recorded six hundred feet of water which is ideal for anchoring our little cruise ship

Isla Gorgona was being studied by a group of scientists for its unique animal and plant life, so these studious types were visiting in shifts, which gave me an opportunity to quiz them. Although this is a nature based paradise, Isla Gorgona was notorious for its secret role as a former penal colony. The island's role as a jail started in 1958 and it was eventually able to accommodate fifteen hundred prisoners, who were transported from the mainland in the stinking cargo holds of freighters. This overgrown Pacific rock was teeming with wildlife, mostly aggressive monkeys and lending credence to its Greek name, a great variety of snakes. To even contemplate escaping from the penitentiary on Isla Gorgona, with its immensely powerful ocean currents, shark-infested waters, poisonous snakes in the nearby jungle and inhospitable coastline, was to contemplate suicide.

The Isla Gorgona penal facility was eerily similar to the French penal colony on an island in French Guiana, depicted in the movie *Papillon*. This movie stars two of my favorite actors, Steve McQueen, in the role of Henri Charrière and Dustin Hoffman, who plays his sidekick Louis Dega. The movie is about the exploits of Charrière (the eponymous Papillon) and Dega, who are forced labourers and multiple escapees. Papillon like so many of McQueen's characters, is an irascible counter-culturist and his ability to plan escapes while under huge mental and physical pressure makes for exciting entertainment. The overt plot of racism and the complex relationship between the two main characters weaves a fascinating story. For movie enthusiasts this is vintage Steve McQueen with Hoffman playing the perfect foil.

In the late nineteenth century, another famous resident incarcerated on Devil's Island was Alfred Dreyfus whose trial and ordeal commenced in 1894 and continued until its conclusion in 1906. The so called Dreyfus Affair rocked France when this young French artillery officer was wrongly accused of treason–France at that time was rampantly anti-semitic and although Dreyfus was exonerated when the real culprit was discovered, he spent five terrifying years in this French Guiana jail. What catalyzed the defense was the famous open letter penned by Emile Zola, titled "J'accuse." Other supporters of Dreyfus included Anatole France and George Clemenceau, who pressured the French to reopen the case and eventually find Dreyfus innocent.

The similarities between these two prison environments are striking, however, one Columbian prisoner Daniel Camargo Barbosa did escape from Isla Gorgona. He was a serial murderer of young women across Colombia and after his successful escape he continued his rampage in nearby Ecuador. Consider for a moment what Barbosa had to overcome to make his getaway. He had to secretly construct a primitive boat that was to some degree ocean worthy. He had to somehow study the ocean currents in camera so he knew where they might take him. He had to secretly plot a marine route to account for the vicious Pacific drift. In total secrecy he needed to cache sufficient food and possibly camouflaged civilian clothing for his arrival on the mainland and above all, he needed critical lead-time to make his escape before the guards noticed his absence. Barbosa correctly surmised that the guards would focus their search on the island, not for one moment considering he would choose the ocean as his escape route and once their land-based search was concluded, they assumed he had been eaten by sharks marauding close to the island. That misconception bought him some time and allowed him to put distance between his tiny boat and his prison. Making his way to Guayaquil in Ecuador, the psychopath returned to his former crimes and soon the police were looking for an entire gang, believing no single person could be responsible for such a monstrous crime wave. Barbosa was eventually arrested in Quito, Ecuador where a medical expert concluded that he was exceptionally intelligent, surprisingly well read, and totally without remorse.

The prison must have been a dreadful place for anyone to be incarcerated and in its current decaying state it looked even more foreboding than some of the archival pictures I have seen. When it was operating there was severe discipline imposed by the authorities and prisoners were compelled to do all of the manual work including upkeep of the infrastructure and maintenance of the farm. The sleeping blocks resembled the wooden tiered bunks we have seen in the concentration camps of Belsen and Dachau, with razor wire separating rows of bunks to maintain order. The washing facilities were crude, open air circular cast-stone shallow baths resembling animal troughs and the punishment block was as severe as one can imagine. In 40°C and high Pacific island humidity, offending prisoners were stuffed into cells one meter wide for weeks on end, compelling them to stand with no possibility of sitting or leaning more than 5 degrees from vertical. Daily life must have been dreadful for the prisoners and with sadistic guards on hand to regularly administer torture it must have been hell on earth.

The jungle is now reclaiming the prison as steel-grey sinuous branches creep out from adjacent trees, embracing the walls and crushing them inward. Several aggressive troops of monkeys have claimed the prison as their walled city, and we were closely followed by furry sentries each time I walked through the gates. The monkeys kept their distance, but with gangs of fifty sizable simians with razor-sharp teeth shadowing us, we would have been foolish to go in alone and unarmed. During our stay on Isla Gorgona, I witnessed several gang fights between these troops, and it was abundantly clear this was their turf and not ours. Back at the administration building, we wandered through the small museum offering testimony to the thousands of criminals sent to this foreboding place. Late that afternoon I was able to borrow a Wifi connection and using Skype, connected with my family back home–sharing this extraordinary island with its extraordinary history.

I used my last day on Isla Gorgona to catch up on my notes and stroll around playing beachcomber. I spied a small residence with an outsize dive flag painted on the wall, indicating that this might be a dive center, and the grizzled Mexican-American fellow squatting outside was the man in charge. Eric had been on Isla Gorgona for years and ran the leanest dive business imaginable. He had a few customers on a good year, which merely generated sufficient money to buy food and supplies but hardly enough to make this Colombian Crusoe a wealthy man. He was welcoming and entertaining and told me about the wonderful aquatic life surrounding the island, describing large pods of humpback whales which regularly cruise the coast.

Eric also told me an interesting tale about a secluded bay along Colombia's Pacific coast. Before the Japanese attack on Pearl Harbour, the country was quite friendly to the Axis powers and turned a blind eye to German naval activity along the coast. While Eric was hosting a recent dive group, they put into a small cove along the mainland looking for fresh water. The bay was small, the shoreline overgrown with mangrove-type plants floating on the water, blocking access to the beach. Launching their Zodiac, they poled ashore to find themselves facing a twenty-foot-high earth Berm, fifty meters square. The Berm was protecting hundreds of World War II style jerry cans with German naval markings. Eric surmised this might have been a resupply base for a German patrol boat and possibly a key-hole hiding place for one of their U-boats.

No cruise ship had ever called on Isla Gorgona and it was not the place for a large capacity vessel, but for a petite, one hundred-passenger ship, it was an ideal place to visit due to the uniqueness of its remote location, its extraordinary prison legacy and the bragging rights for the few people will ever get there. The local coast guard officer discussed how best to bring guests ashore and it was evident that the shale beach would have badly damaged the hulls of the ship's lifeboat-tenders, so I asked if it would be possible to engage some of the workers and build an outsize raft which the tenders could moor against. The raft would be positioned twenty feet from shore and then gently pulled onto the beach, whereupon the guests could step ashore across a gangplank. This was an entirely practical solution to the deep water rough beach landing, and the cost of labour was negligible.

At the conclusion of my work on Isla Gorgona this mission was completed and our return to the mainland was uneventful, the Yamaha outboard performing reliably and rarely missed a beat. The visit to the island was memorable for any number of reasons, but sadly the bankers holding the mortgage on this wonderful expedition ship decided to call the loan just as the recession was biting into their revenue. The ship is still in the water but was converted to an oligarch's private yacht with no mortgage to worry about. What has remained is the vivid memory of this hell on earth for the prisoners who perished there, the extraordinary indigenous wildlife, the power of the inhospitable jungle and the close-yet-remoteness from mainland Colombia.

---

[1] The Full Monty was my original New Brunswick designed Trawler which would have been infinitely more capable of making this short Pacific journey.

CHAPTER 8

Belize and Guatemala- one of the best cruises I have ever taken

On a lazy summer evening at Toronto's Highland Yacht Club, I was sitting on the aft deck of my Trawler, listening to a fellow mariner talk about a hidden river in Central America. Though the river was well identified on marine charts, an optical illusion made it difficult to spot from out at sea, and the approach was protected by a shallow sandbar with only about five feet of water at high tide. The river was the Rio Dulce in Guatemala, and the more I heard, the more I became intrigued. Most of us have heard of the Amazon, the Orinoco, perhaps even the Irrawaddy, and closer to home, the mighty St Lawrence, but the Rio Dulce ("sweet river" in English) was new to my ears. *Rio Dulce ...Rio Dulce* I found myself repeating like a catchy tune. I was unable to get the name out of my head.

Imagine you are a mile offshore drifting along slowly, paralleling the Guatemala coastline. What you see are endless small hills leading your eyes skyward towards the distant mountains. Every hill is covered in dark green foliage, and as you glide by at three knots, they merge into one another and into the mountains beyond. It is difficult to determine exactly where one hill starts and the next one ends and just as difficult to compare the shoreline to what's on the marine chart. The Rio Dulce lies in a pass between two of these foothills, and a competent navigator has to place faith in both the GPS and the charts to make an informed decision about when to turn in. At about five hundred meters, with a decent pair of binoculars, it's possible to identify the town of Livingston north of the river mouth. And by carefully observing the shading between the hills, you can just pick out the Rio Dulce flowing between the trees.

Like most travel researchers, I have several paths to tread before turning in my passport, and cruising on my own boat into a seductive Caribbean sunset is one of them and like many wannabe long-distance mariners, I often dream of heading south from the Florida Cays to anchor in the turquoise shallows of a Central American harbour. Part of the dream is to taste the saltiness of the breeze each day on my lips, to smell the micro-particles of island earth carried out to sea on the wind, and not least–to escape the Canadian winter. Several times I have almost been there on my boat *The Full Monty*, but for one reason or other I was unable to untie the lines–and quite frankly, keeping the dream alive is becoming harder by the day. I find myself cruising vicariously through other mariners' experiences as several boating friends have figured out how to achieve their ocean freedom, and their electronic dispatches have nourished my Sinbad-the-Sailor ambitions and kept me happy.

I have read in some wired magazines that the future will bring travel "without ever leaving home" which I find absurd, despite some amazing technology. I believe they are indulging in wishful, fanciful thinking and fooling themselves. Until they can teleport a human, I will remain a firm disbeliever and don't look forward to being proven otherwise.

If I am unable to bring *The Full Monty* down from Canada to Belize and Guatemala, to slip into the protected water of a barrier reef and anchor in the shallows adjacent to an uninhabited island, the next best thing is to travel on a shallow-draft cruise ship, which has some unique features enabling it to explore where no other ships dare venture. So when the opportunity came up to sample the culturally orientated Central America itinerary offered by Blount Small Ship Cruises, I was particularly interested–because in my line of business, it's advantageous to be ahead of the trend and from time to time look with fresh eyes at an established destination. To suggest that anywhere on earth has recently been "discovered" would be disrespectful to the many indigenous people whose presence predates modern concepts of commercial tourism. I have no intention of falling into this trap–but with the rise of cultural tourism and a far more inquisitive traveling community, many destinations are worth reviewing through a slightly different lens.

Expedition cruising in an unusual custom built mini-ship

Each January, Blount Small Ship Cruises take the *Grand Caribe* down to Belize and Guatemala with an itinerary that includes the Rio Dulce and an entire list of tiny ports and superb cays. Many of these islands and the Rio Dulce itself are what is referred to as the "Yachtsman's Paradise" and the only other way to visit these locations is on your own sailboat or yacht. The main challenge being the shallowness of the cays, and access to the Rio Dulce can only be guaranteed on a vessel with shallow draft.[1]

Belize City

The cruise starts in Belize City, accessible to much of eastern North America with a same-day connection. After a comfy flight from Toronto to Miami, we connected for an equally comfy two-and-a-half hour flight to Belize City where BSSA were waiting with transport to the ship. Belize is a tiny country with merely three hundred and fifty thousand inhabitants, seventy thousand of them living in Belize City and their national population is just three times the size of small-town Kingston where I live. Belize was formerly called British Honduras before gaining its independence in 1977 and as part of the deal the Brits committed a partial squadron of their famous Harrier Jump jets to protect the country's sovereignty. To impress upon their unruly neighbours that it might not be in their interest to encroach on this unprotected nation, several fully armed RAF Harriers fly low and slow along the border each day. This strategy has apparently worked, and

Belize's borders have been relatively calm, allowing Belizeans to get on with life and build their country.

Belize City is not particularly attractive, but we used sea kayaks for a wonderful paddle from the ship's aft end garage, through the working harbour and into the Belize River. This interesting two hundred and forty kilometer long waterway is navigable up to the border with Guatemala, running along the northern edge of the Maya Mountains and being the dominant waterway in this region of Central America, it continues to support a great deal of commerce. My buddies Bruce and Kelly O'Hare and I explored the small fishing fleet moored adjacent to the harbour, peeping into the tiny cat boats rafted against larger schooners, their crews madly unloading the catch from the previous night's fishing. As we paddled under the town bridges, a few young characters were aiming rocks at our tail-end Charlie (me) as we glided by. I had been warned by our crew about this possible exchange, and a few well aimed blasts from my ultra powerful slingshot had them gaping in amazement and running for cover.

An extraordinary river race called "La Ruta Maya Belize River Challenge" runs along this perilous route, west to east along the Macal and Belize river systems. In former times these rivers were the historic link between lovely San Ignacio on the slopes of the Maya Mountains and the Caribbean Sea, via the port in Belize City. The race is run annually, canoes departing San Ignacio about March 4th, arriving in Belize City several days later. The first day consists of forty six miles paddling the Macal and Belize river systems through fast challenging water. The second day is an even more challenging sixty mile paddle to an unlikely named "Double Head Cabbage." Next is the relatively short thirty six mile section with another type of water, this time deep and fast flowing. Last day is mercifully the shortest with twenty five miles of fast paddling–terminating at the Belcan Bridge finish line in Belize City. What makes it interesting is the variety of race classes, designed to be inclusive rather than elite. It is a serious race, though, and each year competitive spirits turn up from all over the world to do battle for honours and cash prizes.

It is surprising what one can see at the rear of some buildings which also happens when traveling by train in Europe and by canal boat in Russia. Similar to other riverfront towns, as much happens behind the buildings in Belize City as on the main street, and paddling slowly upstream we were able to enjoy a slice of mercantile life in this bifurcated city. Paddling along at one point I experienced one of those "déjà-vu" moments and later learned that *The Dogs of War* starring Christopher Walken and *The Mosquito Coast* with Harrison Ford were both filmed here. Returning to the harbour, we found the fishing fleet becoming rapidly animated as buyers arrived and bargaining was in full swing. The crews were equally animated and reacted with friendly greetings as our paddling trio pulled alongside and peered into their holds.

The Belize Cays is typical Robinson Crusoe country, and the Barrier Reef that embraces most of them offers two hundred and ninety kilometres of island seclusion in the most picturesque setting imaginable. The reef has been a UNESCO World Heritage Site since 1966 and is the longest natural heritage site in the Western Hemisphere. For administrative and marketing reasons, the sixty cays are divided into regions–the Ambergris Group, the Central Group, the Southern Group, the Turneffe Islands, Lighthouse Reef, and Glover's Reef. The island names seem to be straight out of *The Pirates of the Caribbean*– Ambergris Caye, Mosquito Cay, Cayo Rosario, Hick's Cayes, Coffee Cay, North Drowned Cay, Gallows Point Reef.[2]

Navigating through the Belize Cays was a significant challenge for the *Grand Caribe*'s skippers, even with years of experience under their keel, they were happy to have a pilot for some of the more intricate sections. Running between cays and being exposed to a beam sea can be daunting for any ship, and our itinerary was always subject to weather and local conditions. Visitors come to the Belize Cays for a variety of experiences in settings ranging from luxury resorts to fully catered tented camp-colonies and in some cases private cottages. We were able to visit the privately owned Southwater Cay and made several bow landings in Glover's Reef Lagoon and the mainland village of Placencia . We also landed at Lime Cay, the small mainland city of Punta Gorda, and Livingston, a pretty water-locked village guarding the entrance to the Rio Dulce. On the journey home we visited West Snake Cay and Goff Cay at the edge of the Belize Barrier Reef.

On a typical bow landing *Grand Caribe* is made ready by the crew as guests wait excitedly to go ashore. Fleet Captain Dave Sylvaria who hails from Brooklyn, is in command, while invisible crew members inside the bow prepare for the landing. On the foredeck, first mate Tim manages the anchor winch, doubling as the surface-spotter for Captain Dave on the bridge twenty feet above. Working as a team, they select the exact location where the ship's bow will nose onto the sand, whereupon assistant Peter will let go the forward anchors. While this is happening, another crew is readying two aft anchors, which will be lowered twenty seconds before *Grand Caribe* becomes amphibian. If they get this right, the bow will be resting gently on the white sand beach, while the rest of the ship, about one hundred and eighty feet, will be floating in the lagoon with two anchors at each end, holding her steady. The ship secured, the magic bow platform can be lowered and Luther's true genius demonstrated. Almost noiselessly, the bow section of *Grand Caribe* opens like the famous "gaping mouth" of a Ford Edsel grill, three sections unfolding into the shallows ahead. Guests walk off onto the beach, and another halcyon day in the Belize Cays unfolds.

One of my passions is ocean kayaking, and although I don't often get to indulge, one reason I opted for cruising with BSSA was their fleet of high quality kayaks. Before we made any landings, we were busy in the ship's garage readying the kayak fleet for a day on the water, and being able to bow-land *Grand Caribe* on these cays was a great convenience. Bruce and Kelly were capable kayakers, and along with several other cockle-shell heroes, we were ready for anything the ocean would conjure up for us. However, as long-distance kayaking is serious business, it requires careful preparation and several precautions, all oriented towards personal safety as well as the safety of the fleet.

Digressing with memories of British Columbia

My most memorable ocean kayak expedition was paddling down the coast of British Columbia, threading between Gulf Islands and camping above the intertidal zone on cliff tops and secluded beaches.

This was an exceptional experience and one which I would heartily recommend. The trick on the BC coast is to paddle *with* the tide rather than against it, so reading tidal tables is a required skill. Each kayak carried food and fresh water, carefully distributed among paddlers so that a single lost kit wouldn't turn us into starving castaways. We carried several waterproof GPS units, an old-fashioned compass, VHF radios, and the best life jackets and kayak skirts we could buy. I believe we were well prepared, but the challenge turned out to be a serious lack of personal judgment that nearly cost two people their lives.

The BC coast has a fleet of tankers moving to and fro in the shipping lanes about five miles out to sea. Their wake is considerable, but at that distance did not pose any threat to our kayaks. The trick is to watch for the rolling bow-wave ten minutes *after* the tanker goes by and then turn to face it and bob over like a cork. The Inuit are masters at this and have been handling their kayaks in challenging Arctic water for ages so once we acquired this skill, the next challenge was learning to sail the kayak. Paddling, while gentle and rhythmic, can become tiring after a while, and flying a pocket-sail was an intriguing proposition, after all if the wind was blowing where we wanted to go, then why not take advantage of it and harness nature?

You can't sail a kayak directly into the wind, nor can you sail it close to the wind, in fact the only safe way you can sail a kayak is with the wind more or less behind you. Once the tiny aluminum fishing-rod of a mast was assembled and slotted into the foredeck, we pulled out our triangular sail made of parachute silk, and attached the upper edge to the mast. There was no structured boom, so we simply held onto each lower edge and stretched out our arms until the silk caught the wind and propelled us forward. It's exhilarating to experience how fast a kayak can sail downwind, however, two of our fleet colleagues failed to realize the impact this tiny patch of silk would have on their kayak, particularly when they got sideways to the wind. Predictably their kayak rolled and threw this tandem pair into the cool water of the Georgia Strait.

Fortunately several of the fleet saw this happen, rapidly dropped sail and paddled over to assist with the rescue. By the time we reached them, the tandem paddlers were cooling rapidly, and while they were not yet hypothermic, they were weakening and unable to right their kayak, let alone climb back in. Fortunately we were not far from shore, perhaps two kilometers out, so we assembled four of the remaining kayaks into a square, lashing them together to form a stable platform. Within this protective zone it was possible to drag the victims onto a foredeck, stabilize their mood, bail out their boat, and slip them back into their kayak. That evening beside a huge beach bonfire and after an overly large dinner, we quietly went over what had happened. There was no drama, no tears, no recriminations, but a wiser and more capable fleet headed out next morning for another ten days of adventure.

Kayaking in the Cays

Cruising on the *Grand Caribe* we were determined to get in as much kayaking as possible, but the limiting factor was the number of beginners. We agreed that it might be elitist to paddle off on our own, and it was safer and more collegial if we formed part of the day-fleet. This did not overly restrict us, but another time we might have approached it differently. Occasionally we launched off the beach, but using the aft garage on *Grand Caribe* was a distinct luxury, with the added advantage of eliminating annoying beach sand from under the saddle. With the rudder pedals and the seats properly adjusted, we waited off to the side while the rest of the fleet kitted up. Suitably equipped with protective headgear, long-sleeve shirts, plenty of water, and snacks, my camera encased in a Pelican box and the portable VHF in its pouch, we paddled off into the distance and went exploring. Our headgear, with fabric over the neck to prevent heat stroke, resembled the *kepis* made famous by Beau Geste, the film about the French Foreign Legion. Apparently these worked well in the Sahara, and they work just as well in the Cays.

Circumnavigating the cays and exploring tiny communities by kayak was great fun, partially because one could paddle up on someone fishing off the dock before they knew we were there. Often when kayaking I remember that wonderful film *The Cockle-Shell Heroes*, about a group of British Seaborne Commandos during World War II who made a daring (for some, suicidal) canoe-based raid on Bordeaux

Harbour to sink several German warships. Silent paddling can also be used to stalk birds and animals on photographic expeditions, and I've enjoyed paddling close to a loon back home.

Coming into Glover's on the *Grand Caribe*, we noticed some distance away a large motor-yacht motionless in the water. I had the binoculars on it for some time before I realized it was high and perhaps not quite so dry on a reef, royally stuck. I recognized the profile of this yacht as a contemporary design, which indicated it must be a recent accident–something we later confirmed with the Belize Coast Guard.

This magnificent motor-yacht was over sixty feet in length, three decks in total, with possibly four cabins and a large fore-deck crane for launching its tender. Two weeks earlier, it had been heading towards the open sea when it went hard aground at full speed. I am not given to speculation, but acquiring the best navigation aids that money could buy would be a fraction of the cost of that yacht, which points to incompetency, faulty systems or both, we decided to paddle over for a close-up look. Kayaking in the open ocean inside a reef is a wonderful experience, and once we had balanced the double-bladed paddles, we settled into a comfy long distance rhythm. Most modern kayaks are either rudder equipped or come with a small dagger-skeg located part way down the side deck. I much prefer the rudder equipped models which I find more restful over any type of distance.

Occasionally we glided through a series of long gentle swells that I would estimate at about eight feet high and perhaps a hundred feet across. This gave the impression of paddling up an incline and surfing gently down the far side. Our modest fleet of six kayaks was spread across two hundred feet of deep blue ocean, occasionally two paddling side by side for a chat as we closed the distance between ourselves and the stricken yacht. From a few feet away, it was apparent how serious the damage was and with a ripped open hull, it seemed fatal. With a million-dollar yacht out here on the reef, in ultra-shallow waters, how could a salvage tug and barge operate with safety?

The movement of the ocean was taking a continual toll on the fiberglass, as the yacht lifted gently with each successive wave, the hull groaning in agony each time it fell back across on the razor sharp coral and I fear it will slip into deep water once the damage is more advanced. Bruce, who is an experienced mariner, paddled around to the far side of the reef and confirmed the damage was fatal. The water around the Belize Cays is squeaky clean, and the thought of how much fuel must be on board started to trouble us. If a salvage tug was unable to rescue the structure, how could a fuel barge ever extract diesel from those tanks? Given the size of the vessel, I estimated they had a carrying capacity of at least a thousand gallons. Knowing how a diesel slick extends on the water after a few drops hit the surface, I shuddered to think what a thousand gallons would do.

We then made another of those amazing bow landings on the mainland in Placencia, one of the southern resort communities in Belize which is colourful and small enough for day visitors to easily feel at home. The low-rise homes and local stores are painted in pastels with tiny gardens surrounded by white picket fences. Visitors to the nearby resort come for water-related activities including diving, sailing, fishing, river running and a visit to the Cockscomb wildlife sanctuary. The sanctuary is of particular interest because this one hundred and twenty eight thousand acre reserve hosts all five of the reclusive Belizian wildcats, including Jaguar, Jaguarundi, Puma, Margay and the magnificent Ocelot. This barefoot resort town is populated by an amazing salad of ethnic communities which includes Latinos, Garifunas, Creoles, Maya, East Indian, Chinese, and Mennonites–a veritable melting pot.

Mennonites in Belize

Central America has a sizable Mennonite population, and nowhere is this more evident than in Belize, where in 2008 they numbered more than twelve thousand. This distinct ethnic community emerged in northern Europe during the latter part of the sixteenth century, and for a time they were horribly persecuted for their beliefs. Many migrated to the United States and Canada in the eighteenth and nineteenth centuries and in the late 1950s a migration protocol was signed whereupon three and a half thousand Mennonite families relocated from Canada via Mexico to Belize. The agreement allowed them to pursue their religion, enjoy specific taxation policies, farm within closed boundaries, and be exempt from military service. In return, this highly industrious community has made a significant contribution to the Belize economy, and they are now part of its human landscape. They speak an amalgamated language that has origins in Germany and the Netherlands, besides speaking English (and some Spanish) and they continue to keep their mother tongue alive. Mennonites generally preserve their traditional mode of dress and use horse-drawn transportation. Passing a Mennonite farm with their fair-haired workers, one could imagine this is rural southern Germany on a bright summer's day.

At last–the Rio Dulce

As *Grand Caribe* crawled down the Guatemala coastline starting the approach to the Rio Dulce, most guests were on deck to absorb the scenery and experience crossing the infamous sandbar. Many long-distance sailors make a visit to this extraordinary river, but the larger boats with extended keels have difficulty sliding over the bar even at high tide. *Grand Caribe* has ample power to push herself across, even if she bounces a couple of times, and it is not unknown for her to tow several marooned sailboats across as a favour.

We were spending the night at anchor off the town of Livingston, and after the hook went down we were into the tender and off to explore. Livingston, which has no road access and must be reached by boat, is the heartland of the Garifuna people, who are descended from a mixture of escaped slaves and southern Maya. Our tender approached the town dock and was secured between a fleet of gaily painted, canopy-covered river boats. The town is surrounded by lush vegetation which is comprised of coffee plantations, coconut groves, and untamed jungle. The main street slopes directly upwards from the quay, arrow-straight for three hundred meters, bifurcating the town into two symmetrical halves. This thoroughfare was a hive of activity, teeming with visitors, locals, vendors and cruise guests from a large ship anchored six miles out in the deeper water of the Caribbean. The economy of Livingston comes mainly from its fishing fleet and coffee plantations. The town is a riot of colour and there was a definite vibrancy in the air, a mixture of commerce and the music of strolling troubadours.

Without diminishing our rich experiences in the Cays, the highlight of this voyage was the Rio Dulce. Early next morning, Captain David Sylvaria was strolling along the upper deck. Kelly was upside-down, balancing on her head, feet pointed towards heaven in one of her yoga postures, and Bruce and I were fortified with mugs of steaming Guatemalan Java. Everyone was gazing ahead of the ship, but instead of the magnificent Rio Dulce, we were staring at a wall of thick white fog. We knew the Rio was directly ahead because we'd left it there the night before, and rivers don't disappear without a thunderclap from heaven. This was a far less heavenly happening–nature repeating what it has done for thousands of years. Until the fog burned off the crew would be polishing the brass, we were fiddling with our cameras, and Captain David was his patient self.

Shortly after we boarded *Grand Caribe*, BSSA rolled out a secret weapon–the on-board camera mentor. BSSA shrewdly discovered that many guests with digital cameras fail to set them up properly when new, and although they are able to take reasonable digital images, the cameras are working well below their capabilities. With the help of "Clicky" (as we called him), this was rapidly remedied, so while we were impatiently waiting for the fog to lift, Clicky patrolled the deck, advising on settings, angles, and apertures .

The Rio Dulce, apart from being a world on its own, is contained entirely within Guatemala and has become a sought-after trophy for long-distance sailors. This waterway system includes Lake Izabal which covers five hundred and ninety square kilometres and the slender El Golfete, ten kilometres long and merely two kilometres across. The combined waterway offers a fascinating variety of experiences, from dramatic jungle gorges and large open Lake Izabal, to narrow tributaries where the ship's tender is the only way to go exploring. There are four other elements to this marvelous destination: the petite Castillo de San Felipe, the developing resorts and marinas, the Pan American Highway, and Casa Guatemala, but one could easily spend an entire vacation enjoying this river system, which for me was the jewel in the crown.

Impatience pays off and by 07:30 the fog started to burn away, so Captain Dave moved his controls to "slow ahead" and *Grand Caribe* slid into the main channel. The riverbank just past Livingston was full of small residences and scores of tiny shrimp boats, some taken over by families of pelicans, others partially submerged, some having seen better days, but still working. The shrimpers hunt mostly at night, and the previous evening we were surrounded by the lantern-illuminated fleet as it made its way out to sea. Most shrimpers returned before dawn, and the remnants were tying up as we wove our way into the first gorge. Captain Dave turned and twisted *Grand Caribe* to navigate the tight bends, and in no time at all we were enclosed in this slender magnificent tropical corridor, lost to the outside world. The walls towered above us well past three hundred feet, covered in mahogany, palms, huge stands of wildflowers, and not-so-evident wildlife. The air was quite still and we were able to hear troops of howler monkeys defining the boundary of their territory–or were they calling up their mates?

The Rio Dulce has a populous indigenous community in villages and small towns along its entire length, and the sudden appearance of *Grand Caribe* around the bend for families paddling tiny cayucos must have been awe inspiring. We passed many fleets of these family crafts floating gently with the current and occasionally a lone cayuco paddling upstream close to the river bank where the counter flow had less strength. We also passed several tiny guest houses with their own steaming hot spring and a fast boat tied alongside. Presumably these were the B&B community of the Rio Dulce.

Casa Guatemala

Casa Guatemala is an inspiring example how the broader community is caring for orphans who are abandoned or abused, some being casualties of the brutal Guatemalan civil war. It was originally called "Casa Canada" because the founders were a Canadian couple who saw the urgent need for a human sanctuary. The civil war was the original motivation for the development of these protected children's homes and their initial focus was to provide a safe refuge where loving staff, good food, clean accommodation and healthcare, become part of the child's life. However, maturing children and scarce resources have altered their mission and they are now committed to an educational and vocational training system that equips their graduates for life in the outside world. Casa Guatemala is home to two hundred and fifty children and is run by volunteers from all corners of the globe.

Blount Small Ship Adventures has been supporting Casa Guatemala since Luther first visited the Rio, and we were now heading to the orphanage for the first of two visits. The plan was to make a bow landing on their handkerchief-sized beach and go ashore and while guests were exploring the orphanage and meeting the children the crew was conferring with staff about delivering supplies on our return journey down river. The dilemma for the cruise line offering support to Casa Guatemala was the issue of banditry, and they advised against leaving a pot of cash with the administration. Far better to decide what food and medicine supplies were needed and purchase them in town for delivery later in the voyage. Springing ahead in this tale, we made a volunteer collection plus a raffle after which the ship's naturalist visited a dispensary and food market, delivering these supplies on our return journey.

Casa Guatemala left a lasting impression on all of us. Our visit was both joyful and a real tear-jerker. Kids are the same wherever you meet them and seeing the parentless children living in this protected sanctuary was both heart-warming and troubling. We met just about every child during our stay and had an excellent discussion with volunteer nurses from the UK, Australia, Japan, the US, and Canada. From the rear of the compound I looked back through the dormitories towards *Grand Caribe*, her nose resting on the beach, and every child was somewhere in that frame. What a contrast in lifestyles for us to contemplate and how inspirational for BSSA to make this visit.

On Lake Izabal we had a chance to launch the kayaks again and explore the shoreline of this remote body of water. The going was a bit tough at times because the wind cascading over the hills caused two-foot beam-swells, and for the first time we were paddling against combined wind and waves. We passed the tiny Spanish fort of Castillo de San Felipe and headed diagonally downriver into a small tributary. This was one of those shallow and narrow vine-covered streams with plenty of depth for our kayaks, so we paddled in looking for wildlife.

The howler monkeys above projected their voices at a volume worthy of an operatic chorus. I managed to see a troop in the canopy and given the size of the animals, the noise they were making was completely out of proportion.

I needed to move past a slender log and pushed left rudder to minimize the effort, but the log moved with me. I was obliged to dip a paddle and "engage first gear" but the log moved yet again. Mindful this was not my environment I moved closer and drew alongside a rather small crocodile. Crocs are not that common in Central America and this may have been a Morelet's Crocodile or even a small Caiman. There was not a hint of aggressiveness in the beast but as he would not move to let me pass, I gingerly tapped him on the nose with the tip of my paddle, whereupon he sideswiped his tail against my kayak and I nearly joined him in the water.

Spanish colonizers

From my perspective, the fact that Castillo de San Felipe exists at all is extraordinary, because of when it was built, who built it, and where it is located. I have tried to imagine how Conquistadores roaming the Central American coastline in the mid-1500s located the elusive Rio Dulce in the first place and how they were able to push inland to establish this commanding fort. They clearly possessed a powerful buccaneering spirit, they were superb navigators, and they were motivated by wealth and power.

They chose a highly strategic location on the precise point where Lake Izabal narrows and flows into the Rio Dulce. For anyone passing by, either by *cayuco* or on foot in the 1500s when the Spanish were in residence, it might have been their last journey on this earth. Not only was this an excellent defensive location but the Spanish possessed highly advanced weaponry for the times. I was struck by the flimsy outer walls of the *castillo*, which may describe how its defender viewed their enemies. Against local tribes, the walls may have seemed impregnable, but against contemporary enemies from Europe, the walls were like paper and could be easily breached by a modest caliber canon. If it was built to offer protection from the original "pirates of the Caribbean," it may have not fared so well against them. The fort became a UNESCO World Heritage Site in 2009 and is preserved as a fine example of the Spanish Colonial period.

With so much richness in the Rio Dulce, we took the opportunity to travel one hundred kilometres inland to the magnificent Quirigua Maya ruins, another UNESCO World Heritage Site dating from the 7th and 8th centuries AD. The Quirigua site is modest in scale, but the quality of carving on the stelae is exceptional, qualifying this as the most significant city of the southern Mayan. There are twenty two such monumental monoliths thirty five feet high with richly carved characters, animals and deities, much like totem poles of the Pacific Northwest, recording significant events in history. The temple and palace are largely in ruins but it is possible to understand the richness by strolling the avenue of the stelae and pausing on the stone terraces above the arena. Our resident archaeologist informed us that the winning side in team games was customarily put to death, which left me wondering about team motives and if modern professional sports leagues could learn a thing or two from these Maya.

We were now heading back to Belize with plenty of picturesque cays and bow landings ahead of us. The weather was as good as it gets, and as Captain Dave was ahead of schedule, we made an impromptu visit to a nearby tributary and once more launched the Glasser. In the highly structured mainstream cruise industry, this type of spontaneous visit would be impossible due to tight scheduling and air connections. With Blount, it was just another day on the water.

Small ship cruising has exploded over the past fifteen years, largely driven by travelers who dislike the impersonal nature of the larger ships. Fewer guests mean less stress when visiting sites and much faster entry and exit from the ship. With fewer guests, the atmosphere was convivial and intimate with full credit to a well-trained crew. The shallow draft meant better access to prime locations and Belize and Guatemala are outstanding destinations for small ship cruising. The only way my smile might have been wider is if I had been there on *The Full Monty*.

[1] Built by an American marine visionary called Luther Blount (1916–2006) in his own shipyard in Warren Rhode Island, the *Grand Caribe* is unique. Luther came out of the same mold as the Wright Brothers, who pioneered powered flight, or George Stevenson, who invented the steam-powered engine. Luther was a driven marine pioneer with an eye to the future of cruising. He efficiently built in the advantages of shallow draft cruising on his intimate scale vessels, introducing thousands of neophyte explorers to otherwise inaccessible regions. He built a fleet of these pocket cruise ships in his New England shipyard with Yankee ingenuity and graft. The *Grand Caribe* is two hundred feet long and forty five feet on the beam and needs a skinny five feet of water under her keel. The most unusual feature Luther invented is the "Bow Ramp" neatly tucked out of sight in the bow of the ship. The ultra-shallow draft and that bow ramp are typical Luther thinking, enabling the *Grand Caribe* to approach an island or a beach and gently rest its nose ashore. Once the ship comes to rest, the ingenious ramp is lowered and guests stroll off the ship–high and dry.

Another Luther feature is the disappearing wheel house and collapsible upper deck. These features enable the ship to traverse the canals of North America, including the Erie Barge Canal between the Hudson River and Lake Ontario, with a mere three inches clearance under fixed bridges. In the tropics my favourite feature is the "garage" at the aft end of the boat. More like a huge carport open the ocean it houses several sea-kayaks, as well as the "Glasser" (glass-bottomed boat) and scuba tanks for dive guests. Predicting that one day the world would embrace small-ship cruising, Luther's design was light years ahead of his time, and his vision was right on target.

[2] The prefixes Cay, Cayo, Caye and Key are interchangeable

Stranded at Timbuktu airport

Timbuktu - straight out of the movies

CHAPTER 9

Not Kidnapped in Timbuktu

The lumbering yet immensely capable Russian Ilyushin 11-18 transport was running up its engines at the far end of the runway in Mali and as the diminutive Malian pilot released the brakes, it surged forward–accelerating out of proportion to its mass and weight. It circled the field twice, finally banking a wing over the dusty terminal building, heading back to Bamako, effectively stranding me and my traveling companions in this Central African outpost, with no accommodation, a hostile administration and a long ride from anywhere–with no transport between the airport and town.

Africa is a fascinating and seductive continent full of stunning beauty, a wealth of natural resources, and complex politics. More than ten times the size of Western Europe, it is bordered by three oceans, several gulfs and contiguous northern states that overlook the Mediterranean. Over the past forty years I have been privileged to visit most of this pear shaped continent and every visit has been pleasantly memorable, with a few challenging moments thrown in for good measure. Africa would not be Africa without the unexpected happening, and for some of us that's part of the charm, although for others it can be daunting. An earlier chapter described one of these challenges in Uganda and the unavoidable "road-conference" with undisciplined red eyed beer swilling troops belonging to Idi Amin, which happily came to a peaceful and relatively calm ending.

My travel on this occasion was to focus on the landlocked sub-Saharan desert country of Mali, which at that time was a political client of both the Soviet and Western spheres, deftly playing both sides of the opposing teams. The basic plan was to spend time in the capital of Bamako, then fly northeast towards the Sahara Desert and spend time in what we tend to call Timbuktu and the locals call Tombuktou. Open a map of West Africa and see for yourself the haunting and daunting nature of this desert country. Mali has no maritime coastline and really only two urban centres and Tombuktou is a long, long way north, even by air, where it occupies a vast region of sand and scrub. To the northwest is lawless Mauritania; to the immediate west are coastal Senegal, Guinea, and Sierra Leone. To the southwest are Liberia, Ivory Coast, Upper Volta, and Ghana and to the east is Niger.

Currently Mali has sixteen million inhabitants. The most recognizable and arguably most cinematic of its ethnic groups are the Tuareg who originate from Saharan nomadic tribes that have dominated the desert trade for hundreds of years. They are also called "blue people" because of the indigo dye used in their desert clothing, which comes in all shades of blue. French is definitely the most widely used language in Mali's two urban centres and therefore communications for Westerners is quite easy.

Mali was once part of an interconnected West African empire that traded in slaves, salt, and gold. It had powerful alliances with many of its neighbours, and with wealth came flourishing commerce, allowing Mali to open a centre of Islamic learning. It was the growth of the technically superior Moroccan empire to the north that over time dealt a death blow to this position of privilege and the development of coastal trade routes heralded the decline of Mali's visually arresting camel trains. Later Mali came under the control of the French, was subsumed as part of French Sudan, and eventually gained independence.

In his book *A Season in Hell*, Canadian diplomat Robert Fowler describes the abduction of himself and his colleague Louis Guay and their harrowing incarceration by the AQIM, which is the Saharan branch of Al Qaida. The region where Fowler and Guay were held is deeply embedded in the desert to the northeast of Tombuktou, across the land border with Niger and to describe this as remote, even in these days of satellites, drones and android phones, is doing the land an injustice. We are looking at leagues of marching sand dunes, deep, narrow, and inaccessible rock strewn canyons, and few landmarks to navigate with, even if you feel inclined to run your own Paris-Dakar Rally. This inhospitable topography is a nightmare for conventional forces to operate within and the AQIM knew this when squirreling away Fowler and Guay. At the time of writing Niger was hosting one of the Gaddafi sons.

As a digression ("petrol heads" will understand), the reason Paris-Dakar no longer runs from Paris to Dakar is the dreadful security situation in Mauritania to the east of Mali. The threats by local bandits, Al Quaida or not were just too serious to ignore, and this awesome test of speed, long-distance motoring skill, and roadside engineering now runs in South America. Some may have heard of the late great Juan Manuel Fangio, the world champion driver who hails from Argentina. He died peacefully in 1995 and would have been thrilled to see this modern version of his Carrera Panamericana, the great South American road race in its new incarnation. But I digress.

I can't say enough to express my admiration for the mental strength of Canadians Robert Fowler and Louis Guay during their incarceration by Al Qaida. From the outset these exceptional Canadian diplomats resolved to survive the ordeal and against the greatest odds imaginable and a constant threat to their lives, they prevailed. Their strength of character and positive attitude gained them the grudging respect of their jailers and their techniques for survival were both innovative and logical, emerging from this hell not only intact but seemingly enriched by the experience. However, I am sure they've had their share of sleepless nights since coming home to Canada, constantly reliving the nightmare of this rogue society. What brings me full circle is that His Excellency Amadou Toumani Touré, the current president of Mali played a significant role in the negotiations leading to Fowler and Guay's freedom. My own travels in remote Mali preceded those of Fowler and Guay but I was relatively close to where the Canadians were hidden and my own experiences came flooding back as I read Mr. Fowler's amazing account.

Bamako, Mali's capital is relatively flat, situated alongside the Niger River with about two million inhabitants. The town site was once dominated by a volcano, now extinct for some time and all that's left of the cone is an escarpment-style falaise[1] gently rising into the distance. Bamako is hot, with a tropical climate year round, typical of sub-Saharan Africa, with monthly averages of over 30 degrees Celsius. It had a number of museums and mosques worth seeing, including the National Museum of Mali, which has an excellent selection of colourful national dress. The Grand Central Mosque and the Bamako Cathedral are close by the fascinating central market or Grand Marché which provides rich pickings if you want to go people watching.

The Niger River provides access for commerce and fishing, but at times it is an angry river, overflowing and flooding the region–the name "Bamako," by the way, comes from a local dialect which ominously translates into "Crocodile River." The town site bears evidence of occupation for the last one hundred and fifty thousand years, which I find extraordinary to contemplate and wonder what my ancestors were doing one hundred and fifty thousand years ago? Similar to other regions with a contiguous waterway, the Niger provided a fertile environment, around which communities thrive, encouraging them to grow their commerce alongside the river, eventually trading with nearby Ghana, Senegal, Guinea, and Mauritania.

I suspect that for 99 percent of visitors, the reason for coming to Bamako is to access a visit to fabled Tombuktou, and as a result Bamako often gets short shrift. However I really enjoyed this bustling and polluted central African capital city and would return in a flash to explore further. Bamako has been steadily expanding as a centre of commerce, agriculture, textiles, and light manufacturing and has recently been recognized as a centre of outstanding music. To my ear, and recognizing that music is a very personal delight, the music of Mali is one of the most seductive sounds I have ever heard. There are many sub-types of Malian music, folk, Moorish, local-ethnic, and European influenced, but all of it has a richness that is engaging and even hypnotic. I particularly love what I can only describe as community singing as large groups of performers weave complex harmonies alongside their marimbas and drums. In the late 1990s,

Malian music entered the international mainstream with performers such as Salif Keita and Sibiri Samake. Now there are thousands of Malian performers, and Bamako is alive with music clubs. Most street corners vibrating to a Mali beat.

I should explain that the purpose of this trip was to take a good look at Tombuktou, to gauge its suitability as a base of operations for sub-Saharan adventure tourism. The plan was to look at the town's infrastructure, determine the approximate cost of opening a modest field office, and research the potential for hiring capable staff. Opening an enterprise of this nature carries its own set of challenges no matter where you are operating, therefore opening a base of operations this close to the Saharan wilderness upped the ante considerably because whatever law and order existed in this region becomes diluted the further north we traveled. I will admit that I was comfortable with the mandate, comfortable operating within this fragile infrastructure, comfortable with the outlook for the firm–but I was uneasy about security.

The night before leaving, I had been urgently contacted by our headquarters with a "slight" change of plan. It seems the firm was hosting a group of legislators on a fact-finding tour through West Africa, and their administrator had fallen ill. The group were landing in Bamako that very evening, and someone in the firm remembered I was in the region and might be able to help out. To cut a story down to manageable proportions, I was tasked with parking my mandate, dashing out to the airport to meet them and taking over their leadership for a few days until we could locate a replacement administrator. Happily, their itinerary included a three day visit to Tombuktou.

To fly from Bamako to Tombuktou, we needed to be at the airport very early, by 04:30 sharp. The country happened to be short of aircraft, and this fine specimen of a robust Soviet era Ilyushin II-18 was waiting to fly us out to Tombuktu–then make an immediate return trip to Bamako–after which it would fly onward to Senegal to pick up some spares. Later that same evening providing the spares were delivered, it was to fly members of government out to Tombuktou–an event that would greatly impact this tale.

The Il-118 first flew in 1957 and became one of the Soviet empire's workhorses both inside and outside Russia. It was a sturdy capable airplane with excellent performance and considerable freight and passenger capacity. In the middle of this warm Malian night and only half awake, I was fully expecting a Russian flight crew to lead us out to the Ilyushin, but instead six diminutive, smartly dressed Malian crew members in freshly pressed uniforms appeared.

Waiting in the deserted airport, (ever the researcher…) I was able to engage the co-pilot in a discussion about his training and subsequent experience flying the Il-118 (try doing that nowadays)–because I was curious about how Soviet flight training was delivered. Was it part of the aircraft purchase deal, and what were his perspectives on aviation in this sub-Saharan region? Given the competitiveness between the west and Russia I half expected him to close up like a clam, but he was happy to tell me about his extensive training inside Russia and it soon became obvious that he had developed a real passion for flying. Evidently his family connections had made it possible for him to become an aviator, and his ability to communicate in flawless French, English, Russian and Arabic was mighty impressive. As part of the purchase and sale agreement for the Il-18s, he had spent several months in Russia, training alongside his Soviet counterparts and being mentored by the factory team. I could tell that he was not much impressed with Russian society and it was evident that he had experienced his share of discrimination while on-the-streets. But this was an elegant, capable, and charming young man who charitably refrained from being too critical of his mentors.

Without fuss or drama, but with copious amounts of blue smoke from yesterday's unburned fuel, the Ilyushin awoke from its airfield slumber, exhausts spitting flames as they put the throttles to the wall and climbed into the cool air to welcome the sunrise at twenty five thousand feet. Most of my thirty five new friends dozed off as we droned northeast across the sub-Saharan desert but as I looked forward through the open cockpit door, my new friend was smiling back at me with a complicit thumbs-up gesture of camaraderie.

On our arrival in Tombuktou, the large yet nimble Ilyushin lazily circled the town and our friend up front dipped a wing long enough for me to see the low profile of its sand-coloured buildings. I was excited, because we were definitely in the Sahara Desert–Tombuktou below us truly looked the part and all that was missing were posses of horsemen in blue robes–shaking their long thin rifles at the Ilyushin. Then right on cue, straight out of central casting, waiting for us in the terminal were our Tuareg handlers, resplendent in their varying shades of blue, tanned faces partially covered with white scarves and long period rifles from the central casting prop-cupboard slung across their chests. With the lengthy introductions completed, it dawned on me that these chaps were also driving our bus into town and I remember feeling disappointed at the thought of this noble camel-riding desert warrior in his new role as a chauffeur. However, in my newly appointed position as chief handler I needed a few moments alone with our desert hosts because in our business it is important to be at least one step ahead of the guests– in fact several steps is preferred and what I wanted was a confirmation of the accommodation arrangements which the lads back in the office had made.

At that precise time the Tuareg disappeared and charitable fellow that I am, I presumed they were in the bathroom or the administrative office, perhaps making a phone call to their office, or perhaps they were checking the bus–which had just left for town and they couldn't possibly be on it–without us. I remember searching high and low through the modest building, feeling like an incompetent idiot, having just flown into fabled Timbuktu and promptly lost contact with our handlers in this several-million square kilometres of inhospitable desert. They had to be here somewhere and in the rapidly warming morning air I could feel myself starting to overheat. At that moment I bumped into the only friendly face I knew, the young Malian co-pilot, and asked if he had seen our blue-clad warriors. Negative, he replied, not in the building and evidently not outside and he had just come down from the tower and was preparing to fly back to Bamako.

I am not given to panicking, but my calculations went something like this. 1) See the Ilyushin fly back to Bamako empty and be happy that you arrived safely. 2) See the Ilyushin fly back to Bamako with me and the observers onboard. (Neither was possible as the aircraft was heading for Senegal to pick up a load of spares). 3) Wave goodbye to the Ilyushin and somehow contact the Tuareg and transport these thirsty people into town for a long, cool drink. Each of these options was now rapidly diminishing and as four big Russian engines growled at full throttle at the end of the dusty sand-covered runway, I knew for sure that we were staying in Tombuktou.

What compounded my angst was the possibility that the Sahara desert terminal might be closing for the day and where would this leave my charges and how could I make contact with the men in blue? The Ilyushin was not due back for many hours, and the few workers in the building were heading out to their battered pickups–presumably leaving for town and a siesta. The counter staff then told me that they had no clear idea where the Tuareg had gone but suspected they had ridden the bus back to town and the least they could do was offer me a lift and with that confirmed, I broke the news to our (by now increasingly inquisitive) guests. I remember the resigned calmness on their faces as I explained what I thought was happening. The negative aspect to all of this was that I had absolutely nothing of substance to tell them other than "Leave it to Beaver" and I would be right back.

Arriving in the heart of downtown Tombuktu late morning my first priority was to locate the elusive Blue Men and sort out some accommodation. In those years, there was only one hotel in this edge-of-the-desert outpost and my driver was able to drop me off at the door. It was now about noon, the sun beating down on the street, raising the temperature to well north of forty Celsius and I was thinking how frustrated the observers must be back at the desert airport, probably contemplating the vanishing Tuareg and now their fearless leader had gone missing. Tombuktou in those days was a marvellous movie-set of a town, dominated by one-storey buildings made of local mud mixed with sand and fibre. Many of the roofs were finished in faux battlement style, squares cut out as if for riflemen to hide behind with drainage culverts set into the walls just below the roofline. At high noon, sensible Malians had taken refuge in the cool of their darkened homes, but the streets were still busy with clattering antique soviet jeeps, battered pickups, and the inevitable donkeys.

Nowadays, there are several hotels to choose from in Tombuktou, including the Hendrina Khan built by Munir Ahmed Khan, creator of the Pakistan nuclear bomb, and designed by his Dutch wife, Hendrina However, in those days there was one game in town, and with fading confidence I strolled through the door and asked for the manager. It's always useful to know who else is staying in a hotel, and I noticed an inordinate number of military personnel in the reception area, some might say guarding, one might say restricting access from the lobby into the hotel proper. At the reception desk I was able to look beyond the counter and was elated to spot our Blue Men in the hotel's administrative office talking to someone I presumed was the manager. At least I had located our handlers, and at least we were in the right hotel. Surely I could now order up some transport and get my observers out of "Camp Changi" and into the cool inner sanctum of Tombuktou.

It is sometimes difficult to suppress anger, but out of necessity it's often practical to do so if you need a positive result. It's equally hard to suppress frustration when faced with an absolutely outrageous situation, but often necessary to do so in the interest of making progress and there was little to be gained from blowing my stack in a desert hotel, when the manager was holding his palms in the air facing towards me. I am sure you are following the trend here; soldiers in the lobby, accommodation unavailable, nowhere else to sleep in town, Tuareg handlers had cut and run, the Ilyushin was now in Senegal and my party had nowhere to sleep.

In my business you are often forced to improvise and while the result may be far from expected, it is often accepted as a welcome refuge by the guests if only a temporary fix. The challenge was that I needed accommodation for thirty five weary travelers in a town with only one hotel and no established tradition of bed and breakfast. There were actually several immediate challenges to overcome. First I had to communicate with my party, so they knew I had not left on a camel train to Morocco. I had to source accommodation for at least one night (maybe more) and if possible locate some food. I had to rearrange our bus transport and ensure we had thirty six places on the Ilyushin back to Bamako. Above all, I had to ensure the group's personal safety and just as important–ensure they knew that I was in charge.

In more recent times, circa 2008, the local Al Qaida branch started kidnapping travellers in this part of the world and in 2009, several tourists were kidnapped in Anderamboukane near the Mali-Niger border, one of them being tragically murdered. As a result the government of Mali moved their annual cultural community festival to the outskirts of Tombuktou, where presumably they could offer more protection for both residents and visitors. Sadly, in November 2011, Tombuktou experienced its first taste of Islamist terrorism when gunmen attacked the hotel in town, kidnapping three visitors and killing one. In earlier days one could enjoy a calm inter-racial cross cultural exchange in this outpost of the Sahara, but it is desperately sad, even tragic to reflect on the current atmosphere of fear, as Robert Fowler and Louis Guay can attest. Conventional reporting focuses on Al Qaida, and for good reasons, however, there is a growing body of evidence that sheer thuggery and banditry is hiding beneath the cloak of terrorist activities, although the line between the two tends to get blurred.

The hotel flatly refused to allow our observers in for a drink and some badly needed R&R, although they handed over a large supply of canned juice for me to take to the airport. From their tactical perspective, the further away our observers were from the hotel the better, because they feared that thirty five capable and highly educated visitors might just refuse to budge once they were in the comfort and safety of the cool lobby lounge. After networking with the hotel management and observing the nature of the military presence, it became apparent that the hotel had been taken over by the government for several nights and the Ilyushin due back later this evening would be carrying these delegates into Tombuktou. So there you have most of the story in a nutshell. Our agency had done its due diligence and made the reservations. Our local handlers in Bamako and Tombuktou had executed the contracted arrangements with precision. The Blue Men were where they were supposed to be–but at that point the government bureaucrats took over and we were cast into the desert to fend for ourselves.

Now the issues were identified and they knew that I was aware of the gravity, the Blue Men became more accessible and we started to work through the options. Charter a flight to fly back to Bamako?

Not possible because of an equipment shortage. Place more pressure on the hotel manager to make rooms available? Not possible, because the government held all the cards (and seemingly the guns). Move to alternate accommodation? Not possible, because there was none. Stay at the airport for the night? Not possible, because the airport was to be closed by order of the military. Stage a demonstration in protest–are you kidding? In short the alternates were evaporating before my eyes, and even the Blue Men agreed the situation was absurd. How could anyone allow thirty five observers to fly to Tombuktou knowing full well there was no accommodation for them? How could even the most irresponsible government kick out thirty five foreign visitors at the drop of a hat? These were interesting topics to contemplate once I was back home, but right now they were not much of a contribution towards finding a solution.

Back at the airport, courtesy of the Blue Men and their transport, I was quite candid with my charges, to ensure they were fully aware of what we were facing. To their credit, they handled the news quite well. I decided to take two approaches in my briefing, the first being "everyone hears the story as a group," after which I conferred with individuals to hear anyone's specific concerns and more importantly, to ensure that the guests had any medication they needed. My interim plan was to keep most of them at the airport but take two of them with me as consulting stakeholders to approve whatever solutions I could develop.

The Blue Men had taken me aside in a corner of the hotel to give me an in-depth briefing about the government, the military, and the nearby barracks. Apparently Tombuktou was host to a significant military jail, and several trials were scheduled during our visit, requiring that accommodation be handed over to "the brass and the wigs" and as there was absolutely no chance of this being altered, leaving me to my own devices to find a temporary solution. "Let's tour the town" I suggested, so off we went in an antiquated Russian army Jeep, the one with the rounded radiator which I always thought looked a bit like the nose of a Canadian beaver–without the fearsome teeth.

Tombuktou closely resembled some of the paintings done by artist-members of the expeditions that had come through en route to the Sahara. Fabulous looking sand-coloured low-dwellings, a dusty 18th and 19th century camel market complete with camels, donkeys, men in multi-coloured robes, background noise of animals braying and the occasional jeep or pickup kicking up the sand as it growled by in low gear. If only we had somewhere to sleep, this would have been a marvelous afternoon experience at the edge of the sub-Sahara.

For some unapparent reason, our handlers thought it useful for me to walk through the market, and I was soon being tagged by sellers of spices, tin engravers, woodcarvers, venders of cinematic desert clothing and–of all things, mattresses. It seemed like a normal day in a normal third world village. Then a middle-aged fellow addressed me in pretty good French and we soon fell into a discussion about my predicament.

In these bazaars, a casual observer immediately identifies an atmosphere dominated by business, but to the careful observer they are actually highly complex social locations, where families and friends of vendors tend to hang out, play with their worry beads and kibitz. The stalls are modest and generally packed to the rafters with goods. There is also a type of bazaar discipline (opposed to bizarre discipline) which regulates the marketplace, so that not too many stalls sell the same type of goods, giving each seller a decent crack at the business. A spice seller at one entrance gate may have fifty stalls between him and the next spice seller. The same goes for the copper merchant or the tailor or the gunsmith. In Souks such as Jerusalem's old town, there are many purveyors of the same type of goods, but that market is substantially larger and can sustain this cheek by jowl competition. In some regions of the world there are bazaars that specialize in one commodity, like the spice bazaars of India.

The fellow who tagged me was the mattress seller, but I would caution you not to jump too far ahead with your assumptions. The grapevine or the local bush telegraph, was working overtime at the edge of the desert and our mattress seller was well aware of our predicament. He knew who I was, he knew I was carrying a wad of cash, he had a fair handle on the number of bodies that might slumber on his mattresses–but most of all he had the kernel of a plan.

Not that long before our visit the convent in Tombuktou had been attacked and burned. I suspect there were fatalities and not necessarily from the fire so he casually suggested that I drive over and take a look. I immediately got his drift and realized this was not an impromptu sightseeing tour of Tombuktou by night. He was suggesting that the convent might be a temporary refuge until we could get sorted out– and then either leave the desert or reclaim our rooms at the hotel. The Blue Men were impressed with this suggestion and we promptly crossed town to the burned-out convent.

The building stood apart from the town and was in pretty good shape considering it was badly charred and smoke stained. I'm not sure exactly what had happened, but a fire had definitely consumed most of the wood in the construction, but as the sand and mud walls were not as combustible the basic two-level structure was largely intact. The window frames were all burned out; thus no glass. The stairs to the upper floor had been reconstructed and were in fine shape, although without a handrail of any sort. The ground floor had fifteen small rooms, presumably bedrooms for the former occupants and the upper floor had ten more bedrooms and several large meeting rooms. The ground floor rooms were arranged on the outer perimeter of the building, leaving a large central courtyard, much like a basketball court or a parade ground, with no obstructions of any type.

A plan rapidly emerged in my mind, and with few hours of daylight remaining to turn this into a reality, I was making decisions on the fly. Brief the Tuareg, develop an understanding with my ad-hoc stakeholder's "sub-committee", commandeer the bus, collect the observers and their luggage from the airport, rent thirty five mattresses, source a dozen pressure lanterns from the bazaar, buy thirty five sets of plates, knives, forks, mugs and spoons–and then go about developing an evening meal of some sort. Word of a well-financed spendthrift of a foreigner spread through the "commission intensive" bazaar like wildfire, and with the help of the Blue Men and the Mattress Man (and their relatives), the plan was rapidly put into action and our position in Tombuktou became less tenuous.

News of my solution did not sit well with many of our observers. They were still at the dusty airport, which (under threat of an international incident) was being kept open for them, while being fed on fruit juice, flat bread and fruit. Admittedly it wasn't the best diet in the desert heat, but it was all I could get my hands on and it was reasonably hydrating and filling. The group were rightfully appalled when the reality of our situation hit home and they were angered by what had transpired, particularly when I shared the administrative paper trail with them and why and by whom the rooms had been commandeered. After a very contentious discussion, it took a huge effort for everyone to abandon the security air terminal and board that bus for Tombuktou. I knew full well that in the next hour I would be going through an even more frantic discussion when they saw the burned-out convent and what we had organized for our communal night in the desert.

It was important to be frank with these thirty five observers. They were educated adults of a mature age, and many of them held responsible positions. I have always believed that when leading teams, the first item on the agenda is the truth, as in "exactly what are the current circumstances and how is that likely to affect us going forward." I applied the same tactic with these guests and the responses were varied. I believe most understood that we were located somewhere between a camel and its dung heap, with few options in hand and those options could easily evaporate before our eyes. Some immediately got the picture. Perhaps they had a more adventurous background and might even have been campers in their youth. Sadly, a sizable minority became very agitated, and it became necessary to play the hard card to avoid circumstances spinning out of control.

If you are an artist, a photographer or a keen observer of landscapes and colouration, you will find the desert colours to be simply marvelous. I have always considered the light in Australia to have special qualities, and it is the same in the Sahara, particularly in the morning and also when the sun starts dying towards the end of the day. On reflection I think that softness appears when an undefined combination of sun, sky, atmospherics, and earth come together. That softness infuses itself on every object in its path and that magic light–as it has for millions of years, was working its magic in Tombuktou. I could not help thinking that if our circumstances were different and if the convent would have been a four-star hotel, we might be appreciating the warm colours of that sundrenched Sahara evening.

The converted convent looked quite romantic in the soft transformative light of the Tombuktou evening. I had our Blue Men place some of the pressure lanterns I'd acquired in the bazaar in some of the windows, and the rest we strategically placed in the courtyard and at the base and apex of the staircase. From a distance it almost looked like a movie set from *Beau Geste*, but in reality it was merely window dressing and a mirage of what the group expected me to deliver. The hard card I had played was a frank talk about what we had gone through to develop this modest refuge, but some of them were still agitated when they realized their sleeping accommodation was a mattress in a convent cell. As the evening progressed we modified the plan on-the-fly, and about fifteen elected to sleep around the fire in the yard.

With a plentiful supply of fresh juice and fruit, along with fabulous sweet flatbread and fresh tea which was available from the samovar we had purchased at the market, and with the utensils sterilized in scalding water, we had the nucleus of a picnic. The next challenge was to create a more substantial meal, and as I was now officially adopted as a rich relative by Mattress Man, this became easier than looking for accommodation. It appeared he could also supply meat and rice and spices and, if our guests were keen, he could even improvise a barbecue and cook some "real food." Years earlier in Tunisia, my host had introduced me to tender local lamb, spicing the meat in whatever came out of his wife's larder. I clearly remember the result was absolutely delicious and I hoped I could persuade my charges to try it.

The barbecue was duly arranged and amazingly just about everyone was in favour, if only as a diversion from the eclectic and impromptu camp-out, and I reasoned it might even shorten the night. Meanwhile I had the Blue Men drive back to the Tombuktou hotel and after a careful look around the lobby they identified my co-pilot friend on the Ilyushin who luckily was back on shift and accommodated at the hotel. The mission was to secure seats on the morning flight to

Bamako, where I knew we could get rooms, as the capital was not that busy and I knew that I had the cash to lubricate the way. Mercifully, the morning flight was virtually empty and as we had no chance of real hotel rooms in Tombuktou for at least another five days, the consensus was to fly west and recover the trip.

The evening under the star-lit Sahara night went surprisingly well, the convent serving its new role as an impromptu hotel. The rooms were not quite as comfortable as we hoped, and the majority migrated to the downstairs courtyard, where we kept a well stoked fire crackling through the night. The barbecued lamb and rice went down much better than expected and with sweet flatbread to dip in the perfumed gravy, fresh fruit for dessert, and sweet hot mint tea on-tap all night, we were in good shape–until breakfast next day.

Next morning the familiar shape of the resting Ilyushin was a welcome sight as we pulled up to the dusty terminal and after the most modest of formalities–they evidently knew what the group had just gone through–we were onboard and soon over the desert en route to Bamako. My wallet was considerably lighter, and sadly, my intimate knowledge of the mattress trade would not been of much use in my career. However there were many lessons to be learned from this experience, not least, how to manage expectations.

CHAPTER 10

Polar Bear Tracking on Hudson Bay

Polar bears are iconic animals, as dramatic and dominant in their natural setting as elephants are in theirs and there is no doubt about their dominance in the polar wildlife chain where being "king of the hill" creates an aura of invincibility. Currently our federal government has designated them a Species at Risk, strictly regulating lucrative game hunting and the sale of polar bear pelts for non-natives.

First Nations communities dispute the scientific studies and are not happy with the position of the government, reasoning the decline of bear populations and the uncertainty of the polar bear life cycle is not caused by over-hunting, but by climate change, accelerated melting of ice fields in the spring and the late fall freezing of the ice where polar bears hunt seals. Late freezing causes a delayed start for the bears to go hunting, and an earlier melt leaves them less time to seek their prey. Polar bears use sea ice as a hunting platform to catch seals and other prey and without stable ice, they have difficulty meeting their dietary needs–leading to physical deterioration and decreased rates of reproduction. There is no easy answer to this situation.

Our firm's response to this was to emphasize the polar bear as a sustainable resource and to develop a program whereby guests shoot with a camera rather than a Remington 30-06. This concept is not new; our sister province of Manitoba has a mature polar bear viewing and photography program which is well developed and very successful. We therefore planned an expedition-style field trip to assess the feasibility of a sustainable close-encounter polar bear program, based out of a First Nation community in northern Ontario. Our idea was not entirely novel and I was recently told that King Edward VIII was instrumental in the switch from guns to cameras .

The commercial season for polar bear viewing is August to October, after which Nanook head out onto the sea ice to hunt seals. Unfortunately due to other commitments we were unable to visit before November, so we took a huge risk on the weather and might have missed sighting the bears. The visit was certainly bone chilling, but we did see polar bears–at very close proximity.

The plan was to fly up to the northern community of Fort Severn– named after the River Severn in the UK, close where I come from, and to head out to the shore of Hudson Bay to see if we could locate these magnificent animals. I asked my good friend Tracy Walter, a respected colleague from my earlier life in the tourism industry to join me for this exploratory visit. Tracy is one of the most incisive people I have worked with, possessing one of those rare and sought-after qualities in the development side of the tourism business, a built-in GPS which instinctively knows what will work and what to steer clear of. If the program was to flourish, I needed to have someone with Tracy's practicalities along to balance my built-in enthusiasm, but Tracy has other qualities that make her a superb traveling companion. She has an infectious giggle that breaks out at the oddest times, she knows her way around good food, and she has the courage to disagree when necessary.

"Are you up for a sortie to Hudson Bay looking for Nanook?" I asked her over lunch whereupon she promptly said, "Yes–affirmative– when do we go?"

I first drove to Ottawa and using the excellent Porter Airlines service from Toronto to Thunder Bay, we flew the Canadian-manufactured Q400, which is the world's most advanced Turbo Prop. Sitting out on the apron, its high tail gives away its military heritage which allows it full STOL (short take off and landing) capability. The Q400 flies fast and quiet and requires a short runway before it is airborne. Porter's success comes from their novel habit of treating their passengers as real guests which is something most airlines have forgotten.

Thunder Bay, our northern gateway, is a cross between an urban and frontier town of one hundred and twenty thousand inhabitants, and the only community of its size on the edge of such wilderness. From here we flew the First Nations owned Wasaya Airline to Sioux Lookout (love the name) and onward to Fort Severn and we presumed that Wasaya must have been talking to Porter, because their pilots are chatty and pleasant and I felt like a real guest. The Wasaya arrival in these remote communities is the event of the day–an added bonus for visitors hoping to observe the local lifestyle. Wasaya mostly fly the Beech 1900 which is a sturdy nineteen seater well suited to short-field operations where combinations of passengers and freight have to be carried.

Fort Severn is located a stone's throw from Hudson Bay. It has about seven hundred and fifty inhabitants but lacks a specific town-based enterprise. Some residents are employed in telecommunications, some with airport maintenance, several work for the band office and about fifty are Canadian Rangers, a newly minted arm of the military responsible for northern security and search and rescue. The town also has a substantial nursing station, with two nurse practitioners in residence. Sadly, there is a high incidence of diabetes in many First Nations communities, and I noticed that the box for spent needles in the Sioux Lookout airport was full. I mentioned this to the police officer we met, who indicated that the majority of needles came from drug use, Oxycontin being the latest fad.

Some background concerning Aboriginal life may help to place this in context. As you may know, conditions in many First Nations communities are substandard when compared to mainstream Canada and the clash of cultures between Aboriginals and the "newcomer-colonists" has not always gone well. A few aboriginal communities have developed well-founded enterprises, but many have experienced difficulty with sustainability, and as a result the vast majority of First Nations live below the poverty line. Aggravating this are a substantial number of land-claim settlements which continue to be disputed, with some treaties dating back to the reign of Queen Victoria and further.

Complicating these disputes is aggressive mineral exploration and the substantial discoveries of gold, chromate, oil, manganese, copper and natural gas–on the same lands that are under treaty dispute. These high stakes are adding to the atmosphere of suspicion as discussions grind on, royalties are negotiated, and access to well paying sustainable work becomes a priority. More recently there has been a massive discovery of chromite in an area north of Thunder Bay called the "Ring of Fire." Chromite is a necessary ingredient for the stainless steel industry, and this discovery holds the promise of wealth and dispute between First Nations and the mining companies.

We had several challenges to overcome before contemplating publicizing this adventure holiday. The town has a very basic six room motel with no services other than baseboard heating, hot running water, plus a stove and fridge in each room. This would be inadequate for polar bear enthusiasts paying a decent tariff for the privilege of roughing it on the shores of Hudson Bay, but it was perfectly adequate for Tracy and me on a research trip to see Nanook. Also, there was nowhere to buy a catered meal in Fort Severn and as we knew the price of local supplies was high, we decided to raid a supermarket in Thunder Bay and flew north to the coast with a cooler of supplies in the belly of the aircraft.

Years ago in Africa I had worked on the design of a platform tent community that would act as the base camp for wilderness safaris and I had this in mind for seasonal accommodation–that is if the notion of polar bear photography looked like it might be possible. However the temperature was hovering about minus twenty when we were dropped off at the motel and discovered the only other resident was a young policeman from Thunder Bay who was on contract to the community as their peace officer.

In planning the expedition, we needed to secure the services of a knowledgeable local guide, preferably someone who might be a delivery partner for our polar bear program. Locating the right person is never easy but sometimes luck plays its hand, and our hand came through while we were networking for another program. We were introduced to Freddy Koostachin, a well-known First Nations hunter, who along with his buddy agreed to act as both lead guide and tracker.

Both our guides on this trip were of Cree heritage[1] and had grown up on the shore of Hudson Bay, acquiring a vast amount of local knowledge as children playing in the community and later as young adults, so who better to have along on this trip and who better to interpret the landscape and its unique animal life? Freddy was a curious fellow possessing the dual quality of shyness around new acquaintances and immediate leadership born from his familiarity of this unforgiving land. I have been around indigenous people often enough to appreciate that their concept of time is often quite different from my own urbanized version of the 24 hour clock. During my early days in the tourism business I must have annoyed many indigenous colleagues with my finger-tapping approach to getting things done and now once more I was obliged to adjust my approach to time as Freddy went about the business of organizing our visit to the land.

We knew it would be dangerously cold, with unpredictable weather and almost no shelter once we were on the shores of Hudson Bay, and we thought we had had dressed accordingly. The plan was to use open Honda and Kawasaki All Terrain Vehicles, called ATVs or Quads, which exposed us to the wind for the duration of our one hundred and twenty kilometre journey. The ambient temperature started off at about minus twenty but rapidly fell as we approached the shore of this historic bay. The wind was blowing directly at us from Quebec on the eastern shore of the bay, and as we rode onward, the temperature descended to between minus thirty, then minus forty and I was starting to feel somewhat inadequate as we motored on with the wind on the nose.

Below the belt I wore high-value thermal underwear, a pair of heavy cord trousers, along with a wind-and-waterproof trouser shell, but after fifteen minutes in the open, this was barely satisfactory and although I started out warm, I was definitely beginning to cool off. Above the belt I wore a similar long-sleeved thermal shirt, a regular undershirt, t-shirt, bush shirt, fleece zip-up and a second fleece zip-up–and on top of that my thick down jacket. Believe it or not, this jumble of clothing was only marginally satisfactory when the wind hit us and I felt even cooler than before. Tracy said that I looked like the Michelin Man but I really needed a thicker heavier goose-down parka with a fur-rimmed hood.

On my feet I wore a pair of waterproof Quebec-built Sorel boots with thick felt liners and inside that a normal pair of thick wool socks. In contrast with my jacket and pants these boots were just amazing and kept me snug all day, although a pair of warmer socks would have been luxurious. On my head I wore a thick wool cap, over which I pulled my jacket hood with a pair of clear glasses to keep the wind off my eyes, but this covering was also inadequate, and my face was cold and uncomfortable. What I really needed was a wool balaclava (Tracy called this a baklava) and a decent hood.

On my hands I wore a pair of thick gloves, which rapidly became a liability. Initially they were modestly warm, but as my hands perspired, moisture migrated through the outer fabric and the surface became frozen solid–rendering them useless for anything that required dexterity. I was unable to use my camera, turn the throttle smoothly, even scratch my nose without lacerating myself with an icy finger–and in a crunch they would have to come off before pulling the trigger of the 30-06. On my part this was a stupid choice that nearly cost me dearly.

The Polar Bear program will not be offered at this time of the year because it is far too cold and the bears are heading up the coast out onto the ice. The months for bear viewing are therefore August to October when the temperatures are warmer and the bears more accessible and less draining of one's energy. However, getting an in-depth look at Hudson Bay in winter was a real privilege, particularly for anyone interested in First Nations settlement and the colonization of Northern Canada and as I read passages from British and French expeditions about forming the Hudson Bay Company, I marveled at how tough and resourceful these Europeans were in order to survive.

Nowadays winter brings an entirely different aspect to life on the Hudson Bay coast. The scenery looks the same, but when the land freezes, travel becomes easier and modern winter roads (accessible by four-wheel drive trucks) are plowed through between Gillam Manitoba and Fort Severn. The key to handling winter is appropriate clothing, plenty of food, warm accommodation and reliable transport. The rest depends on careful planning and luck with the atmospherics.

The chosen path from Fort Severn to Hudson Bay depends on the weather, and the overnight freeze-up enabled us to travel anywhere we wanted. Our path was though a growth of bush with four-foot high thickets and then over several river banks, descending onto a smooth path of solid ice. Running a frozen river is preferable to a land route because the ice is often billiard-table smooth and mostly quite safe and for a petrol head like me–it can be fun. We occasionally felt ice elasticity where the water beneath is pushed along under a mini ice-wave which is experienced by the ice-road truckers, but we didn't break through to the water, and in these temperatures I was happy about that.

After feeding on stories of exploration, reaching the western shoreline of Hudson Bay was quite a moment for me and I paused to reflect on the brave English and French explorers and the fortune hunters, who see-sawed across this unforgiving body of water looking for a safe passage and in some cases the elusive North West Passage. Not far up the shoreline, we discovered the thirty-foot square mechanism of a huge anchor winch, which must have come from a one hundred and fifty foot sailing ship. The power of the Hudson Bay wind has driven this massive structure a good fifty feet onshore, where it will remain until archaeologists decide it is worth saving. One wonders who these seafarers were and if perhaps they were part of the flotilla searching for the North West Passage. I wandered alone through the massive wreck of this huge contraption and could easily imagine the period accented French and English commands from senior officers, cursing and blaming the seamen after their ship ran aground.

The shoreline of Hudson Bay is hard-packed gravel and at this time of the year it is covered in dense snow or ice, with eskers and low lying dunes marching inland. It has a magnificent wild beauty all of its own and the scenery becomes even more compelling the further north you travel–with Hudson Bay to your right and the tundra to your left. I wish I were an artist and could replicate on canvas the repetitive wild landscape of wind-stunted trees, sand dunes with wispy tufts of grass like inverted goatees and a continuous trail of white bleached driftwood, which probably floated from Quebec on the opposite shore. In the distance an odd shape came into view, completely out of context, invading this undisciplined landscape, subsequently forming a perfect square. Eventually we motored past a large hut roughly built out of driftwood at the edge of the shoreline—an escape camp for the boys in the settlement perhaps?

It was at this point that we started tracking our polar bears and we first followed huge, fresh eighteen-inch pad prints that wandered diagonally across the land–a bit like an elephant in Kenya, never worrying about which path to take as long as it points roughly in the right direction. Once on the shoreline, we came upon a second set of smaller pads, which intersected the original set–both animals heading in more or less the same direction with us following close behind. The Honda and Kawasaki Quads performed superbly in sub-zero temperatures. Their engines were only 420 cc capacity, but with six gears and four-wheel drive on demand, they performed like miniature battle tanks. I was impressed that they enabled us to track polar bears with such relative ease and once we had tracks in sight, we could easily locate the animals … that is as long as the gas held out and we didn't break down.

Past the square structure, we met our first polar bear, at about three hundred meters distance on a thinly treed ridge towards the sea ice. He saw us about the same time we spotted him and using the speed of the ATVs we closed the gap, ending the pursuit about forty feet from his molars and judging from his body language, he was not too happy sharing his turf with us. The growling ATVs with multicolored aliens perched on top must have been a new and strange adversary for Nanook, and he was visibly nervous, which struck me as a huge negative in bear-human relations. We circled him slowly, but took great care to give him maneuvering room, observing him as carefully as he observed us.

Each time we backed and repositioned one of the ATVs (which generated additional motor noise), the bear reacted with a defensive move of his body and a wide swing of his massive neck, bracing himself on the crusted snow with his massive paws. Each move was accompanied by an audible exhale of his musty breath and given their diet I was happy the wind was at our back. This bear was not too happy to be semi-hemmed in by our fleet of vehicles and I remember thinking there was a 50-50 chance this might end in a confrontation, so I looked over at Freddy and sure enough he had already un-slung his Remington and was moving a round into the chamber as a precaution. Happily, Mr. Bear had another agenda and he gingerly backed out of the semi-circle and waddled towards open water, swinging his massive head to and fro across his withers to ensure we were not in pursuit.

We left him foraging for a snack, while glancing over our shoulders from time to time–to see that Mr. Bear still had us in view, I guess making sure the aliens were driving away and not circling back for an ambush. It felt as though two sets of adversaries had just had an encounter, with one set looking for a natural history experience–while the other contemplated lunch.

The temperature for a southern tenderfoot continued to be bone-chilling and I wished that I was better prepared for this extended experience-but this was a unique opportunity and I was not about to let sub-zero degrees get in the way. The other issue compounding my discomfort was that my gloves were useless, and I wasn't able to keep them off for more than a few seconds, because the icy wind locked my fingers solid and I couldn't work my cameras. I was obliged to carefully time my photographic sessions and restrict them to a maximum of twenty five seconds in order to grab a few images and it was while juggling hands, gloves, and camera bags that I nearly caused a disaster.

In the excitement of belting after that bear and distracted by concern for my safety while on a highly vibrating ATV–I had somehow lost my gloves. In these temperatures, in this remote location and in these bleak Arctic conditions, losing any piece of clothing could be fatal and with no spares in my bag I had caused a predicament that had inadvertently placed my colleagues in a difficult position. Within seconds my fingers started to seize up and it became almost impossible to keep a firm grip on the ATV–so we immediately turned back down the trail racing against the fading light, looking everywhere for my frozen Wal-Mart specials. Mercifully, after wandering back and forth over our tracks and taking care not to run over them by mistake, we located the frozen solid gloves standing out against the snow, fingers pointing skywards as if in prayer. After my hands and gloves were reunited and after we cracked off the surface ice from the fabric fingers and warmed up my flesh, we were able to continue tracking the Great White Ghost.

We motored along the shoreline for several hours with a deep blue sky overhead and the contrails of an F18 making its way across Hudson Bay. All day we had been keeping a weather eye on a ferocious storm which was well out at sea, about thirty nautical miles due east across Hudson Bay towards the Quebec shoreline. The sky out there was a mixture of angry grey and black clouds and definitely not the place to be without shelter if the storm made landfall. While we were tracking the bears we noticed the elongated paw-prints of rabbits, ptarmigan and Arctic hare and then a short distance away, running perfectly parallel, the paw marks of several foxes who were stalking their prey from a distance. Wildlife in abundance.

I have discovered that in these extreme low temperatures my body needs a constant intake of calories, and I was happy to have packed a supply of sandwiches, granola bars, cookies and a large flask of super-heated herbal tea. We had strapped the flask inside my backpack under the rifle on the front rack of the ATV, and I was happy that it was piping hot even after four hours exposed to the icy wind. The trick is to superheat the inside of the flask for an hour before pouring in scalding hot tea, giving the vacuum a head start to do its job. I did not finish all of the tea and that evening the flask provided a hot drink as a nightcap. I was experiencing a curious feeling of vulnerability in these sub-zero temperatures and realized more than once that I was not too well prepared for Hudson Bay. I had not eaten enough for breakfast, my liquid intake was less than my body was demanding, and the effects of that penetrating cold were being aggravated by my lack of calories.

We motored past our second polar bear, completely missing him lurking in the short grass about one hundred meters from our track. One of the hunters motioned an alert and our ATVs curved around in a crescent formation and went bouncing over the snow-covered gravel–circling to come alongside him. The body language of our second polar bear was similar to that of our first encounter, as he swung the front part of his body left and then right, his massive head each time facing to confront our machines. He was almost like a cowboy in a western movie, swinging his revolver to and fro, covering the bar room ... just in case. At one point I guess we went too close, because Freddy was rapidly loading his 30-06.

The bear turned to face each ATV in turn and I marveled at how he lowered and elongated his body profile, seemingly growing three feet longer each time. That magnificent thick coat made it impossible to see his muscles flexing underneath, which is generally a clue when a large animal decides to lunge, but I could hear the low pitched grumbling from deep inside his chest and clearly he was unhappy with his position and even less happy about the multi colored people astride ATVs invading his turf. Our hunter-guides were permitted to kill two bears on this journey for village handicraft purposes and a single shot dropped this magnificent animal not far from our feet.

It was now about 13:00 and we had been in the open for several hours and were located about seventy kilometers north of town, so we decided to start the long journey back. The timing of a journey at this time of the year is critical, because when the sun goes down you have about thirty minutes before the light fades and navigation becomes challenging. Yes, we could have used a portable GPS to replicate this journey, but when it's a matter of knowing where the rivers are–gauging the state of the ice and the stability of the river banks, we felt it was safer for local knowledge to take the lead. As we headed for the settlement, we retraced our tracks along rivers that had been marginal that morning and were now frozen solid and ready for speed. It's odd how a return journey along the same outward route can deliver an entirely different perspective and it was a treat to see this unforgiving landscape, under the setting sun with a new set of shadows framing our machines.

What had previously seemed a makeshift crude plywood shack now looked more like the Hudson Bay Sheraton and we looked forward to lighting the wood stove and eating a meal sheltered from the bone-chilling wind. Wanting to be a good team-member and showcase my boy scout fire-lighting techniques I was all set to drive inland and hack down a tree for kindling, when our Cree hunters nonchalantly kicked at a small piece of wood and an entire series of bone-dry planks appeared out of the snow-which when doused with a cup of high-test gas soon created a roaring fire. Our impromptu Sheraton buffet on Hudson Bay was more than welcome, as we stripped off and luxuriated in the warmth radiating from the stove. Tracy took off her boots and thawed out her toes. The extra pair of socks she was wearing had made her boots too tight thus not allowing her toes to move and keep warm.

Our day of departure for home was a bit distracting, but gave us an insight into the often challenging nature of life in some of these communities. Our prearranged ride to the airstrip did not materialize, and in low temperatures, with extra luggage and Nanook somewhere in the bushes, walking a short distance was not a realistic option, so Tracy approached the policeman who was resident in our building and he agreed to drive us out. On the way to the terminal, he told us that the previous year the detachment house was burned to the ground by an arsonist with a deadly grudge against the police, but mercifully loss of life was avoided. This had forced the police into the motel where we were staying until the detachment building could be re-established. En route to the airport, this young officer was called on his radio to deal with an armed resident who had barricaded himself and several children inside a house and was refusing to come out. I am unsure how it all ended but as he dropped us at the airstrip we understood the children had been released and he was waiting for a charter aircraft with backup officers before he re-approached the house. Last fall there had been a murder in the same community and while not excusing any of these crimes, it is easy to see how a stressful life with limited work prospects, few diversions, and an uncertain future can drive people to alcohol, drugs and violence.

Looking along the length of the wing as our pilot circled the town I was full of vivid memories, of optimism for the community–yet tinged with apprehension. Would the locals seize this interesting opportunity for a new livelihood or would this remain yet another lost opportunity for our fellow Canadians living in this remote part of the country? Sadly, and after many follow up calls and communications the community is disinterested in taking this further.

---

[1] The Cree are one of the largest First Nations/Native North Americans which are estimated to have two hundred thousand members living in North Eastern Canada, around Lake Superior and Hudson Bay.

The amazing Icelandic horses I almost slept with

CHAPTER 11

Exploring Canada on my 650

In the late 1970's, I decided to take an in-depth look at my new country using two wheels in-line with a motor in between. Four wheels would also have been possible, but with so many open, solitary secondary roads on Canada, many of them with pleasantly curving radii, touring on a 650cc Honda seemed too good to miss. However, because my career was now in full swing and I was unable to make longer term personal plans, my biking adventures were broken up and sandwiched between research and contracting missions.

Canada is a huge piece of real estate, so making a road trip of any distance takes careful planning and my journey from coast to coast to coast using this prodigious Rice Rocket was achieved in component parts, with tent, panniers, and camping gear neatly tucked in behind. My original 650 was a superb motorbike, light years ahead of the pack at the time of its birth–however coming from the UK, I would have preferred to be riding an English bike, basking in the glory of solid British engineering, listening to the clattering of a Norton or Triumph between my knees. Sadly during this era, the innovative engineering community in the UK decided to take a decade-long sabbatical and R&D funds dried up while union labour produced more Friday cars than dealerships could handle. Partially as a result of these circumstances, the loyal commonwealth of consumers steadily deserted British-made products–to become enthusiastic buyers of competitive exciting cars and motorbikes from Germany, Italy, Spain, France, and Japan.

This was depressing for a loyal and self-confessed gear head, but the truth was self evident and I was witnessing the unravelling–worse, the surrendering, of the British automotive industry, car by car, bike by bike, and widget by widget to overseas competitors. From the current perspective of three decades later, the industry has hardly recovered, and the UK is now an island of branch plant factories with premium marques such as Jaguar and Land Rover owned by BMW in Germany and Tata industries in India. However, despite this disheartening state of affairs, the spirit of innovation and superb engineering still resides on this tiny island where most of the current Formula 1 race cars are conceived, engineered, tested, and built. The UK also has an amazing variety of manufacturers within the kit-car industry, turning out an wide selection of fascinating vehicles for road and the track. This crop of current innovators including such luminaries as James Dyson are following the path of their inventor fore-bearers, the likes of George Stephenson or John Logie Baird–but when the volume British automotive horse bolted the barn, the door slammed shut on an empty stall.

My Honda CB 650 was the earliest of this edition with four cylinders, six gears, sixteen valves (four per cylinder), shaft drive, and 650 cubic centimetres of constant linear power. I recently purchased the same model fully 31 years after it was manufactured, and I am still impressed with its power, road-holding, and gearbox.

If I had arrived in Canada fresh from the UK, my senses might have lacked some valuable tuning. However, after being involved in challenging in-depth tourism research I was now looking at Canada through more critical eyes and beginning to realize how much it offered as a nature-based tourism destination. Sadly the need to work for a living rendered my two-wheel blasts of joy into manageable time segments, but each time I completed another segment of my on-again-off-again Canadian road trip, the extraordinary potential of this land became more apparent.

Riding around Georgian Bay

Close to the north of Toronto is fabulous Georgian Bay, a huge expanse of water to the east of Lake Huron, at one time a paddling vacation paradise for indigenous tribes from each the five Great Lakes. Many have suggested that Georgian Bay is so distinctive with its inshore island topography that it should be named the sixth Great Lake, but after a flurry of early interest there has lately been no traction on that.

My first motorbike trip in Ontario found me riding the Bruce Peninsula, crossing by ferry to Manitoulin Island, cutting across a corner of Lake Huron, to discover that for a biker, this is superb touring country, with relatively little traffic coupled with single-lane car free roads. Manitoulin lives to the distinct beat of its residents, and for anyone riding a 650 Honda, this is as close to your personal Isle of Man TT as it gets. This island is a special part of Ontario and most especially for the Ojibwa First Nations people for whom it carries a spiritual significance. I particularly enjoyed the town of Little Current and heartily recommend the Anchor Inn run by my friends Kelly and Bruce O'Hare.

My plan was to circle Lake Huron by riding across Manitoulin Island and eventually making my way down to the Thirty Thousand Islands, which embraces the compact waterside town of Parry Sound. However, as enthusiasts will know, one of the pleasures of motorbike adventuring is the opportunity to wander along a labyrinth of secondary roads, vaguely in your direction of travel in a half-hearted attempt to get lost–knowing full well these roads will always lead somewhere and most often to a warm bed with a decent breakfast.

I had been experiencing an increasing degree of wheel-wobble at the front of the Honda, coupled with lazy damping over the many long dips in the road, and it was evident that my well worn Rice Rocket needed attention. Fate has a habit of intervening at curious times, and just south of Magnetawan on this single-lane road, an identical Honda 650 was heading towards me, ridden by another two-wheeled adventurer from Toronto. He was heading for the same Lake Huron ferry that I had taken and was packed with superb local knowledge, especially where I could get help for my rattling 650.

One of the enrichments that accompany impromptu wandering is the chance to stumble into something special that might not be on one's agenda and the sign on the tree simply said "Icelandic Horses," which instantly rang a bell with me because father had spent part of the war in Iceland and had spoken glowingly about this breed of pocket-size steeds. I can't quite recall a bed & breakfast sign, but given the pounding on my wrists caused by the wheel-wobble, I was ready to dismount for the night, even prepared to bed down with the Icelandics in their barn. The owners who had emigrated from Europe with a nucleus of Icelandic breeding stock, were engaged in raising these amazing animals for domestic and export riders. Icelandic horses are about one-fifth smaller than most standard breeds, almost pony size, but their compactness gives little away in terms of their character and immense strength–while their stamina is legendary in harsh conditions. Icelandic horses have a double coat that allows them to thrive in conditions other breeds would shy away from and they also don't trot like any other horses. They use a fast-stepping gait (Icelanders call it a tölt) that allows them to accelerate like a 650 Honda between 2nd and 3rd gear and this curious movement is one of several gaits bred into the stock over many generations. Visualize a standard horse trotting along with the rider rhythmically bobbing along on the saddle, which is not what you will see from an Icelandic horse. The tölt allows the rider to remain perfectly level without the bobbing up and down and after riding Icelandics in Iceland I can speak with authority about how addictive this becomes. Happily this family of breeders was able to offer a bed and breakfast package (not in the barn), and I spent a wonderful pre-dinner evening in the paddock wandering amongst this ancient breed. I slept soundly that night and next morning in Parry Sound I was able to buy a new set of front dampers for the 650, so with calm wrists and a happy throttle hand, I headed south for Toronto.

Other bikers The *Star Wars* gang and Emilio Sotto

I am a fan of the Scottish movie star Ewan McGregor of *Star Wars* fame and his friend Charlie Boorman who are prodigious long distance BMW motor bikers and have ridden some challenging routes through Asia, Africa, and North America. Their *Long Way Around* is a marvellous account of two friends making their way around the girth of the earth, while their *Long Way Down* is a wonderful tale of their ride through Africa–both journeys undertaken on BMW motorbikes. Recently they released a series of DVDs of their bike trips that are highly entertaining, but Charlie's attack on the Paris Dakar rally was almost his last adventure. These high quality productions were challenging and complex in the extreme, requiring a formidable back-up crew and a set of videographers, during which Ewan and Charlie proved to be outstanding riders.

A contrasting approach to motorbike adventuring is that of the Argentine rider Emilo Scotto who, with no back-up crew whatsoever, toured the world and rode for 730,000 kilometres on his heavy 1980 Honda Goldwing. I can't help reflecting that once dropped, a bike of this weight must be almost impossible for a solo human to pick up rendering this adventurer a brave rider with courage to spare. Scotto outdistanced every other "iron butt" rider by a country mile and the statistics are impressive as he completed this extraordinary ride, which absorbed ten years of his life–without a shred of support and only $300 of initial funding. His ability to focus, maintain his powers of observation, and manage the mental and physical challenges of riding through two hundred and seventy five countries and a distance of 735,000 kilometres propelled him to the head of the long distance field. Born in Buenos Aires in 1956, he had an early career as a writer, photographer and a sometime salesperson for Pfizer the pharmaceutical corporation and oddly enough this ten-year odyssey was Emilio's first time out of Argentina. At the conclusion of his journey in 1995 he had used thirteen Argentine passports, worn out a complete 1100cc Honda Goldwing engine, consumed 47,000 litres of fuel, discharged twelve batteries, and bounced his way through nine seats. Not to diminish his achievement by an iota–many of his journey segments would be impossible nowadays because of localized violence and banditry. But fortuitously in 1985 he was able to motor unscathed through the centre of the Nicaraguan civil war although was arrested as a spy in no less than three African states–Burundi, Chad, and Cameroon. Undoubtedly he was disappointed when denied access to paranoid North Korea, but he did manage to part the Bamboo curtain thanks to the intervention of the Beijing Motor Cycle club, which persuaded the authorities to cancel his $70,000 "entrance fee." Emilio Scotto was not a wealthy traveller, nor did he start out with sustainable funding, but thanks to a polyglot list of backers, including funds raised by a New York television appearance and, surprisingly, $300 in cash from Muammar Gaddafi, he was able to complete his journey with his wife Monica perched behind him.

Colette Coleman and *Great Motorcycle Journeys of the World*

I met Colette Coleman in the shadow of Ripon Cathedral, in that atmospheric Yorkshire market town at the edge of the Yorkshire Dales–excellent riding country and a hotbed of motorcycling enthusiasts. A mutual friend, Debra Taylor, had introduced us as potential collaborators for a Canadian tourism project, and at that time I had no idea that Colette and her husband Steve were such accomplished long-distance motorcycle adventurers and that her book *Great Motorcycle Journeys of the World* is an outstanding how-to guide for nascent and experienced two-wheel riders. Colette describes a variety of motorcycling destinations, each of them inspirational and well known to her. She points out that adventuring by motorcycle is now within the reach of anyone and enthusiasts can either take along their own bike, rent one at the destination, journey as a loner, or join an organized group of intrepid riders to undertake a two-wheel social experience. Closer to home Colette rides a 250cc Honda for local recreation and a BMW for longer journeys–such as her overland odyssey between the UK and Australia.

North Shore of Gitche Gumee

After consolidating my workload in the office, I was ready to head into the fabled northern region of Ontario, locally referred to as "Up North." The North Shore of Lake Superior is a motorbike rider's dream destination, with a superb road surface, an abundance of gently contoured curves and several compact communities. I have always enjoyed riding to Sault Ste Marie, located where Lakes Huron and Superior meet alongside the St Mary's River–and for three specific reasons. It is home to my friend Ian MacMillan and it houses the fabulous bush plane museum which is an exceptional collection of Canadian pioneer aircraft, deftly telling many true and improbable stories of how early aviation opened up the Canadian North. Sault Ste

Marie is also the southern terminus for the romantic Algoma Central Railroad, which to this day runs the amazing Agawa Canyon day-train.

It was here that I was able to leave my bike at a small bed and breakfast for a few days and take the ACR north, but not quite to Hearst. The ACR was one of the few lines in the world that offered "flag stop" service, which simply means that if you stand by the track waving your hands, the train will stop for you. Because of harsh winter weather, particularly the freezing and heaving on the rail-bed, most trains rarely exceeded fifty five kilometres per hour, so hailing the train is definitely not the heart-stopping experience it would be in Europe.

My flag stop at Kilometre Post 206 was to visit Errington's Wilderness Lodge on Lake Wabatongushi and as the ACR clanked to a halt, Albert Errington was arriving trackside in his pontoon boat, ready to motor me across to his island wilderness retreat–known for its inquisitive bears, excellent fishing, ancient lichens, magnificent island solitude, and Doris's fabulous cooking. The resourceful Erringtons have carved a wonderful life out of this wilderness island retreat in the Chapleau Game Reserve which is one of the world's most expansive animal sanctuaries, and it is mystery to me that more Canadians, particularly from the Toronto region, have never visited this paradise on their doorstep. It is easy and affordable to fly into Lake Wabatongushi from Sault Ste Marie, or Hearst, or Frater and as an additional treat the flight is often made on a vintage Canadian-made De Havilland Beaver which is a venerable bush plane on floats.

I was interested in the bears, and next morning Al took me out on his boat to see if we could make contact with these animals which have a sense of smell seven times more sensitive than a bloodhound, one reason that campers are wise to pack their food in bear-proof containers–resistant to smell and powerful claws. We halted the boat thirty feet from a mature female foraging along the shoreline, and as we drifted on the flat water, moved along by the offshore breeze, Al spoke quietly about the intelligence of these animals, a trait that we humans might characterize as "cunning." We then drifted across to an island where we gently stroked the head of soft lichens, imagining the thousand winters, springs, falls, and summers these hardy plants had experienced. I wonder what secrets they could have told us about climate change and how adaptable they have become to cope with airborne pollution like acid rain.

Reclaiming my bike five days later, I rode north from Sault Ste Marie to visit the gold-mining community of Wawa, but mainly because I had heard about an amazing bed and breakfast located on a peninsular jutting out into Lake Superior. It is a long-standing joke with my friend Ron Johnson, director of Business Development at Duluth's port that in all the years I have been visiting this lake with its fearsome reputation for killer waves, all I have seen is calm water and eye-popping sunsets. However as I glided my Honda off the finished surface of Highway 17 and gently motored across a packed earth track, I could hear Gitche Gumee through my helmet, reverberating off the surrounding forest, as the grumbling thunderous pounding of waves hit the rocks. This signalled that Gitche Gumee (as the First Nations call Lake Superior) or Gichigami (as Longfellow preferred to call it) had awakened from its slumber, and Ron was correct after all.

My Honda was behaving well on the earth track and I managed to ride up to the building and carefully stash the 650 inside an empty woodshed for the night. The bed and breakfast was right out of a wilderness tourism brochure and its location on a rocky peninsula was wild and simply awe-inspiring. As experienced mariners know, waves are a result of wind acting on water over a measured distance for a specific period of time, and these pounding waves, building for days across several hundred miles, were demonstrating how devastatingly powerful the big lake can be. That evening, as the waves started to calm down, the dying sun peered through the cloud cover, and the deep rumbling of Gitche Gumee subsided–my investment riding to Wawa fully repaid.

Characteristics of riding and dropping the 650

A word or two about the characteristics of riding this wonderful motorbike may be useful. Leaning the 650 rhythmically through a series of S bends is relatively undramatic because Soichiro Honda had tested his new bike on the track well before putting it on the road and it possessed excellent manners. In fact, many of our current motorbikes and cars have benefitted from extensive R&D paid for by the racing community, without which our suspension, gears, engines, and the use of modern composites would be light years behind. Coming out of Wawa and carefully transitioning from loose-packed earth to tarmac took a weight off my mind, because the bike was loaded with camping gear, and although the centre of gravity was low, the turning movement was slow, and making slight corrections in direction not quite so crisp. On the road towards Red Rock, I was leaning into a decreasing radius left hander in 6th gear, turning about 5000 RPM when a series of inshore islands caught my admiration–about the same time that Mother Goose and her family wandered into my path. Conventional wisdom is to sacrifice a small animal in order to ride safe, but how can you cook such a cute goose?

Thanks to Soichiro's steering, suspension, and progressive brakes, I was able to slide between mother goose and the leading set of chicks, scaring the life out of the avian family and learning more about my 650 in the process. However, the violent twisting motion I initiated while avoiding the birds dislodged one of my panniers, which started leaning out, catching the slipstream. As fellow bike riders will understand–when you experience road trouble, you make all of your correcting movements as slowly and smoothly as possible to maximize the positive and minimize the negative. Therefore slowing and gliding gently to the shoulder worked well for me, until Mr. Honda's front tire embraced the pea-gravel and in slow motion the front of the bike slid out from under me.

When you come off your bike, several things happen simultaneously, some of them instinctive, some self-protective, and some pure reactive, and there is often a deep sense of failure at not anticipating the obvious. My journey around the North Shore of Lake Superior was going so well when this happened and as I was falling I remembered thinking "Will I be able to continue my journey and what repairs will I have to make to the 650"? The highway along Superior's North Shore was lonely in those days and only a handful of cars passed me by, so once I had lifted the bike upright and began working on it, most travellers waved me a cheery hello assuming that all was under control.

Soichiro had built a tough mechanical bike that could take a real pounding and keep performing at its peak long after it has been abused, but metal is metal, and when it meets the unyielding road surface it is generally the road that wins the confrontation. Sitting my Honda upright and surveying the damage, it was obvious that my protruding pannier had fractured its housing when it connected with the gravel, scattering a debris field of camping gear down the banking and into the grass beyond. Further forward, my windscreen had shattered in several pieces and the front fender was bent skyward where it caught a piece of slate embedded in the gravel shoulder. After sitting on a rock for some time surveying the damage and massaging my bruised ego, I thought about developing a plan to get myself out of this mess before night fell and I was compelled to camp by the side of the road. From my third-world travelling days I had developed the art of packing a toolkit that I modified for each trip, so out of the opposite pannier I dug my Crazy Glue, tie wraps, racing (duct) tape and a couple of wrenches. At about that time I realized that my right elbow was hot and clammy which meant that I was bleeding beneath my Belstaff road suit and while the suit had protected me from major damage my elbow has taken a hard knock and needed attention.

There was not much I could do to weld the fractured pannier bracket but the tie wraps easily held the frame in place and it was soon back on the bike, firmly nestling against the chassis. I am continually amazed what modern adhesives can achieve, and very carefully if not too neatly I mated a jigsaw puzzle of five Plexiglas pieces into a semblance of what the windscreen looked like before it fractured, using the tape to hold the jigsaw in place until the adhesive set–after which I would remove the tape to clear my line of sight. The heavy metal of the fender was another issue entirely, but when I eventually unbolted what resembled a peeled banana, Dorothy and the Tin Man were once more looking over my shoulder. As I glanced across to the outer guardrail of the Lake Superior drop off, I noticed that the railing was supported by slender logs embedded into the gravel shoulder. The circumference of the logs almost matched my disfigured fender, and with some careful pressure from my foot on the outer edges and using the log as a template, the banana gradually unpeeled and started to look more like a slightly dented fender.

Starting up after an "off" is always a tentative process, but as there was virtually no traffic I was able to go through all six gears, test the front and rear brakes independently, and then progressively curve left and right, testing the front forks, the suspension travel, and the balance of the bike. Objectively speaking, my "off" had not been one of those Paris-Dakar drop offs, where the bike and rider tumble head over heels down a steep banking–commonly called an "end-over." Those long-distance riders have experienced some mind-numbing accidents to their bikes and themselves and although they have a paid mechanical support team, many of them have sustained horrible injuries and in some cases even death. My "off" was relatively minor, but even a minor accident can have unintended consequences that might not be too evident at the time. However, all was well with the bike and once into Red Rock I was able to attend to my elbow, a minor abrasion that healed within days.

The cops who patrolled close to Red Rock, another attractive North Lake Superior community, were as anal as their cousins in Quebec, and at one point I droned along for an hour in fourth gear tailed by some ticket-hungry fellow looking for a minnow. Happily, his territory seemed sharply defined, and at the county line, still denied of his catch-of-the-day, he blasted past, turned into the next gas station, and accelerated home the way we had come. Once he had gone fishing this allowed me to exercise all six of Sochiro's well-spaced gears and enjoy some of the sweeping curves between Wawa and Red Rock, occasionally glancing at the magnificent views over Lake Superior's inshore islands. At that time the Red Rock paper mill was still operating, and although it seemed to be the only private-sector employment in town, there was a distinct buzz to the place. Sadly, once the mill closed, this pretty location has experienced challenges in charting its way forward into a new economy.

Red Rock is in a magnificent location, tucked away on the North Shore of this fearsome lake, protected from the elements by huge St. Ignace Island. The town, located at the north western end of the bay, takes its name from the colour of the cliffs that dominate the community. Nowadays the former paper-mill lodge is a small inn and the view from the mountain behind across to St Ignace Island has to be seen to be appreciated. There are many magnificent viewscapes around the world and the perspective from this Lake Superior mountaintop is as good as it gets. During World War II, Red Rock was an internment camp for German prisoners of war, and these troubled years are interpreted in a display inside the new marina building. What could these prisoners have thought on their long journey north to Lake Superior: Where on earth were the Allies taking them? How utterly vast was this Commonwealth country they called Kanada, and what fearsome weather would they face in the coming winter? Some of the German visitors today making their way around Lake Superior are relatives of these prisoners. Recently, due to a coalition of motivated interests, the town had a visit from the first cruise ship in its history, sliding through the deep-water channel alongside St Ignace Island. Perhaps Red Rock is discovering a new economic life as a wonderful port of call.

Next day my 650 was idling strong, ingesting cool morning air into its fuel system and riding through a light morning mist, I headed west for Thunder Bay to the home of my friends Paul and Bambi Pepe. Further west, I am sad to report, I rode straight through Manitoba and Saskatchewan, because of scheduling issues, and saw little of either. In contrast, my riding through the Rocky Mountains, Banff, Jasper, and Lake Louise was exceptional because unlike a car, a motorbike gives outstanding views of the mountains and pulling off anywhere is easy. In British Columbia I rode as far as Prince Rupert, eventually taking the ferry across to the northern tip of Vancouver Island for the drive down to Victoria. Memo to self: "Must make that trip again on another Rice Rocket."

Biking the Maritimes

Biking around the maritime provinces of Nova Scotia, New Brunswick, and Prince Edward Island, I discovered a charmingly laid back and welcoming destination full of warmth, personality, and speed-tolerant cops. I first tackled this world-class ride around the Cabot Trail through the Cape Breton Highlands in Nova Scotia, which was a real highlight on my Honda. It was one of the few remaining roads where you could power through a corner laid over at an angle with reasonable confidence there was no traffic coming the opposite way. My side trip through New Brunswick was specifically to experience the extraordinary tidal flow in the Bay of Fundy, where no less than one hundred billion tons of water flows in and out of the bay *twice each day* and you have to see this phenomenon from a cockle-shell kayak to get the true perspective. On Prince Edward Island I distinctly remember not a single vehicle coming towards me for twenty minutes, and I was buzzing along well above the speed limit, but then nothing passed me either. The lack of traffic made me think of postwar Britain or for that matter New Zealand, where cars were somewhat scarce and roads were less cluttered.

Riding through Newfoundland and Labrador was as quirky as it gets (still is) mostly because of the chatty and matter-of-fact people who made the most lasting impression on me. Just about everywhere I rode, Newfoundlanders and Labradoreans engaged me in conversation which was highly animated, endlessly interesting and often generous ("Come stay the night with us laddie"). Newfoundlanders have not always enjoyed the easy life, and before joining the Confederation they were struggling economically and exporting their youth at an alarming rate. It has often been said that Newfoundland's main export has always been its young people, exemplified by the exceptional performance of the Newfoundland Regiment on the slaying fields of World War II and more recently as civilian employees in the oilfields of Alberta. As the fishery and the localized economy failed, the Outports were particularly hard hit when these fishing communities on the craggy shoreline–tenaciously clinging to the rocks, experienced a disappearing way of life, as fish stocks became depleted. Nowadays the discovery of Hibernia oil has blown in the carbon winds of change, and life is improving in this marvellous corner of Canada.

I was able to book passage on the coastal ferry for a glimpse into life on the dramatic northern sub-Arctic coastline of Labrador. With no road access, these tiny communities depend on the coastal "steamer" for the basic necessities of life, from food and furniture to penicillin and pencils. At that time the ferry was an old bathtub called the Northern Ranger and dodging the icebergs in the fog was our greatest worry. With typical Newfoundland black humour, and with fog slithering in through the portholes and icebergs somewhere on our port-side, my dinner companions insisted in retelling the tale of the Titanic disaster. Newfoundland and Labrador also had speed-tolerant cops, so once back off the ferry I remounted the 650 and blasted down the northern peninsula from St. Anthony to Gros Morne National Park before taking the ferry to Quebec.

Motobicyclet in Quebec

Quebec's linguistic and cultural identity makes it quite distinct from English Canada and a fascinating place for bike touring. Quebec also has an epicurean tradition that permits travellers to eat especially well, even in quite remote and modest locations. However, the cops in Quebec were uptight, tailed me incessantly, seemingly fixated on building revenue. And this from the province that produced Gilles and Jacques Villeneuve, the talented father and son motor-racing duo.

Outside cosmopolitan Montreal and the fabulous walled Quebec City with their superb restaurants and vibrant nightlife, the lower reaches of the St. Lawrence River is where a great deal of interest lies and I loved idling my 650 through the picturesque villages of Charlevoix including; Baie St Paul, Isle aux Coudres and Île d'Orléans. During the French colonization of what is now Quebec, immigrants were awarded seigneuries on which to settle and farm and in this region they run straight down to the St. Lawrence River from the heights above. I was exploring the North Shore of the river, biking past many seigneuries, heading for the magnificent fjord of the Saguenay River and a large family of whales. The riding, the landscape and the superb views from the corniche are just magnificent, and to this day when we drive over the same route we re-enjoy the same viewscapes as before. A modest orchard on Île d'Orléans grows plum trees that are said to have been brought over from Napoleon's own garden and planted when the French settled the region. The orchard sells excellent confiture made from the decendents of Napoleon's plums, which provides an interesting taste for the pallet and an interesting image for the mind.

Separatism in Canada–My View

From time to time in modern Canadian history, separatism raises its ugly head and the country goes through a teeth-grinding, heart-thumping period when Quebec Nationalists gain a toe-hold at the provincial, federal, or both levels of the political landscape. For some Quebeckers (not all), supporting a separatist party is their way of tweaking Canada's nose and ensuring that Quebec gets the attention it deserves from the rest of the country. I believe many of these characters are actually closet federalists and their strategy has worked well–and not so well, producing a mixed harvest of strong federal support along with a great uneasiness amongst federalist Quebeckers and the rest of the country.

While there were originally two distinct sides to this debate– on one side the true separatist Francophones and the other side a combination of federalist Francophones and Anglophones, the lines have recently become blurred as immigrants from at least 30 countries (Allophones) have arrived in the country. Many of these new immigrants come from lands with violent sectarian divisions, some escaping continuous religious strife and some from badly fractured societies and utterly destroyed economies–and most of these newcomers have no use for a movement that promotes the breakup of their new country Canada. Also and possibly a surprise to the separatists, many First Nations Communities inside Quebec have no interest in leaving Canada and if they did decide to take their traditional lands out of Quebec, this would greatly reduce the separatist provincial landscape and leave some odd-looking maps.

Of course there are the true separatists who firmly believe that Quebec should be a separate country and leaving Canada is their only option and they are sometimes led by a collection of faux-intellectuals, some practicing law or teaching at Quebec universities, and frequently backed by the talented francophone entertainment industry. I call them faux intellectuals because real intellectuals always seek the truth in an argument–which has not always been evident from Quebec's separatist leaders.

Despite this occasional angst I have immense sympathies for Quebeckers who are worried sick that their unique identity is in danger of being subsumed by a powerful Anglophone culture–and not only from the rest of Canada, but from the neighbouring United States. I completely understand their angst for the erosion of their cultural identity, which inevitably starts with erosion of their language and once language is lost, the rest of their culture would start to unravel. And if this were to happen, in a few generations all that will remain might be pockets of quaint speaking French villages and perhaps a provincial language institute. Keeping Quebec in the Canadian federation is critically important to me because Quebec contributes a rich and vibrant culture that makes Canada what it is–and for me to imagine Canada without the cultural and mercantile contribution made by this province is unthinkable. But how we achieve that while satisfying the separatists may truly be the long-game. The former separatist provincial government in Quebec, just like any other government in Canada, was preoccupied with stabilizing the economy and attending to the hundreds of issues that government has to cope with once in power, but they have just called an election and have lost big time to a federalist provincial government.

More recently I rode my new-old Honda 650 around the country lanes of Eastern Ontario along the route of the marvellous Rideau Canal between Kingston and Ottawa. The canal was built after the initial scare during the War of 1812 when the young American republic was attempting to add Canada to their version of the United States and remains fully operational and a national treasure to this day. The linear power, that lovely soft clattering of the sixteen valve engine and the controlled exhaust note reverberating off the forest wall of trees is as sweet today as it was along Lake Superior almost 35 years earlier.

CHAPTER 12

The Goodwood Revival

As I tramped across a field on the edge of the South Downs at sunrise, a brace of Spitfires screamed overhead, strafing the field before me in series of low altitude passes. Then, powered by that famous 12-cylinder Merlin aero engine, the two Spits roared skyward towards the coast to do battle with the enemy. I wished the cloud cover was higher than its current two hundred feet so I could see them form up wing tip to wing tip, but during the Second World War, our young fighter pilots of the Dawn Patrol didn't have the luxury of choosing their flying weather to defend the nation and neither did I.

It was a spine-chilling moment and an amazing overture to an exceptional day full of surprises which I had been looking forward to for years. The grass airfield I was approaching in the center of the Goodwood race circuit in West Sussex is the same airfield patrolled by these same vintage fighter aircraft during the Second World War and the extraordinary performance of these iconic Spitfires was a fitting prelude to an exceptional three days of British nostalgia.

The Goodwood Revival is race meeting for historic race cars and motorcycles which celebrates the history of motor sport, as some of the world's finest cars are enthusiastically raced by expert drivers and their mechanics. Recently, the Revival has expanded to host a magnificent display of functional vintage aircraft which are as mouthwatering as the cars. To add an aura of aviation exotica Lufthansa brought over their huge restored Junkers Ju52 Airliner circa 1936, which took off and landed from the infield airstrip, thundering low and slow over the track.

The Revival is the brainchild of the highly talented Lord March who, prior to taking over the family estate, was known as Charles Settrington, a well regarded London-based photographer in the advertising profession. Quite a number of titled Englishmen and women have elected to use "civilian" names to make their way in private life, preferring the advantages of anonymity and hard-work over the advantages of title. Over the past 16 years under Lord March's stewardship, the Revival has secured a position as the world's most successful historic race-event, maturing well beyond the sum of its parts. For some (I fall into this category) it remains true to its original concept of a superb historic race meeting with the world's finest cars competing for on-track honours. For others it is the opportunity to dress in period costume replicating and reliving for a fleeting three-day "moment" the eras between the 1940s, 1950s and 1960s, when these cars were new. Above all it is the chance to attend a pre-eminent period nostalgic event and enjoy an inspirational long weekend, in a unique sporting and convivial atmosphere on the estate of Lord March – heir apparent to the Duke of Richmond.

The twelve thousand -acre Goodwood estate has been in the March family for many generations. Located on the edge of the South Downs close to historic Chichester and the seaside town of Bognor Regis, it is about a two-hour drive from London. Apart from occupying vast and productive farmland, the estate is close to several former World War II fighter bases, which were regularly scrambled to confront Hitler's Luftwaffe as they tried to bomb Britain back into the Stone Age. In postwar years this titled family has recognized the need to support the land with additional revenue, so they developed the Goodwood horse-race track, then the Goodwood motor race circuit and more recently the Goodwood speed hill climb – as their on-site medley of income-generating events.

The Revival is accessible by car from all points of the compass, including by air, using its own infield runway and the event team expertly sign-posts the routes and ingeniously reverses the direction of country lanes to handle the inflow of 140,000 visitors and their cars. Parking for general admission is in the fields surrounding the track, (where I first saw the Spitfire Dawn Patrol) but to encourage enthusiasts to bring their cars out to play, parking for classic vehicles is reserved close by the entrance. This veritable plantation of classics is actually a marvelous free car show, with hundreds of each marque imaginable, parked in no particular order. One misty morning with the dew still clinging to my boots, I walked past a valuable pre-war Aston Martin Ulster casually parked in a corner of the field. Nearby was a priceless vintage Bentley and a pre-war Riley and ... well you get the picture. As the planners are parking visitor's cars in farm fields with rain often in the forecast, they have ingeniously constructed "lanes" of aluminum track along which cars clanked to their approximate parking place. We did get rain, the parking fields did get muddy, but the aluminum lanes worked perfectly.

No event of this nature would be complete without a huge cast of period vendors, period vintage hair dressing salons, vintage clothing suppliers, vintage cars for sale, plus vintage Whirligigs, Walls of Death, and in-period fairground attractions. However even a self-confessed car nut needs a respite from three days of continual racing, and this eclectic combination of vendors was an interesting diversion which was well supported by well dressed nostalgia shoppers. As you might expect, nostalgic traditional English fayre such as bubble and squeak, Welsh rarebit, cheese on toast, and bangers and mash could be purchased from in-period outlets alongside the track.

This display of commercial nostalgia had an unexpected bonus for me because in the back of my mind (the motoring bucket list) has always been the thought of building my own race-special and for years I have been contemplating how best to proceed. The Revival had many exhibitors who could help by supplying parts for my project and incredibly, one firm was displaying a restoration of the same car model and year as I was building.

The special I am building will have its entire mechanical side based on a 1955 Jaguar XK 140, using the original chassis as the backbone. It will be powered by the original 3.4 liter overhead cam engine which we refer to as Miss Inline Slimline, using the original Moss gearbox, back axle, drive shaft and clutch. The suspension, steering and braking system will be as shipped in 1954 and the fuel system will use the original twin 1 3/4 SU carbs'. Upgraded components will be a geared starter motor, which will help awaken 817692 and a large capacity radiator which will incorporate a slim electric cooling fan.

For those uninitiated into the passions of the "Petrol Heads", the word "special" used as a noun or a verb can conjure up a variety of mechanical images, ranging from a bag of mechanical bits to something truly special. In my youth the specials we saw were mainly built for speed hill-climbing which is a peculiarly British type of motor sport where cars are time-raced up a twisty section of private road which is generally closed to the public, or on rare occasions on public roads. These specials were generally built around the mechanicals of an existing (donor) car. For example Nigel might used the engine, the gearbox and the suspension from a Hillman Minx, which he would then mount in a chassis, build a body of his own design and depending on his ego he might called it "The Nigel Minx". Reflecting my bias towards a certain comely chef I would have called it "The Nigella"!

When I first hauled 817692 out of a Southern Ontario paddock where she was impersonating a field-planter, it was immediately evident that we had rescued a charming old gal. My timely intervention almost certainly prevented 817692 from been parted out in several directions and lost forever as a recognizable car, or perhaps sold for scrap to be reborn as an iron railing, a bag of nails or a hospital potty! Now - instead of descending into blast-furnace-oblivion the mechanical and suspension components of 817692, including her original chassis will survive for another 100 years and forever be based on what Jaguar in Coventry shipped to Canada in the mid fifties. How fortunate that I was attending the Goodwood Revival and able to meet enthusiasts who were engaged in the same project as mine.

Now in its seventeenth edition, the Revival has matured into the finest historic event of its type while staying close to its provenance of a well-run series of historic car races – with a superb display of antique flying thrown in for good measure. It took some time, but I was now encountering entire families and groups of friends dressed in military uniforms representing the RAF, the Royal Navy, and the Army. We met cadres of Russian officers with their peculiar raised-peak caps, festooned with medals from "battles in their minds." There were scores of American Air Force generals supported by scowling GI's dressed in combat gear and helmets, M16s slung over their shoulders ready for battle. As I lined up for a fresh latte, Dad's Army of twenty British Army World War I re-enactors came marching by, grinning from ear to ear, presumably marching from nowhere to nowhere and in support of this eclectic army of good-humored military poseurs, many visitors elected to dress in period civilian costumes, most of which were stylish, some quite lavish, and in many cases visually stunning. From chatting to my fellow poseurs it appears that costume rental outlets are flourishing in the UK and for the huge numbers of period clad visitors from across the channel and North America (many ladies in furs), getting into spirit of the event allowed them to become part of it.

I suspect that Lord March's team of event planners thought carefully about how to surround the core race activities with appropriate in-period attractions, because racing takes place non-stop on all three days, and any free track time is instantly filled by classic course-cars driven by officials inspecting the circuit. To lighten the mood, these were occasionally followed by a Laurel and Hardy look-alike in a 1920's open two-seater, cheekily engaging the crowd as they drove by.

Opening each day's racing was an extensive on-track parade of Mods and Rockers from the 1960s, the Mods riding their tarted-up Lambretta and Vespa scooters with their distinctive pop-popping exhausts, while the Rockers snarled by on their Triumphs, Nortons, and Royal Enfields. The Mods in their Zoot Suits and the Rockers in leathers were pursued by classic police cars – Ford Zephyrs and Ford Consuls driven by Bobbies with sirens blaring.

Each year Lord March identifies two or three supporting activities to enrich the core race events, and this year's Revival celebrated the Tour de France and then commemorated the World War II Dam Busters raid on the German Möhne and Edersee dams in the Ruhr valley. The Tour de France was celebrated by an extensive on-track peloton of vintage competitive riders on classic bikes led by Sir Chris Hoy, the British Olympic cycling champion - who was wildly applauded as he pedaled by - this tiny island really takes its champion sports figures seriously. Then as the Revival is primarily a historic car race event, the Tour de France vignette was led by a fleet of classic French vehicles including the avant-garde designed *caravane publicitaire*, which originally carried the French media reporting on the race, lending an elegant and "éclectique" touch to this interesting display of Gallic pedal pushers.

The anniversary of the Dam Busters raid was a real tear-jerker for us Brits, as the wonderful lady narrator (who I was informed is Binnie, sister to Lord March) unfolded this amazing story to a totally silent and attentive crowd of visitors around the track. Some visitors were young adults at the time of this audacious raid, some were babes in arms – and some from the Continent were yesterday's enemy on the receiving end of this daring flight. The raid by Allied Lancaster bombers was a success from a destructive perspective, but the loss of many young Allied air crews was a serious blow to this close-knit squadron of flyers. Lord March personally introduced the retrospective of this raid which is still revered in the UK, paying tribute to Canadian air crews, amongst others. In an elegant and thoughtful nod to today's allies, he included the casualties of German civilians caught up in the tragedy of their fanatical leadership.

The racetrack is surrounded by large video screens, and as Binnie narrated details of the raid, original grainy black-and-white footage from the cockpit cameras of the bombers came up on the screens, recording each aircraft's suicidal bombing run towards the dam with anti-aircraft flack being flung towards them like fireworks. Somehow Lord March had secured the presence of one of the few surviving members of those bomber crews, and the entire crowd of 140,000 were on their feet, saluting with caps off as he was slowly driven around the track in a WWII Jeep. A true hero to us all.

Race aficionados will know the Goodwood race circuit is where Stirling Moss, now Sir Stirling, ended his career with a horrific crash in 1962. Sir Stirling was also at the 2013 Revival signing autographed copies of his scrapbook memoirs.

> *On April 24th, 1962, Stirling Moss entered a minor Formula 1 race known as the Glover Trophy at the Goodwood track in West Sussex. He danced at a country dancehall until two the night before, then rose, apparently unaffected, and prepared his pale green Lotus. On the eighth lap he pulled into the pits with a jammed gearbox. By the time mechanics fixed it, he had dropped to 17th place.*
>
> *"What are you going to do?" a friend asked. "Have a bloody go," Moss answered. In his determination to make up time, he flew down straights at 180 mph and hurtled into corners at 75 mph – dangerously close to the limit. "He's pushing it," a mechanic said. On the 35th lap Moss neared a twisty right-then-left turn called St. Mary's Corner at 110 mph. His car veered off the road, streaked across 150 yards of lawn, and smacked into an eight foot embankment.*
>
> *It took mechanics half an hour to saw through the crumpled aluminum and remove the driver's limp, unconscious body. A nurse held his hand much of the time. Blood smeared his face and dripped onto his white coveralls. His right cheek was torn open and his left eye socket was shattered. The crumpled steering wheel had broken two ribs. X-rays revealed severe bruising on the right side of his brain. He lay in a coma for a month, his left side partially paralyzed and his career shattered.*
>
> —*Extracted from "On the Limit" - a book by Michel Cannell*

Racing at the Revival is serious, highly competitive, and occasionally damaging to the cars as well as to the dismounted bruised pilots of hard-ridden vintage motor bikes. The classes race were divided up into logical groupings starting with astonishingly fast pre-war ERAs, then 1960s saloon cars, with Minis chasing Cortinas chasing Alfas chasing

Ford Galaxies – which were built by the famous US race team of Holman and Moody. A class for Ford GT 40s was utterly inspirational, as was the race for "Big Bangers," with Ford Cobras taking on Jaguars while Astons snarled at their heels. There were quite a few celebrity drivers such as Jochen Mass, Tom Kristensen , Brian Redman, Rowan Atkinson (Mr. Bean), Derek Bell, and Adrian Newey (designer for the Red Bull Formula 1 team). For a race nut like me, it really doesn't get much better than this.

The event team has spent a great deal of time honing each day of the Revival, incorporating English dry and often quirky humour where possible. In one corner of the site I saw a whimsical recreation of the French Résistance café from the successful TV series 'Allo 'Allo, complete with an Allied flier and his female French Résistance escort. In another corner was an original street corner blue "Police Box" surrounded by several English Bobbies and half a dozen vintage police cars. I'd totally forgotten that the police used to drive MGs and Sunbeam Alpine sport cars as well as their more boring service vehicles. The attention to detail of these planners was impressive. On the saloon car starting grid, as cars revved their engines, a team of high-street robbers rushed up behind a Mini, opened the trunk, and extracted a dozen "gold" bricks before disappearing into the crowd. At the Police Box there were about a dozen or so uniformed "officers" on duty including a couple of real ones, but while grinning from ear to ear, no one would admit to me which were the fakes. The cars on the starting line were marshaled into position by the Goodwood Glamour Girls clad in 1960s miniskirts, long boots, and (this is Goodwood, after all) … black bowler hats.

The non-stop activities – racing on the track, the aircraft in the air, the witty informed commentary over the PA, the eclectic field of vendors, people in vintage costume and the many cafes and bars – was perpetual motion from opening to close. Several months later, memories of what happened during my three days at the Goodwood Revival remain sharp, rich and vivid in my mind. Quite an event!

Note

Planning to visit the Revival takes some forethought, and choosing the right tickets for your budget and stamina is important. The first two days of the event are slightly less crowded and I recommend walking the circuit counterclockwise to face the oncoming cars. Locating fence-leaning room around the circuit is relatively easy, and frequent visitors take folding chairs to claim their favorite pitch for the weekend's racing. The last day is very crowded, although Lord March closed ticket sales at 140,000, which in my view is about site-maximum. Also on the final day of racing it is useful to have a grandstand ticket, and I enjoyed the Woodcote corner grandstand towards the end of the Lavant Straight within sight of the chicane.

Top: *Aston Martin in the Goodwood car park*

The Goodwood "Char Ladies'

Wartime MG on the flight line

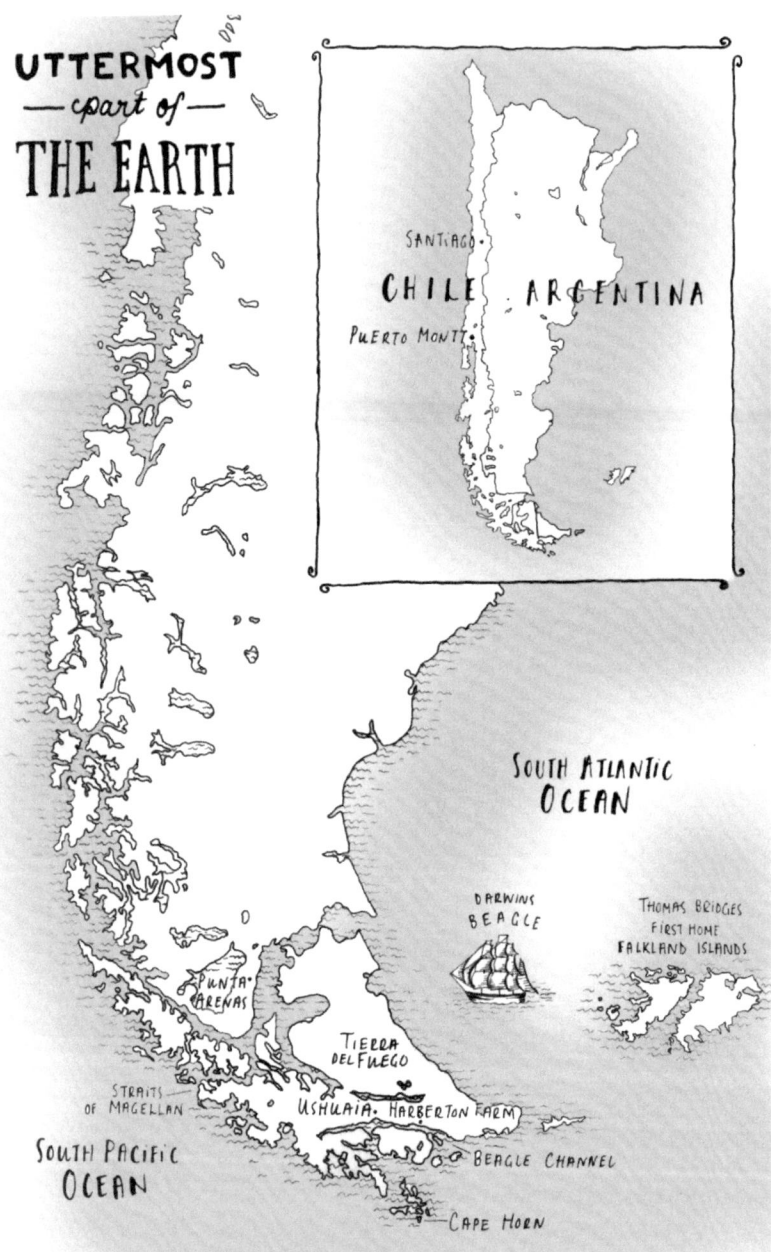

CHAPTER 13

Journey to the Uttermost Part of the Earth

A journey to the end of the earth is not what everyone contemplates for a holiday. My plan was to fly to Santiago, spend some time in the capital, then head south to Puerto Montt and board a ship in Punta Arenas for the coastal sea journey to Ushuaia in Argentina. I had previously made several interesting visits to Argentina and Chile, two countries which I enjoy immensely, but never with sufficient time to explore the southern coastal routes and this was the opportunity I had been waiting for. There was another thought in the back of my mind which was to develop an enrichment tourism experience which retraced the voyage of Charles Darwin's "Voyage of The Beagle," by sailing along some of the same passages and exploring some of the same inlets that he and his associate naturalists experienced in 1831. Darwin spent three years and a few months exploring on land but his sea voyage lasted eighteen months and was an extraordinary defining experience. I knew that some of the coastal passages alongside Tierra del Fuego could be challenging to say the least–with what my boating buddies describe as "big weather," but if that was part of the Darwin experience then why not?

Not long ago I remembered reading about a "Mayday" called by a British sailor making his way down the same coastline we were planning to negotiate. Apparently an underwater fitting on his sailboat had fractured and he was taking on water faster than his electric bilge pumps could sling it overboard. He calculated that he could remain afloat for perhaps another two hours, which was as long as his physical strength would hold out with him acting as manual backup to his mechanical pumps. The description of how a nearby British tanker captain answered the call, but was initially unable to come close enough to the tiny yacht, because of the rolling and pitching caused by the massive beam sea makes chilling reading. The skipper of this six hundred foot long tanker tried several different approaches to come close to this Tupperware yacht and on his fifth attempt he was finally able to place his massive ship broadside to the oncoming waves–creating a temporary pool of calm water close to the yacht, buying him sufficient time for the tanker crew to winch down two gas powered pumps that saved the day. I often think about how impossible it would be to tightly maneuver such a huge vessel in such an inhospitable sea-state, but the skipper of the tanker had substantial keel boat sailing experience and knew that if he could maneuver between the wind and the yacht, it might just work–and it did. The sailor was able to make his way into a quiet cove and using a special epoxy that sets under water he limped into Puerto Williams for a more permanent fix.

Before leaving Canada and representing the biggest coincidence I could imagine, a friend gave me a boat-anchor of a book called *Uttermost Part of the Earth*, written by Lucas Bridges. I took it in hand, smiling an awkward look of thanks for this kind gesture, while mentally calculating the weight it would add to my luggage. This was no ordinary gift though and it proved to be the key to my entire voyage of discovery, rapidly becoming the preoccupation of my cruise. It's a long way down to the tip of South America from where I live, but the advantage of flying in almost a straight line, due south over the earth's crust is the modest time difference between Canada and Chile. In repeated crossings of the Atlantic and Pacific, I have accepted the discomfort that time difference brings to my body, which I find even worse when flying east, but still a nuisance when flying west and waking up for three subsequent days at 05:30. Flying from Toronto to

Chile is a long haul, but at least you get there at a relatively civilized time when everyone is brewing up coffee.

Chile is a magnificent country with attractive people, great food, splendid scenery, vibrant culture, exceptional natural resources and superb wines and it has a really bright future, but was not always like that. During the Allende years in the early seventies, Chile lurched haphazardly towards democratic socialism electing a moderately leftist government with lofty ideals. Colonel Pinochet, a serving army officer had other ideas and with the help of the CIA was able to forcibly overturn the democratically elected Allende government and impose a reign of terror. I remember visiting soon after the coup, purchasing a black-market booklet with transcripts of radio conversations between Pinochet's men and their CIA advisors. This was amazing reading at the time and allowed a foreign observer like me to visualize what was happening behind the scenes and how Pinochet's secret police and military forces were being coached. It is not always possible to obtain this depth of insight into a coup of that nature, but clearly someone of conscience had the presence of mind to transcribe these recordings, which made chilling reading.

Colonel (later President) Pinochet's regime was grippingly captured in the movie called *Missing*, a 1982 dramatic film directed by Costa Gavras, starring Jack Lemmon and Sissy Spacek. It is based on the true story of American journalist Charles Horman, who disappeared in the bloody aftermath of the US-backed Chilean coup of 1973 that deposed President Salvador Allende. The film focuses on the story of Horman's father (played by Jack Lemmon) who turns up in Santiago searching for the truth about his son's disappearance and the unforgettably chilling interview he has with the American consul, who was working closely with Pinochet to conceal the whereabouts of the journalist. What stunned me was the level of complicity that the US government seemed to have with the Pinochet administration, which became clearer when Pinochet was arrested in Spain during a personal visit. The film was banned in Chile during Pinochet's dictatorship and although neither Chile nor Pinochet are specifically mentioned by name, it is clear what this is about.

My research trip was principally to review the Charles Darwin ocean cruise potential and to secure pre-and post-arrangements which are an essential part of the business, so I engaged a local Chilean guide and set off for a look at Santiago. As I toured the city I was unable to blank out the horrific reports of terrifying midnight roundups ordered by Pinochet, followed by the torturing of young Chilean dissidents and I was soon cruising the streets of stately homes where the torturers incarcerated their victims. I also parked outside the soccer stadium where these unfortunate victims were corralled before being disposed of. My guide was beginning to give me odd looks because I was taking considerable time to retrace the footsteps of the Pinochet era and to my astonishment he came out squarely on the colonel's side–advancing a well articulated argument that Pinochet was protecting Chile from communism. Finding someone who would actually own up to being pro-Pinochet was manna from heaven (being the argumentative sod that I am) and from that moment on this particular visit to Santiago became a memorable experience for the guide and me–admittedly in different ways.

I had two days to go exploring before boarding my ship and not too far from Santiago is Valparaiso and the magnificent wine-growing region of Viña del Mar–which even for a non drinker is a memorable treat and not only for the scenery. I therefore acclimatized myself to these southern latitudes by touring vineyards, posing as a wine enthusiast (my family will be laughing at this vision) synchronizing my frenetic North American pace with the softer rhythm of Chile while learning what a fertile region this is. Chile also has an interesting immigrant history and once I was further south, walking the streets of Puerto Montt the positive imprint that industrious German immigrants had made on this coastal city became evident. I had budgeted another spare day for exploration so I decided to revisit a farm which I had wandered through several years prior–about one hundred kilometres inland towards the Argentine border. At that time I had completed a fascinating land-crossing of the Andes Mountains from Bariloche (chocolate capital of Argentina and refuge for WWII Nazis) to Puerto Montt and thought it would be fun to revisit the farm and see what was happening.

As I drove up the sloping driveway of the farm, all hell seemed to be breaking loose as anxious labourers, rifles in hand, were converging on a large central work shed, which was emitting a terrible animal wailing. It appeared that a large and aggressive cougar had been hunting domestic cattle in the neighbourhood and a posse of farmers was able to tranquilize and capture it a few days earlier. I can only assume they had not killed the cat because it was a protected species, or they were planning to sell it to a zoo for a handsome profit, however with only a make-shift holding pen, these fellows were discussing how to contain this beast once it recovered from the tranquilizing effect of their dart. One can imagine that while it was tranquilized and still dreaming of fresh meat, they trussed it up and dragged it into the work shed where they rapidly built makeshift bars. Now the poor huge beast was literally hurling itself at the bars in an enraged effort to break free and from where I was standing, the first workman to get in its way would be lunch. I approached the shed and poked my head around the door to come face to face with this utterly magnificent beast which was hissing, snarling and wailing as it paced along the bars, rotating its head as it passed by, never for a moment taking its luminescent eyes off me.

In reality this was a magnificent mountain lion, about eight feet long nose to tail, with a metallic black coat and piercing eyes. The workers were now becoming quite agitated but when the owner of the farm came along in his pickup, he ordered them to re-tranquilize the cat because he had made arrangements for it to be transported into Santiago. Apparently a wildlife refuge had offered to take the cat into custody until it could be released into another part of this wild country–far away from its current hunting ground.

My ship, the diminutive *Terra Australis*, sailed from Punta Arenas south of the capital. This was the "old" *Terra Australis*, which later burned and sank off the southwest coast of Chile but she was a capable well-founded small-ship, having plied these southern waters for some time, calling at smaller ports–much as we see in the Norwegian Fjords or along the coastline of Newfoundland and Labrador. Capacity-wise, she held one hundred guests in fifty outside cabins, with a crew of thirty three and an atmosphere of conviviality and inclusiveness. The cabins were modest in size but ingeniously designed with picture windows and plenty of storage. Outside my window as we cast off I remember looking at the blue sky and the squadrons of frigate birds dive-bombing the surface fish alongside, but little did I know that in several days that same window would be virtually under water as our little ark rolled from beam to beam, taking a pounding in Darwin's southern ocean.

You can almost navigate these waters using a Penguin paperback of Charles Darwin's *Voyage of the Beagle* as your guide. This book is his seminal account of his exploration to examine the origin of species and he sailed onward from here, naming the Beagle Channel after his boat, eventually recording his extraordinary discoveries in the Galapagos. Take a moment to look at a world map and locate southern Chile and Argentina, and you will soon become familiar with this magnificent and terrifying landscape. This craggy coastline beset with thousands of inlets has few ports of refuge, as our British sailor discovered, there is not much shelter to harbour a lone mariner, where the wind can blow for weeks on end, with nothing to break up its power or its destiny. One must admire explorers like Darwin and Drake as they groped their way around Cape Horn and along this coastline in search of heavens knows what, on behalf of some royal patron back home in England or Spain.

Our modern journey of discovery took us down the Straits of Magellan, into the Cockburn passage and along the Beagle Channel. The very names given to this region in the mid 1830's conjured up images of 16th and 17th century three masted sailing ships, gun-ports open, ready for action, as they felt their way through what we now call Tierra del Fuego or "Land of Fire." It was Magellan who dubbed this archipelago "Tierra Del Fuego" because looking towards land he saw many fires burning along the shoreline–set by villagers hoping to entice the ships onto the rocks to fall upon those who ventured and foundered in this inhospitable territory.

You may remember that an antagonistic soccer competiveness exists between Argentina and Chile which is not uncommon between neighbours. Think England and France, Germany and Holland and the great rugby rivalry between Australia and New Zealand. As a result of a soccer dispute, Honduras and El Salvador actually fought a

100-hour war in 1969, and not long after that the Pope mediated the soccer conflict between Argentina and Chile. Meanwhile I had now cracked open the cover of *Uttermost Part of the Earth* by Lucas Bridges which you will remember I had reluctantly added to my luggage–to discover why the book was chosen by the New York Explorer's Club as one of the one hundred best first-person exploration narratives of the 20th century. To describe this book as the extraordinary biography of an extraordinary family is a huge understatement, especially if you consider their achievements. The original characters whom you will meet in the book are Lucas Bridges and his wife, Janette, both of whom were British missionaries and to describe them as a hardy breed would be doing them an injustice. They were immensely tough, exceptionally resourceful and supremely courageous in the face of adversity and I was to discover those same extraordinary family genes endure to this day.

Their 1870 mission-brief was to set sail for the Falkland Islands and establish a base of operations on that stark landscape. Once they were ready for the big jump, they were tasked with continuing to southern Argentina and Chile to convert the indigenous inhabitants of "Tierra del Fuego" to Christianity. Presumably Bridges was targeting descendants of the natives who set fires to entrap Magellan's ships and who lived wild lives along the inhospitable shoreline of this continent. The story of the Bridges clan reads like a rollicking movie script, and it is astonishing that the Spielbergs of this world have not sewn up the rights and put this story onto our screens. What fascinated me is not so much the couple's unshakable Christian faith and the power of their belief, although it is hard to ignore how this fortified them to overcome the dangerous hardships in this remote land. What really focused my attention was the way in which the Bridges' offspring morphed from missionaries to commerce and in the space of several generations founded a merchant dynasty that dominated Southern Argentina and Chile.

Before leaving home for this field trip I did the usual research reading and planned to make the most of the Charles Darwin connection. I also resolved to be on deck as we cruised through the channel named after Charles Darwin's ship and to read aloud names on the chart to the sea birds, or anything else within earshot–while navigating the Magellan Straits. It was a considerable privilege to be researching a holiday our guests might enjoy, and linking the names of explorers to the itinerary could bring historical and cultural value to this program. Meanwhile the story of the amazing Mr. and Mrs. Bridges was daily adding value to an already awesome experience.

There is a considerable depth to the story of the Bridges family and how they succeeded in this inhospitable corner of the planet, and although *Uttermost Part of the Earth* is often out of print I would urge you to put the title on your used book list when you next visit "Word on the street."[1] After fighting their way from the Falklands to Tierra del Fuego, their ship tossed around like a cork, the Bridges established a toehold on the southernmost mainland of South America. Their mission started with few home comforts and for many years life was hard and often dangerous for them. However Thomas Bridges was a man of considerable practical talents, which came in useful alongside his more spiritual assets and it is worth noting that Bridges was an orphan who was found beneath a London bridge and was nurtured by a missionary family into maturity whereupon he took the surname "Bridges" to reflect where he was found. The mission in Tierra del Fuego thrived, the Bridges family grew in size, and in 1886 they were recognized by the Argentine government, which granted them a tract of land where their sheep ranching enterprise was founded. Harberton Farm (Estancia Harberton) was named after Janette's birthplace in Devon and lies about forty nautical miles west of Ushuaia where my ship was heading.

Our itinerary on *Terra Australis* was to include a number of memorable sights, but in weather-dependent regions it can be challenging to check off all of the boxes in the planned sequence. I set sail aware that my flight from Ushuaia to Santiago was linked to a non-refundable flight back to Canada and while that did not unduly worry me, it remained in the back of my mind and I could have easily done without that.

Once out of the shelter of Punta Arenas, *Terra Australis* started acting like a rocking horse, increasing in pitch as we entered the Straits of Magellan, and we were royally beaten up at the western end of the Cockburn Canal, which connects the inside passage to the rollicking

South Atlantic. On this segment of the voyage our bow was pitching wildly into huge waves and I presume the thrumming sound at the aft end came from the propellers, which were racing as they came out of the water and flailed in clear air. What mostly disturbed my neophyte companions was the combined pitch-and-roll motion of the ship, which entirely confuses the inner ear and throws out the balance mechanism causing sea-sickness. At this point *Terra Australis* was making a run-for-it down this exposed south Atlantic coastline–for the relatively sheltered Beagle Channel, which we reached next morning after a memorable and not entirely sleepless night at sea.

However, the rewards for enduring the sea-state were awesome and over the next few days we were able to visit magnificent glaciers and deep secluded bays, frequently launching our Zodiacs to stalk wildlife that would have been impossible on a conventional and much larger mother-ship. In the magnificent Agostini Sound we anchored facing a huge glacier whose icy mass was cascading down the mountainside, carving chunks of millennia-old ice into the ocean below. Once we were anchored in sheltered water our crew took to the Zodiacs which were equipped with rare diesel outboards–enabling us to land near the Aguila Glacier and explore the nearby lagoon for artefacts. On some previous visit, a "bar" has been carved into a huge glacial deposit by our crew members, and at least thirty multi coloured bottles from the ship's stores were set up complete with cocktail shakers, olives, and tiny tropical umbrellas. Watching and listening to thousand-year-old glacial ice popping and crackling in protest while it cooled down a drink is a memorable lesson in pure physics.

Along this coastline there are some obvious similarities with Canada's Far North, and the maritime coastline also compares with parts of Alaska–although with fewer trees and even fewer people. The glaciers are absolutely magnificent but they are mostly inaccessible for larger vessels and not without danger for a small ship maneuvering in a narrow sound with glacial deposits and "bergy bits" floating around the propellers. The Terra Australis, which was hardly an ice-class ship, experienced some difficulty with this and the experienced skipper had to "back and fill" for over 90 minutes to clear an exit path through the ice for his ship.

With all of this magnificence around me, what riveted my attention on the marine chart, causing me to become quite agitated was a "speck of a bay" on the north side of the Beagle Channel, just west of Ushuia and due north from Puerto Williams in Chile. Was this the same Harberton Bay where the Bridges had established their home, and could I possibly persuade the skipper to alter his course and put me ashore in one of the ship's Zodiacs to investigate?

After an intense discussion, with me being at my persuasive best, the skipper agreed to make an unscheduled stop in Harberton Bay to allow me to verify if this was the original Bridges homestead. After being immersed in this extraordinary story of human endeavour I now identified quite closely with this family and I was prepared to hike cross country from Ushuia if he was not prepared to stop, Apparently he understood my reasoning and I soon discovered these were the original buildings–which had been lovingly preserved as if waiting for the great man to return. My early morning Zodiac was first to leave the ship and because of the interest I had generated retelling this story to my fellow passengers, there were four inflatables following in my wake, packed with curious passengers and crew.

I recall a peculiar feeling as I landed on that lovely crescent-shaped bay and gazed up the gently sloping hill towards Harberton Farm and the plateau above where the original farm buildings described in Lucas Bridges' *Uttermost Part of the Earth* were located. This was where the family built their lives and here was I, an utter stranger from far-off Canada hiking across the paddock to knock on their door and introduce myself. The fact that I shared a miniscule piece of common national heritage with the Bridges lent me some confidence, but that amazing book is what propelled me forward, plus a consuming desire to see just who these people were. There were no dogs to herald my arrival, no donkeys to honk a predatory warning, and definitely no geese to hiss at this stranger invading their turf. All was strangely quiet in Harberton Farm save for the relentless wind that blows in this part of the world, until I knocked and the conversation commenced.

You can't bring a small ship into a tiny bay even in such a remote part of the universe without anyone noticing, but as that door opened

I had an uneasy feeling that I was about to experience my very own "Dr Livingstone" moment. The man in the doorway was smiling a generous welcome as I introduced myself and when I explained the reason for my visit, he was mildly surprised, but extended a courteous wave to come inside and be properly welcomed. This man was one of the great-grandchildren of Thomas Bridges, still living in the same farmhouse along with his family, who are now fifth and six generation members of the dynasty.

He was humbly surprised at my enthusiasm for his marvellous family story and my interest in the adventures of his ancestors. Having devoured every chapter I was able to hold an in depth discussion about the path his family had taken from the UK to the Falkland Islands and their mad-dash across the south Atlantic to gain a toe-hold in Tierra del Fuego. In some respects chatting with this modern Mr. Bridges was a tiny bit anti-climatic but I have to admit that in other respects it was quite exhilarating. My tour of Harberton Farm was a reverse journey in time, to the years when Thomas Bridges faced his momentous struggle in Tierra del Fuego, first to survive and then to grow his mission–but I was curious to learn what had happened in the intervening years. Although the book has wonderful in-period descriptions of sheep farming and merchant trading in southern Argentina, I learned from the current Mr. Bridges that farming sheep became an unprofitable occupation for the family, but happily the farm has survived and is now hosting a few visitors from around the globe. The orphan boy found under a London bridge was the progenitor of this exceptional transplanted family, which has endured to this day, literally at the end of the road in Argentina. For Mr. Bridges it is a story he had lived with for his entire life, but for me this had become my very own Dr. Livingstone moment and being in the company of a real live Bridges was a tangible connection to Lucas and his wife. I suspect the publishers are unaware how commercially viable the book still is.

As the Terra Australis silently turned its stern towards the farm, I leaned on the rail, binoculars in one hand, waving to the family with the other as they waved me back into the Beagle Channel. Leaving Harberton Bay was emotional for me. I had digested every word that

Lucas Bridges had written, travelled vicariously with his great ancestor as he moved from England, to the Falkland Islands and then braved the southern Ocean to rediscover Harberton Farm. That amazing coincidence of being handed this book to curl up in bed with each night might not have been a coincidence at all, but a pre-planned act of destiny that carried me by ship to the door of this homestead.

Our final port of call was Ushuaia, Argentina, and I budget some time for looking around, especially as there was a truly odd "Canadian connection" that might just interest our visitors. During the rule of Juan and Eva (Evita) Perón, Ushuaia became the uttermost part of the earth for their political enemies, and the jails in this port-city hosted many outspoken foes of their regime. Ushuaia is also the departure point for sailors making a run for Cape Horn and home base for the Argentine navy's southern ocean patrol fleet; however the Canadian connection in Ushuaia was quite different and concerns a quintessential Canadian rodent we know and love, called *Castor Canadensis*, better known as the beaver.

During the rule of the Peróns, the Argentine economy was on a financial roller-coaster, to say the least and this power couple went looking far and wide for techniques and opportunities to boost the economy. Economic development (my field) is an interesting science, but the Peróns were thinking way out of the box, reasoning that if specific best practices worked in other countries, then why not in Argentina and specifically why not in Tierra del Fuego? Their thunderbolt of a (scatter) brainwave was to import large quantities of *Castor Canadensis* and thereby introduce a new industry to this deprived region–by harvesting the fur from wild beavers. For some naive reason beavers must have seemed like an attractive proposition to the Peróns, perhaps recommended by a shrewd Canadian with a vested interest.

Beavers are relatively long living and can survive up to 20 years. They are semi-aquatic animals, which allows them to live both under water and on land. They grow to an average of 35 pounds, and there is evidence that at one time certain species grew as large as black bears and if you have ever seen the front teeth of a beaver, a bear-size specimen must have been absolutely fearsome. Beavers produce one litter each year of between one and four offspring.

Sadly this tale does not have a happy ending, but it teaches us once again that we can't tamper with nature and get away scot free, because all of our species are part of an interconnected global consumption chain and taking beavers to Argentina where there are no natural predators introduced a dangerous imbalance. Imported in 1946, the beavers did exactly what they do in Canada–which is to build dams to stop water flowing, and with no natural predators these beaver colonies grew to epic proportions as they built ... even more dams. Between the dams the beavers created massive rodent colonies, which then produced even more beavers, eventually interconnecting the dams that drowned many of the valuable forests in southern Argentina.

I spent several days wandering around Ushuia because I wanted to get a sense of this southern outpost where the Peróns shipped and incarcerated their political enemies, and also to drive into the beaver-deforested region and see the destruction for myself. Nowadays there is frequent air service from the capital into Ushuia, but in the days of Juan and Evita it must have seemed like an eternal journey for their enemies to "The Uttermost part of the Earth." Locked up in their confined ship's quarters while on this journey south must have been part of the punishment which the ruling class meted out to its enemies.

I wanted to see what our *Castor Canadensis* had done to the local forests and quite close to town it became evident that importing these busy critters might not have been a good move for the Peróns. There were still huge beaver dams along every river I visited, with massive piles of rotting trees being woven neatly into yet more dams with presumably beaver lodges beneath the water. History has not been too kind to the Perón family, but our much loved national rodent was hardly to blame.

This visit had been, full of cultural surprises, exceptional landscapes and endless discoveries. Chile and Argentina are both magnificent countries, brimming with warm, charming people and distinct differences in their national characters. Time spent travelling down here is never quite enough and I would have loved to linger longer in many ports-of-call. There will always be a next time which can't come soon enough.

---

[1] Word on the Street is the accomplished street level book festival in Toronto, which has grown into an event worth visiting from afar. For book lovers it is a wonderful opportunity to mingle with like minded book worms and for those interested in a rather unusual festival this is well worth attending.

CHAPTER 14

Rescuing Jean Marc and Suzanne

CANADIAN SAILBOAT HIJACKED IN COLOMBIA

"A Canadian husband and wife team were hijacked and badly injured while sailing off the Colombian coastline." The six o'clock CBC news was droning in the background as I gunned my car up the hill above Highland Yacht Club in the Scarborough Bluffs. Our trawler *The Full Monty* was sleeping on the hard adjacent to the clubhouse and I had been checking the winterising of my twin diesels because I had been travelling overseas immediately after haul-out, and the last surprise I wanted was a split engine block on those costly Ford Lehmans. I was not really focused on what was being reported on the radio until I heard the words, "Canadian husband and wife", "hijacked and badly injured", "Columbian Coastline". News of their ordeal was fighting its way to the surface between last-minute Christmas advertisements, but before I had time to focus on this news snippet, it was gone. For two compatriots to be in trouble in Colombian coastal waters was bad enough, but boaters will understand how deadly serious this could be, as Colombia struggled with the twin curses of murderous drug cartels and murderous political terrorism–which were conspiring to destabilize their country. During my drive home I tried to recall what I had just heard: "Canadian–sailing–husband and wife team–struggling with their attackers–boat completely stripped–attacked with a machete and badly cut–left for dead–untied their shackles–Canadian consul onsite to assist–serious accusations."

It was three days before Christmas and being a late shopper, presents were still to be sourced and many loose ends required tying before the holiday season arrived. Christmas has always been my absolute favourite time of the year and although I am not a Christian, this is a treasured tradition that my family had embraced since we were tots in the UK, therefore the special Christmas spirit was rapidly affecting our every move and all was well with our world–but clearly not with these two anonymous Canadians in distress somewhere off the coast of Colombia.

I tuned my car radio to every station I could find, hoping to hear these un-named Canadians were safe and unharmed and preparing for a warm Christmas in far-off Colombia, but frustratingly I was unable to find out much more, so when I reached home I called the CBC Toronto news desk which confirmed what I had heard. This story concerned a Canadian husband and wife sailing team, and yes, they had been hijacked, but more than that they were unable to say, but they suggested I call the Montreal news desk where the story had first broken in French and was subsequently picked up by English language CBC as relevant (if sad) Christmas news.

The Montreal CBC staffer on duty was amazing and able to confirm most of what I had heard, plus a great deal more that did not make its way on air. The couple, despite serious injuries, had somehow made it back into Cartagena and were recuperating while giving interviews to local media; in fact they were not only giving interviews, they were aggressively and with considerable skill working the media and getting publicity for their plight. By this time we were more than passively engaged in this story and in the three days left before Christmas, I was able to put together the skeleton of a plan to try to assist this couple, and at least ensure their safe passage home. But first I needed more details, including how they made their escape, what happened to their attackers, and the extent of their support network in Colombia and Canada.

Jean Marc and Suzanne had spent a lifetime building careers in the public service. Suzanne was involved with health care administration in the Province of Quebec while Jean Marc had risen to the rank of police chief in the town where they lived and being accomplished sailors, they formulated a retirement plan which would bring their dream to reality. After all, why work so hard to build a retirement nest egg if you can't enjoy life to the maximum by pursuing your dreams? Like so many boaters (me included) Jean Marc and Suzanne occasionally dared to dream about cruising in tropical water, smelling the scented breeze coming off the land, while their boat swung lazily at anchor a few feet from shore in a secluded lagoon.

This is a dream I know intimately but have yet to realize despite years of saving, planning and carefully honing my boating skills. Cruising in your own boat can actually be an affordable lifestyle once you have made the initial capital investment, acquired your floating home and equipped it with the necessities of your new lifestyle. This lifestyle itself can vary widely from a quite modest existence with few toys on-board, perhaps a simple icebox instead of powered refrigeration, and basic navigation equipment. I can relate to the latter, because even though we used the latest in chart plotting-GPS driven instruments on *The Full Monty*, I always carried a full suite of paper charts along with a simple compass, a set of dividers and my primary school wooden ruler. I did this because I love the sense of history that manual navigation brings to a boating lifestyle and the fact that it is closely related to what the early navigators did to move their vessels around the globe.

A considerable number of families circle the globe in their boats, and not all of them cruise in gleaming half-million dollar yachts. Not long ago a family from Russia arrived in the Great Lakes on a sail-powered dhow that appeared to be more suited to the Arabian Peninsula than Lake Ontario and they were definitely cruising on a tight budget with few of the gadgets one would associate with crossing oceans. Many local sailors were initially happy to assist with equipment, food, and friendship, but sadly the family pushed the hospitality well beyond what was acceptable and they are now pursuing their budget-restricted dreams elsewhere. Others go this route with more style and a few years back while sanding my deck in lovely Kingston spring weather, I watched two young chaps climbing over what I had written off as a derelict twenty-foot, badly rusted steel sailboat. They were there again the following weekend and most weekends during the spring and early summer, attacking the rust with four bare hands and a few power tools. Occasionally an older chap wandered down to talk with them, and what emerged was the story of two young local fellows pursuing their dreams with modest amounts of disposable income and virtually no capital or cruising cash flow. They were not unlike thousands of others who have a burning passion to sail into the sunset and taste the briny coming over the foredeck onto their parched lips. On a hand-to-mouth budget, these characters made it all the way down to the Bahamas, through the Inner Caribbean and back safely to Kingston. I followed their blog and lived vicariously on their experiences as they sailed from lagoon to lagoon.

The Montreal news desk at Radio Canada was able to fill in a few missing facts but not much beyond the hijacking itself, plus the current whereabouts of Jean Marc and Suzanne. The Canadian consul in Cartagena was offering whatever assistance was possible, but what puzzled me most, was the pair were now back in Cartagena onboard their own boat and making a huge effort to keep their plight in the spotlight. This left a host of unanswered questions and if we were to help in any way, I would need to enlist the support of other boaters, perhaps an aid agency or two, and possibly an airline–who would all be curious to know what happened before they agreed to help. How the Mayday call was picked up remains something of a mystery, but at one point a Quebec-based radio ham was patched into the conversation and it was he who first alerted Radio Canada. Putting two and two together I realized that the Mayday call was probably received by and bounced around various agencies including the Colombian Coast Guard, the US Coast Guard, and our ham radio enthusiast–losing valuable time as the agencies processed the information and verified the call's authenticity.

Once I established contact with "Gregoire the Ham" (we called him Monsieur Jambon) in Quebec City, I was able to get a clearer picture of where Jean Marc and Suzanne were and that evening I managed to speak with Jean Marc from a phone in their marina. On the other end of the line I discovered a highly articulate and motivated observer who was able to clearly and succinctly outline what had happened to his boat and the implications this had for their lives. It might be useful to start at the beginning of their ordeal.

After retiring and arranging their affairs it was time for Jean Marc and Suzanne to get serious about chasing their dreams. Most cruising families take a few years before actually cutting their lines, to carefully plan their new life afloat–which can be highly complex, often with implications for their extended families and friends. If there are children along on the adventure, the family often arranges to "home school," and if they are in port for an extended stay, they may enrol their children in a local school to socialize them with others of similar age. The boat has to be made ready for the extended life afloat and equipped with whatever one can afford by way of equipment and necessities. Budgeting is a critical component in the planning process, and banking, while fundamental when ashore, can be complex and frustrating for those who go cruising. Lately this has become easier with the advent of the Internet–and the availability of banking machines that dispense local currency in remote ports means you no longer having to carry a huge stash of cash, making one less of a target for potential thieves.

Itineraries have to be planned, navigation and weather patterns have to be integrated into the "cruising plan" and each boat should have its own security modus operandi to cover the occurrences which can affect a small vessel. Failure of the boat itself can be minimized by careful maintenance, but failure *does* happen and will require a response. Fire at sea is perhaps the most terrifying type of failure and if the fire cannot be contained then abandoning ship is the only recourse–and that requires a protocol. Weather can be your friend or your foe at sea but with careful planning and regular training even the most foul weather patterns can be survived, but weather also needs to be incorporated into the overall safety plan. Security from other humans has now been added to the list of concerns and as Jean Marc and Suzanne experienced off the Colombian coast, every cruiser needs a security plan that can be activated if the ship is under threat. An interesting divergence of opinion occurs when it comes to protecting one's vessel (and its occupants) from those who would take it from you. One camp in the sailing community advocates carrying weapons and being fully prepared and capable to use them when necessary. The other camp is firmly against carrying weapons, arguing that you will always be outgunned if marauders decide they want your vessel, so why start a gun fight you will inevitably lose–along with your life. A great deal has been written on this topic and I have first-hand knowledge of a lovely couple who are alive today because they were able to defend themselves when attacked when at anchor adjacent to a lonely cay in the Bahamas. From talking with them I am convinced what kept them alive was their well-thought-through training (which they regularly practiced) and the effective weapons they were carrying on board. The key component of their plan was to somehow get a call through to the authorities, which they were successful in doing–and in no time flat a US Coastguard Falcon was circling above, chasing the pirates away.

Liquidating their assets to buy their thirty four-foot sailboat and equip it with high-quality equipment for a new life afloat, Jean Marc and Suzanne set sail for the briny. Like most Canadian cruisers heading south, their goal was to miss hurricane season and then cruise in the Caribbean for some time to see where life might take them. Adjusting to the pace of a cruising lifestyle is an adventure in itself, which affects people in different ways and unless you fall into the trap of being structured by the airline schedules of invited guests, your days often start early and night also comes early as the sun slips below the horizon. I have often experienced the definable beat of the cruising day and I can imagine Jean Marc and Susanne leaving high-pressure careers and adjusting to the rhythm of the voyage as they made their way south. Once you have honed your passage-making techniques, settled into a comfortable routine and gained a degree of confidence, you are mentally equipped to tackle the entire globe, either transiting the Atlantic and heading for the Mediterranean or attacking the Pacific and heading south or due west.

Jean Marc and Suzanne had decided it would be a treat to spend Christmas in the outer Caribbean–a substantial change from the sub-zero temperatures of Quebec, so as the winds were fair and the waves were cooperating, they made good haste and approached the coast of Columbia with time to explore. Cartagena is one of the prettiest ports in the Caribbean and Colombia is hard to beat with its vibrant culture, superb scenery, excellent wildlife and a well-developed cuisine. Colombians are also a generous, welcoming people and I have spent many happy hours in this country, both professionally and on holiday. For cruising yachts and their crews, Cartagena offers excellent marina facilities with in-harbour anchorages and professional services on tap. The local marine engineering is first class, and their attention to the smallest detail when handling expensive yachts is well known amongst the cruising community. The only down side at that time was the appalling conflicts between the Narcos and the government and between the anarchist guerrillas and the government–placing great deal of stress on public security services and a huge drain on the treasury as the army was constantly on alert chasing these gangsters. These conflicts regularly manifested themselves in public displays of terror by each of the factions and it was not uncommon for innocent persons to be in the wrong place at the wrong time–never to be seen again by their families. My close associate had her executive assistant kidnapped under these circumstances, but mercifully, he reappeared, walking down a rural street three years after he was taken, during which time not a single indication that he was alive escaped from his jungle-captors. However, the tourist business, a huge net earner for the economy, was largely unscathed by these manifestations of violence, and with this social news as background, Jean Marc and Suzanne sailed happily into the Cartagena Marina for the Christmas holidays.

Having spent time with this couple I can tell you they are resourceful, bright, generous, highly competent and by the way–tough as nails. You don't get to be chief of police by being a shrinking violet. Suzanne was also an experienced administrator and together they were excellent judges of character. They sailed into the Caribbean fully aware that lonely anchorages come with peace and tranquillity 99% of the time, but when night falls, there's always an outside 1% chance that security can "go south."

After several weeks at sea, island hopping from anchorage to anchorage, Jean Marc and Suzanne were happy to be tied to the dock, making acquaintances with fellow boaters and getting to know the local service personnel. Their boat was in need of minor adjustment and the cruising commissary was badly in need of replenishment so part of their time was spent sourcing parts and learning from other boaters where the best priced food was located. It was at this time that Jean Marc noticed the mangled corpses of several wrecked sailboats towards the back of the marina, some out under the baking sun with others poking out of containers parked against the security fence. Many of these boats had suffered a high degree of trauma, with fractured hulls, broken spars, and shredded rigging while some of their fittings were ripped out of their housings, as if by a superhuman hand. Jean Marc surmised they had been inside a series of dropped containers or perhaps the victims of a runaway mechanical grader that set its sights on these pretty fibreglass hulls. However being an inquisitive sort of fellow and given his past career, which entailed a high degree of forensic snooping, he slowly picked his way through this nautical graveyard, looking for clues to what had caused the havoc. There was no obvious sign of human trauma and a total absence of activity by the service personnel amongst these wrecks. Even more astonishingly, every boat was made by Dufour the famous French sailboat manufacturer who coincidentally manufactured Jean Marc's boat. Walking through this mess of spars and masts and tangled rigging, Jean Marc made a note to himself that if he ever needed spare parts for his beloved sailboat, here was a handy wrecker's yard with anything he might possibly need. It was a thought that was to haunt him.

The couple explored this magnificent UNESCO World Heritage Site and sampled some of the petite bars and tavernas until their thoughts eventually returned to their core passion, which was to experience the Caribbean, drop their anchor in as many crescent shaped lagoons as possible, and sample the local culture. They consulted their marine charts and reviewed the many opportunities westward along the Colombian coastline in the general direction of Panama, reasoning that with Christmas around the corner, it made sense to buy a small turkey and celebrate the season and the debut of their newly acquired retirement, in some picturesque anchorage.

Highly competent navigators, and by now experienced and capable boat-people, what they lacked was local knowledge of the Colombian coastline, and they were unsure where to choose an anchorage. As many boaters will agree, there is absolutely nothing like local experience in unfamiliar water, so they approached Norman, the friendly Anglophone marina manager for advice, which was a prudent way to save time and ensure the safety of their boat in a region not known for the accuracy of local marine charts. Many remote locations on earth still use British Admiralty charts from when "Britannia ruled the waves," and although the Colombians have updated their hydrographic charting, their depth soundings aren't always accurate.

Norman produced a lined pad with a vintage carbon between the sheets and drew a detailed chart, indicating several "indented coves" not visible on the larger-scale published charts of the coastline. He took the time to hand-draw a chart, which related accurately to the topography of the landmass and he inserted a basic distance scale at the bottom of the page, half an inch on the chart corresponding to half an inch on the scale, which gave Jean Marc and Suzanne a reasonable degree of confidence that he knew what he was doing. What was especially gratifying was that Norman was willing to spend half a morning with them talking through the options of each potential anchorage, but he was adamant that if they wanted a picturesque lagoon, a friendly close-by village, a supply of fresh water and secure holding for their anchor in a blow, then only one anchorage had all four assets–which is where he penned in an X.

I have often been in unfamiliar ports and after making landfall, which is a magical moment in itself, what is most welcoming is when someone offers advice which comes from personal experience. At its most basic this can be a recommendation where to eat that evening, or where to purchase clean moisture-free fuel for your boat, or which museum to visit first because it closes early, but especially where to tie up your ship for the night. An unfamiliar port can be daunting for an arriving skipper and there is no value that can be placed on sound advice, thus being taken under Norman's wing with a solid recommendation (X marks the spot) where to spend Christmas was a welcome gift that arrived early. With a new float-plan under the belt, Jean Marc and Suzanne set about the business of making ready to leave the marina, securing their movable belongings, double checking their fuel supply, and headed out to sea for the eight-hour passage to "Christmas Cove."

The Colombian coastline west of Cartagena is dotted with villages and the occasional small settlement, which made it easy for the couple to sight-sail their way towards their destination. Norman's improvised route indicated several landmarks which they were able to identify on their marine chart and on a topical map of the region. It is far easier to make landfall in daylight, so as the light was failing Jean Marc chose an interim anchorage and dropped their hook in twenty feet of water about a hundred meters from the shoreline. This was not the X-marked cove that Norman had recommended, but the holding was good and their anchor set with relative ease as they reversed the engine and embedded the flukes in the sandy bottom. All was well with their world as the sun slid silently across the western shore to disappear beneath a stand of ragged palms. Anchoring is a special part of the boating experience and there is nothing quite like swinging on the hook, as opposed to being tied to a creaky transient finger dock at the swampy end of a marina. Suzanne took a fix in two separate directions to determine if the boat was swinging within the acceptable anchor-arc, or dragging? Happily the flukes were well established in the sabulous bed and they were at ease.

Solo anchoring for the night inside a remote lagoon can be a mixed blessing. On the one hand you have the magnificence of an unpolluted sunset and often a million dollar view, but this also carries the uncertainty of not knowing one's neighbours ashore and perhaps having to stand alternating watches. Jean Marc and Suzanne had not joined one of the flotillas that were buddy boating along this shoreline, so it might have been prudent for them to stand watches throughout the night–just as they would have done if crossing a busy shipping lane. Dinner was prepared, a glass of wine ready and a citrus candle positioned upwind to act as a smudge to dissuade shore-born mosquitoes. Bed comes early in the tropics, because when the sun goes down it rapidly becomes dark and with that comes drowsiness induced by a combination of one's circadian rhythm, good food, excellent wine, and the effects of a day at sea. Sleeping at anchor is also a special experience and the gentle movement of the boat is sure to beat any sleeping pills on the market.

Jean Marc was unsure of the exact time he first heard the low thrumming of twin diesel engines and at first he was unsure if he was dreaming or awake. Noises of any kind travel amazing distances across still water, especially from low pitched diesels (ask any WWII submariner) and he was trying to determine if this was a passing fishing fleet paralleling the lagoon entrance or a singular vessel in close proximity to his own. He sensed that Suzanne was also awake and it did not take them long to determine they had company in the lagoon as the Dufour rocked gently, telegraphing that another vessel had circled them and was creating a modest wake. Without a word, Jean Marc and Suzanne were on their feet.

The components of a cruising security plan have several elements which under ideal conditions should work together. Identifying the precise issue is the first rule, because that allows you to assess the gravity of the situation and decide how best to respond. If you are able to identify a personal threat, the second rule is to get to your radio and put out a Mayday call, which, depending on how remote your location is and the atmospherics at the time, may not be heard by the authorities or other boaters. You have three ways of making that call, depending on the boat's equipment: VHF Radio, which has a primary range of about twenty Kilometres, Shortwave Radio, which can be tuned to offer global reach with some delay and a Satellite telephone which can instantly reach any location on earth and works like a mobile phone. But the Canadians were unable to reach any of these options in time to make the Mayday call, because as they approached their cabin hatch the attackers' boat was bumping gently against the Dufour, and three men were swinging onboard, in no mood for negotiations. An almighty struggle took place in the cockpit with the attackers swinging machetes at our Canadians. Jean Marc and Susanne were severely cut as they tried to defend themselves and fend off their assailants; they put up an almighty battle, but the attackers had the advantage of surprise, and before long the couple were thrown to the floor and tied up, bleeding profusely from cuts to their heads, shoulders and feet.

Although Jean Marc's injuries were severe, his police training locked in and he was immediately recording what was taking place and his attackers would have been horrified if they knew what his mind was processing. Suzanne was also badly injured and bleeding heavily, but with the advantage of life experience and having worked her way up to a senior administrator, she was also able to focus her mind on the scene. Jean Marc later confided to me that he was convinced their attackers were planning to dispose of their bodies by loading them into their fishing boat and dumping them far out at sea.

What happened next was perplexing and completely at odds with what Jean Marc and Suzanne expected. After a brief search for cash and shiny bling, the attackers were carefully examining the Dufour's equipment, scurrying to and from their fishing boat, returning with crowbars and an assortment of wire cutters and tools. First they detached the radio and navigation equipment, carefully snipping the wires, leaving plenty of space to avoid damaging the units. Next they dragged out the dual voltage refrigerator and rolled it into the cockpit. Next came the diesel heater, the desalinator, the radar screen and, from high up on the mast, the circular radar antenna. Piece by piece their attackers dismantled the boat, eventually unhitching the boom and laying it on the foredeck–presumably to haul onto the fishing boat once the rest of the disassembly was completed. The Canadians were in shock from this violent physical attack, but as they exchanged glances their minds were working overtime to analyse what was happening, why it was happening, and what might happen next–particularly to them. Most of what they had read about pirates targeting recreational boaters was focused on drug runners stealing boats to run narcotics or being attacked because they were in the wrong place at the wrong time or witnessing narcos going about their business. The other aspect of piracy was pure financial gain by those who would steal their boat, their cash and belongings. But the characters who were ransacking their boat fell into neither of these categories. They did not seem to be narcos, nor did they seem to be pure cash-hunters: they appeared to be stripping the Dufour for the component parts and not much more. What exactly were they up to and who were they?

There was a village nestled about two hundred and fifty metres inland from the shoreline, with a jetty that might have accommodated two small boats. The modest fishing fleet that home ported on that jetty had put out to sea well before the couple arrived and the returning vessels coming around the headland rescued the Canadians from certain execution. The pirates started to panic and as rapidly as they arrived, they were on their way, leaving the lagoon in the opposite direction to the incoming shrimpers. Whether or not the fishermen saw what was happening is open to conjecture, but likely they did–and in a country assailed by narcos and political terrorists, they turned a blind eye to what was happening and motored straight past the Dufour to the jetty.

The diesels of the escaping pirates were being pushed to the limit, but as they rounded the eastern headland the engines faded and the night gradually fell silent. Not quite believing they were safe Jean Marc and Suzanne struggled to free themselves, eventually succeeding with the movie cliché technique of grabbing a knife and cutting each other's ropes. Their loss of blood combined with shock and the physical fatigue from their struggle hampered their movements. The piracy attack had crippled their prime mode of transport and inflicted a variety of injuries that were unlikely to be life threatening–but were definitely life impacting. Fortunately most of the cuts were congealing and once more their capabilities kicked in and they began taking inventory, determining what had been stripped from the boat and what was remaining that would help them reach safety. They were unsure exactly what they were escaping from and unsure where they could escape to, their binoculars were gone, along with their passports, watches and with any means to communicate with the outside world. Could they count on medical help from the village? It was hard to believe no one witnessed the attack taking place two hundred metres from the shoreline. Surely with all the shouting at 03:00 on a still night, someone must have heard what was happening and called the police.

The other issue was how to get ashore. Their Caribe Zodiac and its 9 HP Yamaha had been stolen and an inflatable life raft had gone the same way and there was not a single lifejacket left onboard for them to use. While swimming was an outside option, Suzanne thought she had seen sharks in the outer part of the lagoon and with bleeding bodies the thought of human shark-bait was unappealing. Considering the methodical way in which the pirates had semi-stripped the Dufour, Jean Marc was stunned to see the engine ignition key dangling in place beneath the Plexiglas engine control panel. He felt sure the brawny pirates would have eventually dismantled their compact Yanmar diesel had the shrimpers not returned to their jetty, so how on earth had they missed the ignition key in such a prominent location? He thought at one point he had heard the pirates talking about fuel (*carburante*, in Spanish) and wondered if they had drained the tanks. The house batteries had been pillaged, but his starting battery, cached behind a temporary bulkhead, was still connected to the Yanmar and with this discovery came an entire change of scenario.

Their first thought was to pull up their anchor and head straight for the jetty to seek help, but there were a few items to consider before making that move. Would the villagers be sympathetic and offer them help? Why had they not already done so–or were they intimidated by a potential retaliatory visit from the pirates? Was there a police post close by and might they also offer help, but why had they not already done so? Might there be a local telephone to call for assistance–but who would they call? With as much courage as they could muster Jean Marc and Suzanne upped anchor and motored slowly to the jetty. They had noticed that the crew on the closest shrimper had thrown out a kedging anchor[1] before they tied to the jetty and the amount of "scope" that required told them there was plenty of water adjacent to the mooring.

It was apparent there was only room for one boat along each side of the jetty so they nudged against the closer of the two shrimpers and rafted against its starboard side. Once all lines were secure and after checking there was no one onboard, they clambered over the side and hiked over piles of stinky netting to the jetty. The village was quiet and there were none of the typical village stray dogs looking for a handout and a complete absence of strutting cockerels that grace the dusty sidewalks of most Central American villages. At twilight there had been definite signs of life behind the curtains on the shanty windows but it was odd that not a soul was about, which lent tension to their quest for help. The obvious thing to do was to chose a house, knock on the door, and inquire if there was a police post in the area and if they could make a phone call.

However after three separate doors opened in response to their knocking and three sets of villagers recoiled in horror at the sight of the blood-covered sailors, it was obvious that no one had the stomach to render assistance. Suzanne later reasoned the thought of retaliation might have been top of their minds so the couple retreated to their boat to consider their next move.

By this time, as Jean Marc explained it to me, their spirit of defiance was returning, and for the first time they were feeling capable of planning their way out of this predicament. Once they had discovered the tanks were full of diesel and the Yanmar still intact, they realized that even without sails (their spare set had also been pilfered) they could motor along a reciprocal route and pick their way back into Cartagena and the safety of the marina where Norman had been so kind. With this as "the plan" they decided it was important to make haste. The villagers might be in cahoots with the pirates, and they had absolutely no idea if their attackers were waiting around the headland for another crack at the Dufour.

Whatever would happen next, the pirates would be contending with a different type of crew as Jean Marc and Suzanne discussed the defence options at their disposal–which included a plastic signal pistol and a large inventory of distress shells which the pirates had missed. It is not generally realized that signal pistols and their shells, which are designed to be used as a life saving device, can be used as formidable weapons, and their ability to burn bright and fierce can be employed with devastating effect. Jean Marc had also noted the pirate boat was a miniature period trawler with a high freeboard and an upturned bow, designed to handle waves during inclement weather. However, it was also an antique boat, built before fibreglass was affordable. Thus the shells in the signal pistol might be effectively used against this tinder dry hull if the opportunity came for another round of this conflict. In a life and death situation, their boat could also be used as a weapon of last resort as a battering ram.

To conserve fuel, the journey back to Cartagena was agonizingly slow at three knots and eight long hours later the lights of the city loomed across the night sky as they chugged into the outer harbour, motored past towering cranes and into the empty slip they had left only a day before. When a security guard came scurrying down the pier to see who was arriving unannounced, Jean Marc and Suzanne's blood-stained clothes told him all he needed to know and before he was back inside his hut, they were sound asleep with the knowledge they were safe at last–or so they thought.

Next morning a crowd assembled at the entrance to the pier where they were secured and as the Canadians poked their heads out of the hatch, they realized that news of their predicament had spread through the boating community. The condition of their boat told part of the story and it was obvious that a mighty struggle had recently taken place. On the starboard side of the Dufour, a green scrape extended about seven feet to either side of the midpoint where the pirate boat had been tied on during their battle. There was no boom attached to the mast, there was dried blood around the cockpit and the fabric of the seats was stained dark brown from their bleeding. Below deck there was relatively little damage because, after the refrigerator has been taken out, the rest of the job focused on doing as little damage as possible to the components being pilfered.

Jean Marc was visibly angry. His retirement plan had been dangerously disrupted, his life and that of Susan had been placed in jeopardy, and at this point he was unsure what the future would bring. He immediately contacted the Canadian government to ask for consular assistance and as news spread he was approached by the local media, agreeing to an interview on Colombian national TV where he related the story of their hijacking, and in detail explained the injuries they had suffered. He had also been in contact with Gregoire, the ham radio operator (Monsieur Jambon) who alerted Radio Canada in Montreal, which is how we picked up the news.

At this point the story took a dramatic turn when one of the Columbian news reporters asked what the attackers looked like, whereupon Jean Marc dived into his boat, emerging with three detailed sketches which he had created while motoring to safety. Once more he was able to draw on his experience as a police chief, where at one time he trained officers to create visual profiles of criminals from identikits.

He had sufficient artistic skill to put elements of the dominant facial features together and come up with three realistic images. Whether or not they bore any resemblance to the actual brigands was up for discussion, but the sight of this articulate ex-cop on national television painting a vivid verbal picture of his ordeal along with graphic portraits of his attackers rapidly became exported to the United States, Europe, and Canada.

After they originally arrived in Cartagena Suzanne had made friends with a French family who were cruising across from Europe to North America and were stopping over in Columbia to wait out the winter. This family of four–a couple with two children, had heard about the tangled mess of French boats in the back of the marina and as they knew Dufour from France where the boats were made, they took a close interest in the wrecked fleet. Hoping to trade up to a larger boat to accommodate their growing children, they too made enquiries about buying one of the lesser damaged boats and were told by yard workers they were not for sale. Norman had other plans for them, they said. What "other plans" could there possibly be other than a sale, so they arranged to meet Norman the next day and press him for more details.

After they mentioned this to Suzanne, she decided to do some research herself to determine which ship the containers had fallen from, however, the port authority officials knew nothing about containers full of sailboats falling off a ship in their harbour, nor did they have any manifests that listed sailboats being shipped through the port. Returning to the marina empty handed, Suzanne wandered through the back of the marina, looking for clues to the provenance of the wrecked fleet and perhaps a clue or two about their previous owners. She really needed Jean Marc with her because he had dealt with many different types of forensics in his career and she needed the benefit of his professional experience to bubble the real facts to the surface.

Norman didn't turn up for the meeting with the French family. In fact he had been absent from the marina for several days and calls to his apartment yielded no reply. Meanwhile Jean Marc was receiving considerable media attention, and the story of the hijacking ordeal reached Cartagena's major tourism markets, to the horror of local hotels and suppliers as tourism in the region started to plummet. Travel is a fickle business and the US market in particular can be described as highly "situation sensitive," which means that the flow of American visitors reduces to a trickle with the slightest whiff of violence in the region. Not only was there a whiff–there was an almighty stink brewing.

The Canadian consul sprang into action as best they could, offering a variety of options available to Canadians in need of help overseas, but what was peculiar was the sustained pace of media interest and the way in which Norman was gradually being pulled into discussion about the hijacking. A young man who at first appeared to be a reporter asked Jean Marc about how they decided where to spend Christmas, whereupon Jean Marc opened his log book and pulled out the excellent hand-drawn chart Norman had provided for them. The young man then asked Jean Marc about the make of his boat. "Does it not seem peculiar you are cruising in the same make of boat as the wrecked Dufours in the back of the marina"? he asked.

There was intense discussion amongst the transient boaters about what was actually happening. The French family were puzzled about Norman's reluctance to sell any of the wrecked boats, Jean Marc was puzzled about why Norman's motives were being questioned and everyone was puzzled by the appearance of a dozen federal soldiers who took over marina security from the affable (and ineffective) chaps who patrolled the entrance. Then news from Europe started trickling through to the French family, possibly casting a light on the mystery. The wrecked boats might just be the remnants of a Bare Boat charter fleet beaten up by a hurricane blowing through the Antilles a couple of years before and with these new facts, a picture was emerging that brought everyone's thinking back to Norman.

With the aid of Jean Marc's forensic skills they made a more detailed survey of the wrecked fleet and were able to determine from half-removed decals and leftover brochures that these were indeed part of a rental fleet and it seemed plausible that Norman might be restoring them in order to establish a rental fleet in the marina. Everyone knew that the cost of buying replacement parts from France was astronomical, and it might be easier to send a trio of brigands to hijack a passing Dufour and dispose of the owners in the bargain. That might explain Norman's sudden disappearance–but why were there federal soldiers guarding the marina, now augmented by an armoured personnel carrier equipped with a large machine gun turret?

The amiable young man who they had presumed was a reporter was in fact a plainclothes cop, who took Jean Marc and Suzanne aside to place them fully in the picture. The detective believed the Canadians had been deliberately set up to spend Christmas in a lonely lagoon, after which Norman hired a gang of bandits to pursue them and strip the Dufour to restore one of his rental boats. Jean Marc recalled that the hand-drawn chart was created in duplicate by the carbon sheet beneath the original–which might just be how the hijackers knew their exact route and were able to tail them. Murder may or may not have been part of the deal, but thanks to the returning shrimpers, that did not happen. Jean Marc had been able to identify the robbers on national television where his sketches turned out to be remarkably similar to a known set of thieves. The police were now actively seeking these characters.

But why the federal troops at the marina entrance? Given the proclivity for violence in Colombia at that time, the police were taking the precaution of ringing the marina with fire-power in case the hijackers wanted to dispose of Jean Marc and suppress the evidence. In fact the police actively encouraged the Canadians to leave Colombia with or without their boat, because they were unable to guarantee their safety while in the country.

So close to Christmas, we were raising funds, canvassing boat clubs in the Toronto area, using the Christmas spirit to shamelessly ask for donations of spare parts and cash. The good folks at Highland Yacht Club where we had many excellent friends and a broad circle of acquaintances rose to the occasion (as they always did) with generous amounts of funds and spares, and in no time flat we were assembling a care package that Air Transat generously agreed to ship to Cartagena on one of their holiday charters. My contact with Jean Marc was now frequent and less frantic, but resupplying him for his journey became the last of his concerns as this adventure lurched towards another nasty turn.

Cartagena relies on a steady inflow of visitors to feed its tourism facilities, at that time recovering from years of neglect and still suffering from a nervous clientele. With news of the hijacking ordeal playing on television in their major tourism markets, this fragile economic recovery was in jeopardy and a source of distress for everyone employed in this core component of their economy. The last thing Colombians wanted was for this news to remain on the front pages in their major markets and somehow this story needed to be ended. As we were shipping components down to Jean Marc, news broke that three men had been found dead at the edge of a village, summarily executed and dumped at the side of the road and grainy media images indicated they were the same characters that Jean Marc had sketched. This revelation was now preoccupying the boating community and a nervous atmosphere prevailed and many visiting cruisers were making plans to head out to sea.

Our plain-clothes cop again urged the Canadian sailors to leave the country at once, because chatter on the criminal street indicated some form of retaliatory action was being planned against them. The result of our panic appeal to resupply the Canadians meant that technically they were now able to sail away in their boat, but Jean Marc was in no hurry to leave the relatively protected safety of the marina and risk being outside Colombian territorial waters where there were no federal soldiers–so I agreed to facilitate their safe passage to somewhere other than Colombia.

On the one hand it was apparent the Colombians were making a huge effort to secure their safety, and I was impressed with the depth of concern displayed by the locals involved in the case. On the other hand I can well imagine what was in the minds of the Canadians as they talked this through in the privacy of their boat cabin. They had worked hard to enable this retirement adventure and they had plumbed the depths of their character, stamina and physical strength to survive the horrible hijacking. Now they were faced with putting out to sea, knowing that a retaliatory action might be waiting for them, and this time the fire power aimed at their tiny Dufour might turn out to be fatal.

Given what Jean Marc and Suzanne were facing in Cartagena, some form of rapid extraction plan was called for. In my line of work it is the list of contacts that makes the difference between success or failure and my network of contacts extended deep into the US. The lads in Washington immediately understood what was happening and these experienced anti-drug experts had seen it all before. The scale of the US operation to suppress the flow of drugs from South America to the US mainland included a broad range of hardware at their disposal: fast pursuit aircraft, slow reconnaissance aircraft that could remain on target for extended periods, skilled personnel, and a number of large fast vessels. One of their strategies in the battle against the narcos was to ring-fence the breadth of the Caribbean with highly portable assets to prevent unfriendly commodities from migrating north. This strategy was relatively straightforward, but their real successes came from understanding the enemy and accepting that narcos, while an unsavoury lot, were often highly intelligent and utterly ruthless in the pursuit of their trade.

I sat down with these fellows with a marine chart on the table to review the facts as I knew them. They had already heard a great deal about the hijacking from their own resources and when news of the bodies filtered through to the room, I did not need to explain what Jean Marc and Suzanne were up against.

Five days after my contact with Washington, a large US Coast guard vessel coincidentally made a courtesy call to Cartagena, where liberty time was granted to members of the crew. Sailors are often a jolly bunch of fellows and by the second day, word had spread through the broader community that crew from the red and white ship were spending their hard earned pay in the bars and tavernas of town. By the fifth (departure) day, there was no doubt who was in port, and when the large white ship with the red diagonal stripe on its hull left port, a modest line of sailboats bounced along in its wake–which for some reason was uncharacteristically slow until well clear of Colombian water. Once clear of the coast and well out of small-boat fuel range from Cartagena, the red and white ship veered back on course, while the flotilla headed for Panama and into a new cruising adventure.

Later that winter we made another family visit to Quebec and had the pleasure of a fine leisurely Greek meal with Jean Marc and Suzanne to celebrate their freedom. Up to this point our contact had been entirely over the phone, and meeting this courageous couple face to face was one of those seminal events which would remain with us for the rest of our lives. During dinner I could sense that Jean Marc in particular was curious for me to fill in the many open gaps in the communications between us, but I suggested that might be reserved for another time–to which he nodded in agreement, understanding that some of my contacts were better left unidentified–so we ordered desert.

As we left the restaurant and made our farewells, we noticed there were three police cars idling in the parking lot. I sensed that Jean Marc and Suzanne were still nervous, and I am unsure if they truly believed– that we were whom we were.

---

[1] A kedging anchor is often used to pull the boat in a particular direction rather than used in the traditional sense and in this case was being used to hold the boat off the dock to protect the vessel from the rough dock wall.

CHAPTER 15

Sniper Takes Over

I have always had an interest in how nations prosecute their conflicts with other nations and how collisions of ideology are sometimes resolved by face-saving compromises and protracted debates, while others resort to skirmishes and warfare. No one in their right mind could accept warfare with another country as an acceptable way to advance a nation's ideals, but as we have seen in World War II, it is sometimes necessary to take up arms and actually declare war in order to prevent the spread of an antisocial racist ideology driven by an out-of-control leader and his henchmen. There is no doubt that economics plays a huge role in the motivation behind many wars, but let's save that huge topic for another time and perhaps another chapter or two. I also find it morbidly interesting to understand what compels national leaders to send their young men and women to the battlefield, knowing for certain that many will never return and in particular what those same leaders have to do in order to encourage their constituents to fight. Being a self confessed "petrol head" I am also fascinated with the type of mechanical devices used in modern warfare and slightly amazed at the current cross-over in electronic technology and gadgetry from playtime to wartime. However, no matter how intelligent we allow our weapons to become–at the end of the day the role of a human will remain irreplaceable and the challenge we face is exactly which role will we assign ourselves, and what link we will play in the chain of events alongside the technology which will serve us best. Consider for a moment the current expansion of pilotless drone warfare, which is not an entirely accurate description, because these aircraft do have pilots who are located several thousand Kilometres away–shepherding the drone by remote control. This in my view is a clear example of how humans are able to design a weapon for modern warfare while designing a safe built-in role for a human controller–who resides in an air conditioned control room in the home country. There will soon be a vigorous debate concerning the legality or at least the ethics of waging war from a distance, but I have a specific interest in how direct human intervention still plays a role in modern warfare and a chance meeting allowed me a glimpse into how relevant this remains.

One of my friends took retirement from a life-long career as the station manager for a western intelligence agency in Namibia and after a spell in international banking he is enjoying his new responsibility-free career, living and working for a boutique tour operator in Windhoek. On a visit to London I happened to meet his brother, who was stationed in Kenya the same time I was traveling there during the mid eighties, but unlike his banker-brother, Edward was a career artillery officer and his Kenya posting was on the artillery training range close to the Somali border. Over dinner we exchanged experiences of that wonderful country and I casually mentioned an interest in military affairs and in particular for recording my reminiscences of the people and places which impressed me most. Edward was an excellent dinner companion with a broad range of eclectic interests and an exceptional collection of contacts inside and outside the military business, so as we were paying the bill he asked if I would be interested in meeting an unusual character and as I nodded in the affirmative I had no idea just how unusual and interesting Joseph would turn out to be.

Soon after Edward arranged for me to meet with Joseph, whose role within the military was a sniper–which most of us will be familiar with from past conflicts and the many movies where this somewhat peculiar specialty has been portrayed. I wanted to try and get the inside story from Joseph about how the sniper community went about its business and how they were used as components of the strategic and tactical battlefield plan. I was aware of the purposeful cloak of mystery beyond which we are rarely allowed to peek and if anyone could demystify this, now might be the time for me to have an honest and non prejudicial attempt with Joseph during several discreet country pub dinners.

Joseph was not originally fixated on becoming a sniper and his career in the military was to some degree defined by his affinity for machinery and his ability to keep it working. He initially trained as a master mechanic in one of those military educational trade programs and on graduation was attached to a heavy mechanized unit, travelling alongside a tank regiment, supplying ongoing service and repair work as required. His particular unit was also designated as a hands-on training facility, helping graduate mechanics gain practical experience in the field–prior to qualifying as shepherds to these heavy wolves of warfare. Joseph soon found himself putting in massive amounts of overtime as teacher and mentor, which he was able to claim as extra pay coupled with substantial time off–and as Joseph had always been impressed by the snipers attached to his unit he decided to enrol in Sniper-School, using his time off and contacts to gain admittance.

The role of a sniper in military doctrine goes back to the origins of conflict and one can assume that even Neanderthals used some form of individualized surprise attack to disable their foes and principally secure fresh meat. Much later, we have evidence from the 14th and 15th centuries that specialist bowmen were used in this role and between then and now, the art and the science of sniper craft has been refined and redefined as war craft has matured. In the Boer Wars, local marksmen-farmers were able to pin down regular troops with devastating accuracy and take considerable advantage from their intimacy with the bush-land of South Africa. During World War II, German, British, and American forces trained snipers for scouting roles in advance of their main forces and there is evidence of a single effective marksmen pinning down hundred of regulars before he was overrun and dispatched. In the Pacific War, Japanese snipers were often consigned to a line of trees adjacent to invasion beaches, creating the illusion of robust substantial defences as they overlapped their fields of fire.

In a world of rapidly expanding technology, investing time in a sniper school seemed a trifle old fashioned and I was interested in Joseph's reasoning for joining this elite band of characters and in particular if the role has changed over time and his answer was as straight forward as the man himself as he went about separating myth from reality. In contemporary conflicts there are ever-expanding roles for a sniper to assume, but the ability to cleanly hit the target from a concealed location and then disappear into thin air remains an important part of the role. In addition, because the success of their mission and often their lives depends on superior field-craft, they are now tasked with a variety of missions which can include high-risk deep penetration, laser tagging of targets, and broad-ranging reconnaissance, both urban and rural–when only sandals in the sandbox can deliver the intelligence. This was far more complex than I imagined and allowed me to slip a few probes into the training he received.

Joseph explained that most regular armed forces offer considerable training in the complex art of sniper operations and comparing notes with colleagues in allied forces, this varies from country to country, but Joseph's training was multifaceted, including field-craft, camouflage, the use of advanced weaponry, ballistics, target interpretation, communications and laser tagging. What was interesting to hear is that sniping is not exclusive to regular armies and many irregular forces (terrorists included) also employ these specialists who are often highly skilled citizen-marksmen with modest formal training and frequently using outdated weapons. Sniper deployment is something of an art and varies depending on the conflict, the terrain, the weaponry, and the military affiliation of the operative. In earlier times, snipers were also called marksmen or sharp shooters, a term taken from use of the American Sharp Rifle. American Civil War sharp shooters played much the same role as now, frequently operating independently in the field for long periods of time and coincidentally I learned the word *"scharfschütze"* in German conveys the same meaning.

We tend to think of snipers using specialized rifles, but we need reminding that indigenous people were highly effective performing a similar role using bows with arrows and crossbows with bolts. In fact a high profile contemporary ally in one of today's modern conflicts allows its special forces to use silent ultra-high-powered crossbows to deliver ordnance...seemingly out of thin air–and what a surprise that must be for the enemy! No matter what their role and no matter which weapons are used, well-deployed snipers can cause considerable angst amongst civilian and military communities, and for that reason these specialist teams remain a formidable weapon in any arsenal. By the way, Hollywood sadly supports the urban legend that snipers only seek human targets, when a great variety of technical targets are eagerly sought out by snipers. For example, unobtrusive damage to the antenna of a supersonic fighter may not be evident when taxiing for takeoff, but could be devastating at Mach 1. A fractured oil pipe or a shattered gas line may be undiscovered for days in a seldom-inspected location, but can be deadly when repair crews are ambushed by snipers as they travel to repair the break.

Joseph also reminded me that the word "sniper" comes from the bird "Snipe," which the British hunted in India. This is a smallish avian which flits around quite erratically, so successfully bagging one is a considerable feat of marksmanship and would earn the title "Sniper." However, as he pointed out, the broader meaning of the word describes the selective identification of a target–which can vary according to the overall strategy. Therefore, as language is a dynamic art form, "Sniper" is no longer the exclusive pervue of the military and is now used in offices, schools, or even medicine, to identify targeting a colleague–generally for negative purposes.

In the world of warfare, these specialists are used to disrupt opposing forces and destabilize their operations. They can target regular troops and where possible, senior officers, often described as "high value" targets, which is why officers sometimes cache insignia to make identification more difficult. Snipers can also target civilian populations, as in Sarajevo during the sickening Balkan conflict and it becomes particularly interesting and demanding when they are are deployed against each other in an effort to neutralize their effect. The most graphic example of this type of conflict is in the movie *Enemy at the Gates*, which depicts a classic sniper-on-sniper hunt in the bombed-out Russian city during the battle for Stalingrad. This battle pitted the revered Vasily Zaitsev, a Russian peasant crack-shot, against an experienced German game hunter, while the movie skilfully demonstrates two different approaches by counter-posing the Russian peasant worker against the privileged German gentry. Zaitsev is basically a country boy with a natural flair for marksmanship and his ability to eliminate German hierarchy as they wandered about the conflict zone was nothing short of intimidating for the enemy. To eliminate this highly effective adversary the Germans secured the services of a titled game hunter who rapidly became obsessed with the cunningly successful Russian, and with their roles constantly reversing as their deadly dance unfolded, one can see how tactical and lethal a game this was. The Vietnamese were experts at using highly autonomous opportunistic snipers who were largely self sufficient, living off the land, occasionally sustained by food handouts from friendly villagers. They roamed the forests close to US bases, targeting personnel inside the wire, especially pilots of slow flying Huey helicopters who might be landing or departing from missions. Similar "sniper-scouts" were used by both sides in the second Boer War and the film *Breaker Morant*, while not specifically focusing on snipers, gives an excellent flavour of the role.

Joseph was quick to point out that these craftsmen are equally effective in both offensive and defensive roles because a sudden and selective attack by an operative can have a disturbing effect on the overall rhythm of a conflict, disrupting plans, pinning down a disproportionate number of troops, and forcing a degree of improvisation by regular forces with possible costly consequences. They can be deployed, either with pre-planned mandates or in more random, autonomous and opportunistic roles and in some regions, snipers are deployed in two-person teams, which enables partners to alternate roles of spotter and shooter and also to keep a weather eye on their rear. When deployed in pairs, these teams generally alternate roles to preserve their eyesight, which can be strained after long periods gazing through the scope.

Deployment can vary greatly according to the conflict, the terrain, the mission, and the available technology, but the goals are invariably similar, which is to insert snipers with zero indication of their presence. Their covert activity will become evident enough at the location and time of their choosing, handing them a temporary devastating advantage but until that time they remain an unidentified hidden field-asset biding their time for maximum effect. For insertion purposes they are often hidden within a patrol and conveniently left behind in the field as the patrol returns to base. The insertion technique tends to vary in complexity according to the nature of the conflict and the terrain in which they are working. For example in an urban setting, teams of operatives may have pre-researched a preferred nesting location, which is then incorporated into the footprint of the patrol, which has the advantage of hiding the deployment and giving the sniper team the cover they need to perform. In some respects an elevated location may be preferable, but it can also be easy for the enemy to target–so the best locations will often have the advantage of elevation combined with an ability to hide their nest from detection. By the way, insertion of deep-penetration sniper teams by air into a rural setting can be just as effective as being left behind by a surface patrol and its success depends heavily on terrain, technology, and target acquisition. Before a sniper team is deployed, the basic mission will be outlined at a senior level and then ratified once they are in place, and will be either specific or opportunistic–but the targets may not necessarily be identified. For example, to disrupt mine-laying activities along a notorious stretch of highway, several snipers using ultra-long-range rifles with intersecting fields of fire can cover a significant arc and dissuade irregulars from laying sub-surface mines.

There is a basic formula to establishing a secure position, but depending on the circumstances, sniper teams can also double as spotters for roaming allied aircraft and calling in air strikes if necessary. Remote teams can also be inserted within striking distance of a base, whereupon they might target specific leadership for elimination. Nowadays insertion and recovery of sniper teams can be handled by long-range helicopters, thereby greatly reducing casualties. Captured operatives have traditionally been given more brutal treatment than regular soldiers, and for this reason, a career in this field carries greater risk and demands creative extraction planning.

Exploding melons, washing mysteriously falling, and donkeys on safari

One of Joseph's sorties was particularly satisfying, because they needed to send a precautionary message to the enemy that signalled their presence in the region while highlighting their vulnerability at the hand of our forces. To make this possible, the team was air dropped some distance down the backside of a long falaise which dominated one side of a broad sparsely cultivated plain, inhabited by a few tiny hamlets comprising less than ten mud dwellings each. They flew a circuitous route and landed a few hundred feet beneath the summit, rendering the already throttled back muffled engines of the hilos quite inaudible to the villagers below, but necessitated a two-hour tiring climb to gain the required vantage points where the teams would establish their nests. We are talking about five teams of three specialists, distributed along the ridge of the falaise, spread just under three kilometres apart, which would protect a good twenty kilometres of otherwise vulnerable highway. The plan was to safeguard the road running beneath the heights above, by sending a message to anyone thinking about planting an I.E.D. along the dusty hard packed stretch of gravel that the cost of doing so would be high and it might be better to take their trade elsewhere. A series of allied patrols were scheduled to pass by over the next several days and to send a message to any hostiles who might be in the region it was decided to try for a series of ultra long shots at a series of unusual targets, not generally assigned a high value by anyone plying this trade.

 Through their scopes the teams identified several wagons of large green melons, which presumably were in transit and overnighting between their growing fields and a nearby market. The setting sun behind the falaise turned the floor of the valley into an artificial sea of gold, while shrouding the hill tops in the glare of the sun's outer edge. This was the perfect time for a series of well placed mischief-shots, as the snipers took full advantage of the failing light to destroy several of the lower placed melons, allowing the crop to gently roll out the back of the produce carts onto the sand beneath. After that was accomplished they turned their sights on the courtyard of the closest hamlet to discover that washing has been left out overnight, propped up by a single stick to raise the fresh clothes above the surface of the sand. It took several shots before the stick was neatly bifurcated into smaller components allowing the washing to sink slowly out of sight. The rusty latch which restrained the animal byre door was up next in this makeshift shooting gallery and once relieved of it's rusted bar, several donkeys were able to push open the doors and wander towards the dwelling looking for a hand out of food. The message was well received by the villagers who decided that a passive relationship was preferable at this particular time leaving little doubt they would resume as soon as the invisible snipers moved to another location.

In an urban setting a sniper deployment might be based in a static location and with the advantage of elevation this can have a devastating effect for an extended period of time, and choosing a heavily damaged building with a clear view of the city is preferable– with a clear escape route if possible. This technique would enable someone like Joseph to hide his shooting platform towards the rear of the building, maintaining a clear field of fire through blown-out rooms. Setting up the platform towards to rear of the building and wrapping his weapon in dyed burlap effectively blends into the linear outline of the damaged structure, rendering him virtually invisible. The downside is that once he starts hitting targets, regular troops and opposition counterparts will immediately begin a search for his location, but being well-hidden and highly skilled he will be able to continue for some time and possibly escape on his own schedule. Muzzle flash has been somewhat reduced by modern technology, but depending on his target; a certain amount of scientific triangulation can be done by opposing forces. For this reason multiple sniper teams can confuse opposing forces by staggering attacks, rendering accurate triangulation even more difficult. The teams can also use noise from ambient artillery fire to mask the crack of their high-powered rifles, and coordinating this firing sequence along with temperature, wind and distance is part of their game.

Technology is now playing an important role in this game of hide and seek and some time ago an allied force developed an automated anti-sniper weapon-system specifically for urban warfare, which temporarily caused these highly specialized soldiers to alter their strategies. This system employed a number of fix-bases with pre-located and automated sniper rifles which were linked to a complex control system. The anti-sniper rifles were arranged in intersecting arcs, which combined to cover an entire 360 degree field–virtually an entire neighbourhood. The "eyes and ears" of this computerized system acted much the same way that human eyes and ears work. The main difference was their high-fidelity ability to "see more and hear more"—in fact far more than a human is able to. When this system identifies a faint muzzle flash and associates it with the noise of a sniper rifle, the counter weapons system immediately fires back at the source of the attack. This does not work one 100 percent of the time, but it was sufficiently effective to cause urban operatives to alter their tactics.

Sniping in a rural environment calls for a mobile approach, which requires different types of camouflage and operational tactics. One of the earliest camouflage suits was called a "ghillie," which comes from the Scottish Gaelic word for servant or lad and also describes a Scottish gamekeeper's hunting blind. Tropical jungle warfare requires a vastly different camouflage from a northern forest conflict, while desert camouflage differs greatly from bush country. Snipers in rural settings are generally mobile units whose success is aided by their ability to meld into the natural setting and to reappear when being extracted and occasionally sniper teams will establish a temporary fixed rural platform, which will be used in a slightly different way from their urban colleagues. Camouflage is absolutely necessary in this game, and it has become a highly developed combination of art, science, and nature, which has resulted in some remarkable guises. Taken out of context, these guises look crude and simply defy logic and it is only when "viewed on location" that their extraordinary capability becomes evident. In fact the French art expressions *"trompe l'oeil,"* fooling the eye and *"coup l'oeil,"* swiping the eye, come to mind and just as this refined art form has developed over the years, so has the parallel art of camouflage. Various consumer science periodicals are even hinting that the "Cloak of Invisibility" made famous by Harry Potter is now close to a reality, but I seriously doubt this. If this does becomes a reality, the entire nature of warfare will change and sniper teams may well be redefined.

At this point Joseph commented on the crossover between military and civilian police snipers which has been happening for quite some time–in fact most police forces have highly trained members who are superb in this role. In 2008 John Allen Muhammad, the retired Marine sniper, and his sidekick Lee Boyd Malvo took on new roles as murderers of civilians in the suburbs of Washington, DC, and nearby Maryland. Muhammad was a highly trained sniper who used a Bushmaster XM-15 .223 calibre rifle, fired through a tiny hole in his car–murdering ten innocent civilians as they went about their daily lives. Unlike the military, police snipers are only deployed in exceptional circumstances such as hostage-takings or violent stand offs where firearms are evident. There are others differences in the roles of military and police snipers and generally, policing operations are conducted at relatively short range of between fifty and one hundred meters and in some cases are able to destroy the assailant's weapon with a well-placed sniper shot.

I wanted to know more about the entire process of firing a precision rifle at ultra-long range and Joseph gave me a master class in how the laws of physics impacts this environment. First it is important to have a thorough understanding of the science which impacts the gun, the bullet, the person on the ground, the weather, the altitude and the target, and once they have this firmly in their head and aided by computerization, a specific shot can be planned. This is easier to understand if you compare what happens when throwing a pebble by hand at a tree. After the pebble leaves your hand, it travels through the air, gradually slowing down, and eventually falls to the ground. If a powerful wind is blowing directly against you, the pebble slows earlier and travels less distance. If a powerful wind is directly behind you, the pebble travels further before falling to the ground. If the wind is blowing from the side, the pebble will be blown slightly off course before dropping. The same happens to a sniper's bullet and if the distance to the target is say, one thousand metres, the bullet will be vulnerable to wind deflection, air resistance and power loss during the entire distance of its travel. Therefore for the shot to be successful, he or she has to consider all atmospheric conditions plus the laws of physics–of which the wind is only one element. Fortunately, through constant practice in varied conditions and knowing the performance characteristics of his rifle and the weight and profile of the bullet, the sniper can make the compensatory inputs and be right on target. A well-trained marksman will be calculating wind speed, local temperature, height above sea level to determine the density of the air, and the geometry between the target and himself.

There are specific calculations which have to be carefully made and in the latest extraordinary longest recorded shot of 2,475 meters, the bullet will have been in flight for exactly six seconds after the trigger was pulled. Moreover, if the sniper had contended with a slight 5.5kph cross-wind the bullet would arrive at the target 9.2 meters to one side– in other words it would miss. These formulas are highly dependent on the power of the Sniper rifle combined with the loading of specific bullets. From a historical perspective there are documented records of some well known snipers and recorded comments of sniper type activities dating back to 16th century Japan. In the recent past and during the current century, well-known practitioners of the art were evident on all sides of the conflicts, with some of the most prolific recording in excess of one thousand victims. Lyudmila Pavlichenko, a female sniper in the Russian army, recorded three hundred and ninety kills in her logbook, more than the famous Vasily Zaitsev mentioned earlier in this chapter.

Until recently the longest-distance sniper kill was an astounding 2.430[1] meters held by Canadian Captain Rob Furlong of the PPCLI. This has now been surpassed by Captain Craig Harrison from the British Household Cavalry, who shot the aforementioned 2,475 metres, to destroy a Taliban machine-gun post. In other words this shot was a distance of almost two and a half kilometres or marginally under one and a half miles. What is remarkable is that Captain Harrison made two consecutive kills, one directly after the other to silence this Taliban machine gun. None of this would be possible without a superb long-range sniper rifle, in this case a BMG–Browning, using a 50 millimetre shell. This combination is also used by a number of agencies including the United States Coast Guard and the Washington DC Police Department. With this formidable weapon, the U.S.C.G. is able to destroy an outboard engine on the back of a drug-runner's boat, while the police are able to do the same to the engine of a felon's car.

My dinner with Joseph was exceptionally interesting, mainly because he was a thoughtful fellow with a decent sense of humour and a grounded sense of proportion. He was candid about his work which carried recorded evidence of having saving many compatriots' lives and he was devoid of the hate we see in the movies, preferring to accept that his foes were blinded by ideology and had lost the ability to reason, if they ever possessed it in the first place. It has been suggested by one of my colleagues that some of the combatants who are killed by snipers might be innocents working as enforced labourers and in some cases under the threat of violence against their families, and while there will always be some who fit into this box, I am convinced the vast majority do what they do because of their beliefs and in embracing this career they also embrace the deadly consequences of their trade. Operating in the modern war zone can be frustrating for those who were educated by a 20th century doctrine, which is built upon on 19th, 18th and 17th century conflicts where war was to some extent codified and both teams mostly played by the rules. Nowadays for some combatants, some of the rules are impacted by the threat of publicity on our nightly news by the BBC, NBC, CBC, and CNN broadcast teams.

---

1 To be absolutely clear, the record of 2,475 meters is 1.53 miles, or 2,475 long strides– which is a long way to ensure accuracy.

Lotus Seven – Pittsburgh Grand Prix

Mini Cooper - Mosport

CHAPTER 16

Racing Toward My Seventieth Year

I freely admit that one of my enduring passions has been motor racing–in fact anything to do with the extraordinary activity they call motorsport. As far back as I can remember this has been part of my life–along with a relationship with that remarkable magazine devoted to this discipline-fittingly called "Motor Sport." In my early days it was father who inspired me with his spirited driving and uncanny ability to place his underpowered van or car exactly where he wanted it to go, while pedaling furiously along the highway. I often remember saying to myself, "there is no way he will ever make that gap in the traffic"– and be completely amazed when the gap stayed open, the oncoming car moved slower than anticipated and the car he was overtaking obligingly maintained its station on the road. This was not an occasional occurrence, it was father's modus operandi on public roads and anachronistic though it may seem in 2014–this was how motoring enthusiasts drove in those days. Our famous trip through France to the Côte d'Azur was another example of his exceptional driving ability on public roads. In those days the optimum route south took us over some pretty interesting Swiss and French mountain passes and witnessing my old-man doing his stuff in a right-hand-drive car on French roads was watching a virtuoso at work.

My formative "low-earner" days working in the UK allowed me to buy a modest Austin Healey Sprite and "Rallycross" the car with some success on various tracks roped off in farmers' fields. My memories of belting across slippery fields with absolutely no barriers to restrain my car, was a defining experience for a late teenager and I credit Rallycross for incubating my comfort zone when motoring sideways in races with my car seemingly out of control. This particular form of racing was a peculiarly British type of motorsport that was popular at the time. Cars lined up behind each other and were released at timed intervals–the official idea being to set a faster time than your competitors–but those of us with an ounce of competitive spirit knew the real game was to try and catch the fellow ahead.

I was also very interested in karting and especially the British geared karts powered by motorbike engines that resembled miniature formula cars. My early "Keel Kart" was a modest and rather conservative chassis (under) powered with a Villiers engine, which at 2.5 inches above the ground seemed like the fastest thing on earth and with only 110 pounds of steel to push along I thought this moved the kart at a great clip. At least that was the impression as I lowered my lap times on the local kart track and came to grips with this little rocket. A call from a buddy in Bradford encouraged me to enter a race on a cinder-oval where dirt track bike racing took place, so we changed the rear sprocket to provide appropriate gearing for this flat out speed experience and I borrowed an old Belstaff Jacket to protect myself from the flying cinders and what an interesting experience this was. Thanks to racing my Healey in Rallycross events I was entirely comfortable sliding through banked corners and soon found myself running on the front row with three other karts–with the added bonus of dust-free laps until we caught the rest of the pack and overtaking the back markers became a necessity.

My appetite now whet for karting I took the plunge and purchased a Spanish Bultaco motorbike engine to re-engine my kart–which took the performance of this modest race machine to another level entirely. The Bultaco was a sturdy high revving 175 cc power plant, the same capacity as the British engine, but the power delivery was entirely linear and just kept building as I took it through the gears. Having tested the Spanish engine at my local track I entered many races in and around Yorkshire and learned a great deal about inch-close racing with other wannabees in the sport. For some reason at that tender age I came to the early decision that I was not interested in earning my living in motor racing, preferring to keep this as a passion-hobby and to continue my involvement as a spirited and competitive amateur-privateer.

Once my career started to move I was frequently working overseas which brought some unique perspectives to rapid motoring. Living in Lugano was a marvelous opportunity to enjoy the famous Swiss Mountain passes in my highly capable and well modified Judson supercharged VW Beetle, which terrorized many of the locals in their Fiats, Beemers and Ferraris. The Beetle was relatively low powered, but its gearing was perfectly suited to mountain driving and the Judson Supercharger converted this Clark Kent into a veritable Superbug! At one time I was employed by a British firm and sent out to Tunisia where my motoring adventures continued with a company supplied, pneumatic suspension Citroen DS 19–the one with the most peculiar single spoke steering wheel. This curious and to some extent technically advanced French car, was perfectly suited to the ultra-long, ultra-fast, ultra-straight Tunisian highways which had been built during the Roman occupation and were living proof that the Romans never built a corner unless absolutely necessary. In later years the DS was replaced with an ultra-tough Peugeot 403 which has been immortalized in another chapter of this book.

When I emigrated to Canada motorsport was definitely on my mind, but the need to grow my business and raise a family cramped my style for a number of years–until we had that mostly under control and it was time to resume my passion. Meanwhile taking every opportunity that was available I kept close to this unique sport, and sustained my passion while establishing the foundation which my family needed in "Upper Canada."

Returning to competitive motorsport posed other challenges and running an international travel company with the need to be frequently overseas on research field trips made this a case of careful scheduling to ensure I was in town when race dates were published. One of the side benefits of working overseas is the opportunity to visit race circuits in other lands, not all of them famous Grand Pix venues and I remember a particular visit to Barbados when we were contracting a brace of new hotels and discovered that our local agent was also a race enthusiast, which was evident from the copies of Autosport, Motor Sport and Road & Track on his back seat. As is so often the case, one thing led to another and two hours later we were belting like madmen around the remains of the Barbados motor race circuit–long forgotten, somewhat overgrown, but with sufficient sun-drenched pavement to make it interesting. A charming elderly day-watchman prevented us from spending more time on this relic of a post colonial race circuit, but the memories are strong of this surprise in the sun. In later years on a field trip to Monaco I rented a Lambretta and drove the grand prix circuit for two hours solid, but was embarrassed to continually lose my way, as I took the wrong turning at "Casino," "Rascasse" and "The Swimming Pool." Duh! Twenty laps later I more or less understood the route of the track, but passing the same traffic cop twelve times in two hours did cause a raised eyebrow of acknowledgement as if to say, "I see you Monsieur and know what you are doing." He must have seen this so many times before from wannabe race-tourists such as me.

I decided to re-enter competitive racing with historic cars rather than contemporary ones and acquired a rapid Lotus Seven powered by a 1500cc Ford engine, which I raced on the Eastern North American circuits in Canada and the USA. The "Seven" is a unique classic race and road car which was designed by Colin Chapman the engineering visionary, who pioneered the system of skeletal space frames using modest diameter tubes–which were not very robust. What gave the "Seven" its remarkable structural integrity was the thin steel body panels which when riveted to the "space frame," transformed the flimsy set of tubes into a strong stiffened structure, capable of handling great amounts of engine power. Chapman was lauded as a constructor-genius by many, but he was also criticized for under-engineering his race cars to save weight, with both positive and negative results for his drivers. The Seven was sold in the UK as a road going kit-car to avoid taxation and is still in production today under the Caterham brand and by various look-alike manufacturers. Racing a Seven is a wonderful experience because the car is so well designed it more or less goes just where you point it. On fast tracks such as Mosport and Watkins Glen I have enjoyed many tussles with more powerful and considerably faster Corvettes, E-Type Jaguars, the odd Porsche 911 and on rare occasions an Aston or Ferrari. The strategy is to recognize that with such long and open straights these machines with engines often twice the size of the Lotus, will often blast past me in a straight line–but due to their weight and their terminal speed, they were compelled to start braking for the next corner much earlier than my Lotus. I often played a ten lap race of cat and mouse…or tortoise and hare with these monster classics, seeing (also hearing and feeling) them blast past me, only to re-pass them by diving inside before the entrance to the next corner. During a ten lap race on a track with ten corners and perhaps ten of these classic cars, the amount of passing and re-passing was incredibly entertaining.

After my Lotus Seven we raced a giant-killing Mini Cooper S, the 1275 engine capacity model with all of the go-faster bits I could afford–which we added to its already lively engine. The Mini when first released was deemed to be just as revolutionary as the Lotus, because of the unusual design of the car. Instead of placing the engine in the traditional position (front to back) it was placed sideways in the car and the gearbox instead of being behind the engine was located underneath it. Not only that–the Mini was front wheel drive instead of the traditional rear wheel drive and because it was designed by a genius, the Anglo-Turkish engineer Alec Issigonis, it was dimensionally tiny outside, but could accommodate four adults inside plus luggage in the rear located trunk. In many respects it was an unlikely race car but in-period and in the right hands, it was a true giant killer, humbling Corvettes, Mustangs and larger machinery on both short and long race circuits. My mini was insanely fast and out of the box it was proving to be a front runner on all types of tracks.

Driving techniques as distinct from race-craft can vary depending on which car you are using, therefore racing the Mini was quite different from racing the Lotus–and mainly because the former is front wheel drive, while the latter delivers power to the rear wheels. With the Lotus one could carefully chose whatever line was appropriate for the next corner and by carefully placing the car, it would generally take that line with some drifting induced by pushing the loud pedal and feeding in more power to the rear wheels. Racing the Mini, you threw the car into the corner, causing the entire vehicle to slide sideways–to the point where at the entrance to corner you were at an acute angle to it–but the more you pushed the loud pedal the more the Mini's front wheels would pull you through the corner. The open Lotus was relatively quiet, but the mini resonated like a steel matchbox and wearing ear plugs was prudent.

One of the significant achievements in Chapman's Lotus workshop was the development of the single seat Formula Junior and I managed to secure one from a fellow in Brighton UK. I remember the day it arrived outside my home, sitting on a transport truck with one of those sliding pallets on the back and once down at eye level, encased in a temporary garage of 2x4 wood framing, it looked eerily similar to a caged animal that badly needed to be exercised. As you might expect the unpacking caused quite a stir and before long word got around that a cigar shaped race car was residing in my garage. Sitting in this slender Lotus formula car cockpit and being considerably slimmer than as I am now–I remember the feeling that I was somehow part of the Chapman's Lotus tradition which for a motoring historian is a satisfying feeling. The "Junior" was a sheer pleasure to drive and as predictable as a train on rails. I managed to race all three cars on each of the classic tracks in Eastern North America and it takes only a few moments to recall vivid memories from each corner on those tracks. The cars, the characters, the tracks, the magnificent scenery have now blended into a wonderful mélange of years well spent in the sport which I have adopted as part of my life.

Last October I was driving from Kingston to Ottawa, along quiet secondary roads, through small rural villages and for the tenth time over as many years, I drove past the same field, glancing over to a shape which was partially covered in soft fluffy snow–the kind that landed and then blew away in the slightest whisper of wind. I knew this was the remains of a noble Jaguar XK140 which had been left to die–acting as a planter–not quite in Flanders Fields but an Ontario field which was gradually draining the life out of its body. I am unsure exactly what event acted as the catalyst for my next move, but on my return trip I met the owner of this "wreck," eventually signing adoption papers, after which my family instantly grew by a factor of one amazing.... field-find.

I am sure you have experienced that curious cerebral process, where the human mind still beats computing power–whereby we synthesize a complex idea in the space of a nanosecond, where the concept, the process, the issues, the critical path, the vision and the end-game, pass through your mind, neatly wrapped up and delivered by "Mind-FedEx" as a done deal. Which is exactly what happened to me while I was parked alongside that field and I knew the end game of this process was to acquire that 140 and build my own historic Race Special, which I have now branded the "Kingston Jaguar." In the chapter about my visit to the Goodwood Revival I have described what type of a race car a "Special" actually is and over the next eighteen months, with a short hiatus for work and recovery (W&R) I gradually disassembled my field-planter and then just as gradually, but with great care, forethought and I like to think precision–re-assembled 817692 into a Jaguar XK 140 based historic race special.

Which brings me more or less, to my seventieth birthday...

This 600HP monster I was driving on this third mile oval was quite different to my other race cars and with several other monsters inches alongside me, the noise reverberating off the cement walls seemed an integral component of this amazing engine–which I believe was more sensory than actual. Racing this close to a cement wall was alien to any racing I have done previously, but once I was through the first ten laps it was considerably less intimidating than it was made out to be and in a fleeting moment between radio messages, I caught myself thinking the cement offered a measure of safety from the drop-off on the other side of this boundary The radio crackled as I dove for the inside line and somewhere above the steep banking I could hear the clerk of the course announcing the last lap was about to commence. This was my 30th lap of the 1/3 mile oval and although the car was in great mechanical shape, my body badly needed to re-hydrate with large quantities of cool liquid.

This exceptional experience was gifted to me by a young friend who works in the motor-trade. Over a twelve month period I helped him through the complex process of acquiring the service garage which he had been managing, and as the former owner was agreeable to selling the enterprise, if they could just figure out a fair deal for both parties this might work. Finally after a period of due diligence a deal was struck and as the two parties are still friends they seem to have chosen the right formula.

One of the large auto-parts-firms which sell garage supplies offers the owners and mechanics of their customer-garages a place at a race school as an incentive–and when my buddy approached them with this proposal, they generously allowed him to re-gift the session to me. The experience of a NASCAR style race school with its own special brand of race-culture was a type of motorsport I was keen to understand and while my memory is intact and I am able to make comparisons with my road-circuit racing I will try and paint a picture of what it was like. The track which we used is a banked 1/3 mile oval–which is the typical of the tracks you see in old US fairground race movies–about the same size and style where American stock car racing got its start. Similar tight speedway ovals are in competitive use to this day in many North American communities and what they call "Outlaws," huge 600 HP Silhouette racers use a similar track, but covered in tightly packed dirt!

The banked turns at either end are joined by two short straits which I would guess are about 120 meters long. The entire track is ringed by thick cement walls which are far tougher than the cars, and the last thing I wanted to do was "kiss the cement" and bend one of these valuable monsters. The asphalt is unlike what we race on and it is considerably stickier than a public road surface and works in tandem with racing slick-tyres to create exceptional g-r-i-p.

The cars were genuine NASCAR style machines and although they looked like road cars (mine was a Charger)–they are "silhouette racers" rather than showroom cars that have been worked over. To develop these projectiles they start with a custom built tubular frame using robust wide diameter tubes with considerable wall thickness, they locate a 600 HP full blown race engine inside the frame and cover it with panels that are molded from a real Charger to create a "look-alike" or "silhouette racer." The engines are immensely powerful with what they call "short-gearing"–and on this 1/3 of a mile oval, they reach each banked corner in an incredible three and a half seconds. That is three and a half seconds of 600 horsepower flat out–after which you need to brake as hard as possible to reduce speed for the next banked corner. The race-going public is mostly fooled into thinking these are road cars–but nothing is further from the truth. To attract auto factory sponsors these race cars have to resemble the cars in the showrooms–and the way the race teams achieve this is to make them into monster look-alikes.

Racing them is a bit like watching a herd of bull elephants suck in a belly full of water, which is then squirted out of their trunks at maximum velocity! There are no doors in the conventional sense of the word, just an opening above the door panel through which I had to climb into the car–one leg first and then rotate my body to slide down into an ultra tight bucket seat. Once in place the "dresser," for want of a better word, leant into car and fiddled around my crotch (I had requested a female dresser but was studiously ignored by my "team")–in order to secure the four-point full race harness. After that, an apparatus called a "Hans Device" was slipped around my neck between my shoulders and the lower level of the helmet to prevent whiplash and neck trauma if an accident occurred. Trussed up like a Christmas Turkey in Loblaw's, I glanced around looking for the instruments to see where was the emergency fuel shut off and the electrical shut-off and try as I might I absolutely could not locate the foot pedals. I suspect the dresser was becoming annoyed when I buzzed him on the radio to come back over to the car, but that evaporated into a grin as he removed a timing board that had somehow found its way into the car and under the pedals. The cars have four gears, the first three are for getting started, but all racing is done in 4th–which means that once you are in "top gear," it's a matter of "gas and brakes and gas and brakes" for the entire 30-60 lap race.

In terms of technique–coming out of a corner you have to have the car pointing reasonably straight before touching the gas pedal, because if you don't–the car will head straight for the wall which you will spoil your day. In fact coming out of the corner you need to feed in the gas ever so gently until you can confidently unleash 600 horsepower in a straight line. The reason for this is that the cars have a combination of solid axle and rear wheel drive, which means that they want to go in the direction where they are pointing–therefore pointing the car where you want it to go is highly important. I should mention to make them easier to turn to the left, the frames are built offset rather than straight and they run with 15 psi on the left side tyres and 30 psi on the right– all of which encourages the car to turn left (as it should)!

The reason these cars have very short gearing is to enable the driver to use all of their power and reach maximum revs and to achieve as much accelerated speed as possible on the short 120 meter straights– after which three and a half seconds later you have to shut it all down and get on the brakes real fast. It's worth repeating–that after using all 600 horsepower when exiting a corner, you have no more than three and a half seconds before you get back on the brakes–and almost melt the brake pads to slow the car for the next banking.

The sequence and rhythm goes like this…

Three and a half seconds flat out
Brake like hell for the banking
Very gently turn left
Slowly feed in the power until the car is relatively straight
Three and a half seconds flat out
Brake like hell for the banking
Very gently turn left…etc

After thirty laps of furious activity, tremendous sideways G force, mostly on my upper body and a growing thirst for a swig of Gatorade, I was ready for a breather–after which…it was more of the same–shaving off fractions of seconds each lap, to reach my eventual best of 18 seconds which I felt I could lower to 15 seconds over time. Out of sixty drivers I managed the third fastest and quietly smiled at the unhappy faces of the twenty year old mechanics when they realized my age was north of seventy. I enjoyed the experience–the power was simply amazing, the techniques were really interesting, the entire set up was biased towards sheer brute force, but while I found turning left not in the least boring, after a few laps it became incredibly monotonous and I was yearning to turn right and drift through a series of chicanes. Looking back in my rear view mirror I have even more immense respect for the guys who really go fast on these ovals–but I have to admit to preferring my road-racing at Watkins Glen, Mosport and Road Atlanta.

Now the magic seventy is behind me, I am working hard on completing The Kingston Jaguar and look forward to racing it on some of the US tracks in 2015.

The Trawler Caper

CHAPTER 17

Delivery Cruise of the Trawler Caper

From Owen Sound to Toronto Down the Trent Severn Waterway

I was at the helm of my new trawler as we cast off from the Georgian Yacht Club in Owen Sound and nervously groped our way through the fog–peering at the green antique radar screen through one of those eye pieces you may have seen in World War II movies. The "sweep" of the scanner which was ten feet above our head refreshed the screen at four second intervals, the rotating head picking up scores of blips where yesterday none were evident. We knew there was a fishing derby scheduled for the outer harbour of Owen Sound, and I had some idea how many boats we would have to contend with but the atmosphere on the bridge was in a word–tense. As skipper my role was to ensure the safety of the crew and my newly acquired "little ship," but looking through the wheelhouse windows into the dense fog, knowing we were considerably larger than any of these day-boats, I was aware that our bow would slice any of these competitor's boats in two and my responsibility instantly increased by a factor of 200–the number of boats we saw on the entry list.

We had seen *Caper*, a very salty looking vessel in "Boats for Sale," but were new to the trawler world and not quite aware of what she was.

The owners had seemingly become stressed about the slowness of the market and were "reverse auctioning" the boat, dropping the price each month until it sold. I joined the bidding process and eventually bought *Caper* from Paul and Donna Capel, who were experienced boaters and exceptionally helpful to me, sharing their knowledge and completing my education. But first they rapidly brought me up to speed with the design and build of *Caper* and the awesome capability of the vessel, and their family adventures aboard her.

Caper is a wooden constructed forty foot long Cape Island trawler built by Camille d'Eon, a Nova Scotia based commercial boat builder. Cape Islander boats have a bold sea-going heritage which comes from the severe requirements of the Maritime Atlantic fishery. The looks of a Cape Islander are not entirely cosmetic as you might gather from their "salty" timeless design, with a high upturned bow, broad beam and separate wheelhouse. Countless Maritime fishermen have taken to the sea in the exact same hull as *Caper*, and after cruising her across the Great Lakes in all types of weather, we can personally attest to her capabilities. On acquiring *Caper* we resolved to keep her good maritime looks while equipping her with the best we could afford.

Caper's most endearing design feature was the separate raised wheelhouse which can accommodate five people spread out on captain's chairs, which was especially good for night-running, because ambient light from the lounge would not interfere with our night vision. Sleeping accommodation was mostly in bunks under the raised bow plus a large sofa-bed in the lounge and on the covered aft deck where I loved to sleep. The galley was also in the lounge with an older but quite efficient propane-powered stove that we eventually replaced. Motive power was delivered by the amazing and legendary 318 gasoline V8 Chrysler engine, which is as silent as it is miserly. There was a usable upper deck but mostly for observation–as steering was done from the wheelhouse. For a single screw boat[1], *Caper* would stun onlookers by virtually turning in her own length, and when the prop wash hit her large rudder, she just leaned into the hill and carved a tight turn. However I was more interested in her ability to take rough water, because the Great Lakes are famous for what we call the "short high chop" which can build high waves with troughs close together.

This type of relentless sea-state where a boat slides up a wave and before she can settle, is hit by the next wave, is exceptionally tiring for crews and stresses even a well-founded boat. In the ocean we have often experienced twenty foot high waves, but the troughs have been a hundred and fifty feet apart which give the impression of driving up a gentle slope and sliding gently down the far side. In the Great Lakes the short high chop is what we disliked most.

As we were concluding the purchase, friends mischievously reasoned that if Canadian beavers eat trees … and they are made of wood, would beavers also consume wooden boats, so in retaliation to these comments and to dissuade these charming rodents we studied the Gougeon Brothers epoxy technology which introduced me to an entirely new way of thinking about wooden boat repair. Their "West System" is basically a marvelous way of preserving wood, by using exceptional fast setting epoxy, primarily designed to protect against deterioration and lend strength to a wood structure. With a coat of Gougeon Brothers' best chemicals spread along my planks we were sure that our wildlife would take their incisors elsewhere–so we invested in several liters of this two-part black magic, thinking beavers beware! By the way the Cape Island name has now been adopted by many boat builders, because from a marketing perspective the name has always been synonymous with stability and toughness. In glossy marine magazines the list of so-called "Cape Island" boats grows by the day and Martha Stewart apparently has her own Cape Islander picnic boat …I guess for her picnics.

When the purchase was complete, we started to dream about the trip home so I budgeted time off from work, assembled a series of crew members, and planned to savour each day of this fascinating journey, along with the characteristics of the Cape Islander and the uniqueness of our route.

The Seiche–Great Lakes weather phenomenon

My delivery trip home required some familiarization at the helm, getting used to her handling characteristics and her maneuverability, so for several weekends I commuted to Owen Sound while I got the hang of *Caper's* mannerisms and learned her idiosyncrasies. All boats have the same basic modus operandi while sitting at the dock and one can argue that when you spin the wheel over to the left–the boat will naturally follow. But I can assure you that when boats leave the dock, many of these similarities tend to evaporate and before I brought *Caper* home I needed to learn as much as I could about her capabilities because we may just hit a patch of rough weather.

We were new to the relationship with this Cape Islander and in retrospect *Caper* may have been wincing as I figured out how much helm she needed and how little gas was sufficient to place her where we wanted. Paul had retained his slip in the Owen Sound Yacht Club, so we spent many days backing her out, drifting into the stream, practicing "touch and goes" in the empty slips and learning how this quite large boat would behave. I never enjoy being observed when learning a new craft, and remember my early days racing cars, trying to get the hang of a four-wheel drift while more experienced racers were sliding around me at twice the speed, glancing over at this wannabe race driver. Eventually my helm time on *Caper* started to pay off, and Paul continued to mentor me until we ran out of time.

Part of my familiarization during these weekends was to sleep onboard *Caper* and start using her systems–so when we cruised home I was not scrambling to figure out how everything worked. I had given considerable thought to this and not only because the dynamics of this converted commercial fishing trawler would be quite different from my other boating experiences. In one respect the slow motion that characterizes trawler type boats can be a distinct advantage when maneuvering in tight marinas, but getting used to a slow-motion boat meant altering my DNA need for speed and recognizing that "slow" was one of the reasons I had moved to a trawler. There were other requirements on my familiarization list such as mastering the electrical system which Paul had self-engineered and accessing the under-floor engine compartment which took some getting used to. The electrics were a tad rudimentary and were high on my list of improvements when I reached HYC, while the under-floor "Iron Duke" 318 Chrysler was one of the most attractive and endearing features of this boat. However daily checking the propeller coupling and various engine related functions would mean lifting the center floor panel in the main salon–which dictated where we could place carpets and furniture.

Paul and Donna were superb hosts and could not have been more understanding and willing to show me the ropes but what really impressed was their willingness to accompany me on local maneuvering trials around the tight confines of the Georgian Yacht Club and alongside the grain terminals in Owen Sound. Given my steep learning curve I decided to make the most of my four weekends on *Caper* before starting my journey home and to absorb as much as I could from this delightful and highly capable boating family.

One night while I was slumbering onboard, one of those famous Great Lakes storms erupted, with massive peals of thunder rumbling in from an obscured horizon to stall somewhere above my head with lightning whizzing around us in circles and as a consequence I didn't get much sleep. Great Lakes storms are famous for their pyrotechnic effects, often remaining in a localized area where they put on an amazing show of electrical power. Years later I was at the end of Navy Pier in Chicago under a glass domed auditorium with a similar Great Lakes storm over my head and being on land several hundred feet out in the lake with a thin layer of glass between me and the lightning was a hair raising experience. But this was nothing compared to what was about to happen, because at 02:30 I was awakened by a different sort of noise, this time it was not the Donner and Blitzen kind but a creaking and groaning as though pizza home delivery from Hades was rising up beneath us. I shrank deeper under my duvet trying to ignore this racket, but the groaning refused to disappear and was actually getting worse, so I thought it best to make an appearance and face off with Gandalf's wrath and whatever was causing this sound.

My appearance on deck turned out to be a tad exhibitionist. I whacked my head on the bunk and eventually confronted the ladies on the boat alongside with blood streaming down my nose and my pyjama fly wide open, but after making completely inadequate explanations, I focused on the mess and could hardly believe what was happening in the club-marina. For a reason which was unapparent at first blush, the gunwales of at least twenty sailboats had slipped under the floating docks and being fully ballasted they were now pushing upwards, trying to bring entire docks with them. The collective stress of wood on fiberglass was producing a groaning and grinding like a wreckers yard and the tangled mess of masts and rigging was not pretty.

What happened in Owen Sound was a phenomenon called a "Seiche," which occurs when a storm system pushes large masses of water in one direction and significantly alters the level of the lake at the other end–not unlike a bathtub when your kids slosh water from one end to another. The groaning I heard was caused by sailboats that had sunk lower when the Seiche sucked water out of the basin and were now trapped under the dock fingers as they tried to re-surface when the water returned. Not quite dressed for the occasion I nevertheless sprinted across to the phone and soon car lights were sweeping down the hill as Paul raised the alarm and marshaled his fellow club members. The challenge we inherited was to somehow lower each sailboat in the water by loading the gunwales with as many bodies as we could harness–and then carefully pry each of them out from under the dock as we released them from the wood. If we were unable to restore these boats to an even keel and if the trapped gunwale was pushed deeper into the harbour, they were in danger of taking on water through their windows and entry doors with disastrous consequences for the owners. We had to use massive crowbars on some of the dock surfaces and even destroyed a section or two before we had each boat stabilized in its mooring.

Crossing Georgian Bay

Paul rounded up some friends who were up for an early spring trip and I was happy to have a delivery crew of good-humored and experienced Georgian Bay boaters for the run across to Midland. The plan was to leave quite early, cruise across Nottawasaga Bay, and landfall in Wye Heritage Marina where I would park *Caper* for a week and return to work. Before casting off I spent considerable time planning this journey and had assembled a great many materials for the boat, including a new set of Trent Severn strip charts and a brand new Hand Held Garmin 45 GPS (my first). *Caper* was well provisioned with sufficient food to reach Australia if my navigation was faulty, so we could have motored on for several weeks before stopping–but that was not the plan. As you have read, we left Georgian Yacht Club in thick early morning fog and with yours truly at the helm, Paul glued to the radar and Ed sitting Buddha-like with legs crossed, becoming drenched on the bow and groped our way up the sound. *Caper* was equipped with one of those World War II radar units, with the antenna turning above the wheelhouse and a black rubber eye shield to gaze into. This pale green display was impressively sensitive, and Paul soon identified what looked vaguely like the Spanish Armada, spread a full 90 degrees across our bow.

Out of the mist–Radar pays off

Owen Sound hosts a few professional fishing derbies, and we were now picking our way through scores of sixteen-foot aluminum fishing boats, with anxious-looking competitors staring wide-eyed as we silently emerged out of the mist–*Caper's* 318 Chrysler engine providing silent motive power. I need to pay homage to this slow-revving V8 which was an extraordinary invention and here we were fully twenty years after its birth, moving stealthily across Southern Nottawasaga Bay with it purring away beneath our feet. With the benefit of extensive local knowledge, Paul confidently proclaimed that we would emerge in thirty minutes–and right on cue (don't you hate that confidence) the fog lifted, the sun broke through and we turned *Caper* east towards Christian Island. Our plan was to run directly for the mid-point of this island land-mass and then drift south around the peninsula towards Midland Bay. In retrospect I should have taken more ownership for our navigation, because we encountered even more mist and ended up closer to the north end of the island, eventually having to correct a few degrees to make good our course.

Superb heritage attractions

This part of the Great Lakes has a marvelous colonial heritage, and several sites are well worth mentioning, because they encapsulate the history of Canada's beginning. *St Marie amongst the Hurons* historic village in Midland is a recreation of a Jesuit mission, accurately depicting life one could expect in 1639. The village is extensive, showcasing an accurate picture of the tiered relationships between missionaries, fur trader Samuel de Champlain, and the Huron tribes. Dutch explorers ascending the distant Hudson River were aggressively selling firearms to the Iroquois, who launched a large-scale attack on the Huron in 1649. The massacres, the torturing of Jesuit priests, the subsequent burning of this site, and rampant disease are all part of Canada's early history.

Across from the village just east of the town center is the *Martyrs' Shrine* dedicated to the memory of eight Jesuits who lived, worked, and died here some 380 years ago. The grounds are beautifully landscaped and offer a tranquil respite from the pace of life–that is if you plan your visit to avoid the crowds of visiting pilgrims. The opening of Upper Canada and the development of trading outposts required Britain to build a series of defensible garrisoned communities from one end of the country to the other. In the lower Great Lakes, a necklace of forts allowed British ships to feed these colonial outposts and here in Georgian Bay, *Discovery Harbour* was an essential northern link in the chain. In 1793 Sir John Graves Simcoe acknowledged the strategic importance of Penetanguishene Bay to this colonial strategy by establishing the fort. This harbour was originally a supply-link between York (now Toronto) and the upper Great Lakes posts. But with the War of 1812, thinking changed and a naval dockyard in Georgian Bay became a defense against the young American republic as it morphed into a strategic outpost and shipyard, assuring the flow of supplies and men to British outposts and their First Nations allies. By 1817 construction had started and the arrival of HMCS *Tecumseh*, HMCS *Newash*, and supply vessels *Bee*, *Mosquito*, and *Wasp* declared that Britain's outpost was ready for business.

Titanic appearance of the SS *Keewatin*

For many years the former Canadian Pacific Great Lakes ship the SS *Keewatin* had been residing in a Michigan Creek, carefully looked after by its American history enthusiast owner and thanks to a Toronto based entrepreneur and the amazing Eric Conroy, this important piece of Canadian maritime history is now back on home turf, residing in Port McNichol a short drive from Midland. What interested me most was her build provenance, having been constructed in Gavan Scotland merely five years before Titanic, bearing a serious resemblance to the style of the ill fated ship. Keewatin is one tenth the size of Titanic, but visitors will marvel at how well she is preserved and how authentic she is dressed as a showpiece of the former Canadian Pacific fleet.

The Trent Severn Canal

A week in Midland was a good time to reflect on the journey and practice more "touch and goes" until my friend Tom Hope joined us for the shakedown cruise. The design of *Caper* was attracting quite a bit of attention from other boaters and I soon realized that she presented a romantic notion for sailors, who came over to chat about where we were heading. The silhouette of the Cape Islander seemed to represent a vessel capable of going virtually anywhere. With the cruising kitty replenished after a week back in the office, we were now ready for the mid-part of our delivery cruise down the Trent Severn waterway and at this point I made our first navigation mistake, which was tagging along behind a vessel, which supposedly "knew the way." I did this out of laziness and found myself in an ever narrowing and increasingly shallow channel with my new trawler looking larger every second. We were heading nowhere fast and as our "expert" up front also got the message, I used *Caper's* amazing ability to spin her on her own axis and resolved to paddle our own canoe from now on.

The route to Florida

The Trent is a wonderful canal linking Lake Ontario to Georgian Bay and the upper Great Lakes so we could think of no better way to go boating from one lake to another, as did the delivery skipper of a Chicago-based sixty footer who obviously thought the same. This chap was repositioning the owner's yacht from Chicago to Florida, and the Trent Canal system combined with the Erie Barge Canal in New York State was the shortest route to take. Later in this transit while playing tortoise and hare with us, he took a tragic shortcut that ended up costing him a bundle as he whacked a rock with his starboard prop and limped in for repairs. For us this was a valuable lesson in staying between the Red and Green channel markers and circumscribing the imaginary circle if the markers were near a bend. The delivery skipper cut the corner and was last seen talking to Aetna about an insurance repair to his shafts.

Big Chute: an extraordinary experience

In the development of most canals it is often necessary to connect different levels of water, and the conventional way to achieve this is by building a series of locks. At Big Chute the challenge was not only to transport vessels over an escarpment–which a conventional lock system would have done quite well. The issue was to prevent invasive species from migrating between Georgian Bay and Lake Ontario and in 1911 building Big Chute was how they did it. To use this marine railway, you first park your boat on the Blue Line adjacent to the lock and wait until you are called into the chute carrier. Meanwhile from where you are parked you can see this massive open railroad car descending the hill, packed with boats of all shapes and sizes. Once this is in the water, the gates of the carrier slide open and out the boats cruise–after which it's your turn to climb the mountain. The railroad car is open front and back, so as you enter, attendants are climbing the structure, working hydraulic levers to cradle your boat in two large straps. Once you're secured, they repeat this with another ten boats, and when everyone is happy, four mineshaft electric motors start winding inward, and huge cables haul the lot up the hill.

Over before it was started

As we approached Orillia we were listening to Peter Gzowski on CBC when the 15:00 news reader mentioned something about the Trent. We weren't really listening, but Tom thought they mentioned high water and the dreaded "closure" word and the dock-master in Orillia also mention the "C" word and it was apparent that we were about to get another week of enforced vacation. Seemingly the amount of spring runoff coming into the system was so great that it caused navigation issues and rather than jeopardize the locks, the authorities decided to close down for a week.

***Caper* gets a facelift**

This enforced rest in Orillia was an opportune time to start restoring *Caper*, so after a visit to the local hardware store and armed with paint stripper, tools and a gallon of best "white," we started the year-long restoration of *Caper's* exterior. This was great fun as we scraped, sun bathed, listened to Jimmy Buffet, showered, ate well, and then started over again, day in, day out for a week in Orillia. I suspect the locals were a bit perplexed with all this frantic work, but owning a unique trawler with undeniable provenance, we felt that we owed it to *Caper* to spruce her up before arriving home. Eventually the Trent system normalized enough for us to continue, and we backed a very smart-looking *Caper* out of Orillia and headed south for Lake Ontario.

The Kirkfield Lift Locks

The second engineering feat on this amazing canal system is the lift lock at Kirkfield further south close to Peterborough, which joins two levels of the canal. Imagine two huge square bathtubs each capable of floating forty boats. One tub is in the same level as your canal, and the other tub is sixty feet below at the level of the other canal. The side of each tub is attached to a huge cement pylon on which the tubs slide up and down. Now imagine each tub filling with boats from both levels of the canal–and when that's completed, the lockmaster spills a few more gallons into the upper bathtub, making it heavier, whereupon the higher tub sinks while the lower tub rises. I am surprised when re-reading my log of this journey to realize how little we knew about these locks. We arrived at Kirkfield, were soon whisked high into the air, and gently continued on our way in the lower segment of the canal.

Lake Ontario: Trenton and the Murray Canal

We overnighted in Trenton, mostly because we had been pushing it quite a bit and badly needed a good night's sleep. We also needed supplies for the galley and fuel for *Caper's* 318, so we paused, refreshed, and headed for the Murray Canal which is an excellent short cut between Lake Ontario and the Bay of Quinte, leading to Kingston and the Thousand Islands. Unfortunately the bridge keeper was ill that morning and did not report in for work so we waited with a small armada until a replacement technician swung the bridge and let us through. I have always received mixed signals from bridge keepers on the Murray who are often curt with their replies over VHF radio. Sometimes they are helpful, but mostly inconsistent with their attitude. We deposited the obligatory toll in their well-burnished brass cup and headed East into Brighton Bay.

Who put smoked glass in the windows?

Our run down Lake Ontario was mostly pleasant until we were abeam of Cobourg, where we picked up two-foot swells coming south from Rochester. This rolled *Caper* around a bit, not too unpleasantly, but I was happy that we had familiarized ourselves with her characteristics and the weary crew was soon nodding as the motion rocked them to sleep. Our journey was more or less uneventful until Oshawa, at which point the sky started to darken and although I had carefully noted the marine forecast I found myself wondering if I had made a mistake. The voice on channel 22 definitely said the winds would be variable, and the two footers from Rochester arrived more or less on cue, but at no time did the anonymous voice on the VHF mention storm clouds–or worse and I wondered what sort of weather we were heading into. My alternates were Port Hope, Whitby, Newcastle, and Frenchman's Bay, but I really wanted to make the Highland Yacht Club in the Scarborough Bluffs, where my son Daniel was waiting to handle our lines. I tuned the VHF once more to channel 22 and listened for a weather update. "Two footers from Rochester, winds variable–stable for the next 24 hours." Perhaps there was such a thing as localized weather, so I turned on the radio and channel-surfed for the CBC, where I got the land-based version of "two footers from Rochester, winds variable–stable for the next 24 hours."

The Culprit

With the crew of *Caper* in another world and no one to talk to, I started discussing the weather with myself (not always a positive thing) then quite by accident I noticed our anchor had worked free from the deck housing and needed a kick back into place. *Caper* was on auto-pilot, so I confidently stepped out of the pilot house into bright sunshine! What was going on here? One moment a darkening sky, the next bright sunlight–and then it hit me. *Caper* had smoked glass on her pilothouse windows, and in the late afternoon failing light I had the impression we were heading into weather. One of the first pieces of structural work we did was to remove those sexy smoked-glass windows and replace them with panes of mild tempered clear glass.

Arrival at Highland Yacht Club

The run along the north shore was more or less as expected and excitement mounted as we approach the Bluffers park entrance marker. My son Daniel was getting a bit worried because I had grossly underestimated the time it would take from Trenton to HYC, but he was there when we arrived, and deftly handled our lines as we introduced *Caper* to her new home on the famous O dock, slip 10. The arrival of *Caper* was a milestone for me and our first boat at Highland Yacht Club. Our club-mates were curious about what we had acquired, and I was happy we'd taken time to spruce her up ready for mustering next morning.

---

[1] Single screw boat refers to the fact that *Caper* has one engine and one propeller–but it was as maneuverable as any boat equipped with two screws. As mariners know, maneuvering a boat in tight quarters with two propellers (twin screws) is infinitely easier than using a single screw. In a boat equipped with twin screws, the skipper can move one screw into the "go-forward" position and the other screw into the "reverse" position which effectively "twists" the boat around its axis. The technique is to keep the rudder in the central position, effectively rendering it neutral and to let the twisting effect of the two screws turn the boat. *Caper* had an extraordinarily large rudder which helped the single screw to turn the boat on a dime.

Our capable Oceania Trawler The Full Monty" at rest in Kingston"

CHAPTER 18

Multiple Passages to Manhattan on Trawlers Caper and The Full Monty

I was watching the massive bow wave of the powerful tugboat coming towards us and knew that if we met under the bridge we would be in big trouble. The tug was not pulling its usual string of barges, and released from this massive dragnet it was able to make a good twelve knots and create what appeared to be a ten foot rolling wave along each side of its hull. Our speed downstream was a shade under eight knots, and after estimating our closing path it was evident that we would meet under the navigation arch towards the eastern edge of the span–which would cause us no end of grief. A bow wave of that magnitude in open water was ordinarily a non-event, because you could turn into it and take it on the bow as opposed to on the beam, thereby minimizing the rolling effect to the boat. But in the tight confines of the narrow arch of this bridge, it could push us violently towards the starboard abutment with potentially disastrous results. There are well defined maritime rules governing the passing of vessels which we are always careful to observe, but in my world, size overrides everything and I was not about to test the other skipper's courtesy and cope with the consequences of a river collision. Sizing up the potential confrontation, there was an obvious solution for us to take, so for the next ten minutes we turned elegant lazy two hundred feet circles in the Hudson and only when Mr. Tugboat had powered through the bridge did we think of passing through. This was not the first example of bad seamanship and discourtesy on the Hudson River and we rapidly became familiar with the "me-first" attitude in this part of the world.

This tale is a blended account of several passages onboard our trawlers *Caper* and *The Full Monty* between Toronto and Kingston on Lake Ontario and one of our favorite destinations–Manhattan Island and New York City. This route is an exceptional boating destination for the novice wanting to acquire experience with mid-range passage-making and for experienced mariners hoping to explore the lesser known gunk-holes along the Erie and Hudson canal systems. At one time the Erie Barge Canal was a powerful mercantile waterway bringing produce from the American Midwest via Manhattan to Liverpool in the UK. It was dubbed "Clinton's Ditch" after Senator DeWitt Clinton and canal-side towns experienced boom and bust cycles as localized industry grew and fell on hard times.

Hélène and I were originally sailboat enthusiasts, but after years of waiting for the wind to arrive and with demanding jobs, we became attracted to the predictability of power. Reading about this type of boating was facilitated by the excellent publications in the Nautical Mind bookstore in Toronto, and ever so slowly my heading altered and I gravitated towards the world of slow boats and miserly fuel burn. Much of the slow boat philosophy I have read about is akin to that of sailing, where the journey is as important as the destination and with similar planning for both disciplines, so having made a decision to leave my sails behind, I knew that a trawler was in my future. At that time, perhaps by coincidence, there was an awakening in the recreational boat building industry, and a number of small-volume, high-quality builders were offering gleaming renditions of boats we could only dream of. I had no issue with the products they were offering. The issue was my ability to pay for a gleaming new trawler, so we researched the used market and considered converting a work boat into a family cruiser.

Caper, the Cape Island Trawler

The last chapter describes *Caper* the Cape Islander our exceptional first Trawler on which we traveled safely across the Great Lakes and down to Manhattan and let me again rave about the virtues of this exceptional boat and pay homage to its Nova Scotia Lobster boat provenance.

The Full Monty: Taiwanese Tupperware Trawler

Our second trawler *The Full Monty* was a twin diesel fiberglass vessel which emerged from the Marine Trader line of boats–and the same friends who talked about beavers eating *Caper* were now referring to *The Full Monty* as my "Tupperware" Trawler. A variety of these Taiwanese fiberglass trawlers were built from similar molds and customized by various assemblers who then branded them accordingly. In earlier years the Brits called this "badge engineering," whereby basic car models from the same factory and assembly line were tarted up and rebadged to suite their various brand requirements. *The Full Monty* was a handsome two-deck boat with separate twin sleeping cabins, each with private head and shower. The upper deck had a practical steering station with fully enclosed Mylar screens, fabulous visibility and plenty of seating for a quiet dinner. The main steering station one deck below was rarely used because the visibility was so much better from up above, the only drawback when steering in heavy weather was the movement of the boat, which makes visiting the head interesting and a challenge. The four-cylinder Ford Lehman diesels were tough and lumpy and never really ran at the sweet-spot of larger sixes. They were economical, though, and barely audible from the upper deck.

The trips and differences

Our plan was to make another memorable visit to Manhattan, enjoying the scenery along the north shore of Lake Ontario, then crossing to the south shore to enter the Erie Canal which leads to the Hudson River. En route to our destination we played Leonard Cohen's "We'll Take Manhattan" to get into the mood as we slowly progressed south. Sharing this type of boating experience is always a pleasure and having crew members onboard makes for a memorable trip, but the planning is often complicated as they can rarely start and end with you. This means having to meet at an agreed location at a precise time and then repeat that again when they leave, so my preference is to have crew onboard from start to finish.

The two trawlers differed in many aspects but were similar in others. *Full Monty's* twin diesels propelled her marginally quicker than *Caper*, but they burned the same amount of fuel, and I can't speak highly enough of the tough little 318 Chrysler on *Caper* and how easily it propelled that forty feet Long Cape Islander. I can hear comments about the danger of carrying copious amounts of gasoline on a wooden trawler and I agree with most of them, but suffice it to say that we took more than the usual precautions with gasoline and lived to tell the tale. Both trawlers looked very salty, *Caper* like the lobster boat she was, and *Full Monty* the perfect impressionist recreation of what *Caper* represented. I loved the separate wheelhouse on *Caper*, the ideal location for a skipper to pilot the ship. On *Full Monty* the main steering station was inside the cabin and less conducive to steering with a full house behind you. *Full Monty* had a much better equipped galley with excellent refrigeration, good storage, and private sleeping arrangements.

My plan was to use these trips as training runs for a more dramatic escape from my working life, but so far I have been unable to make that happen. That plan is to embark on a lengthy trip through the Caribbean and Central America, using the capability of a slow economical trawler to check out of life's mainstream for several years. Perhaps one day–who knows?

Caper-Bluffers Park to Cobourg, Belleville, Bay of Quinte, Murray Canal, Picton, Kingston

The agreed hour to cast off *Caper's* lines has arrived, so untying as "O" dock slumbered, we fed fuel to the 318, backed her into the channel, and headed for the open lake. Reviewing the marine weather forecast, we planned for a calm morning on the water and the Scarborough Bluffs were soon disappearing over our stern while the dome of the monastery to port lingered for a few hours. Lake Ontario is featureless on this stretch of the north shore, but that was not my preoccupation. I was entirely focused on the boat's systems to ensure they were pointing at the right temperature, the right depth, the right bearing, and the right pressures for the passage ahead.

The long-range forecast was excellent, and *Caper* soon picked up swells out of the west, which were moving one knot faster than we were. The crew noticed this as our stern was being gently pushed towards the shore and they also noticed the pick-up effect as the two-foot swells cradled *Caper* and gently carried her forwards–not an uncomfortable feeling and one which might shorten the day. Our ancient auto-pilot was the grooved "belt and gear" type attached to the wheel, so the constant wheezing of the mechanism soon had everyone asleep except the skipper, who was recording the course on his chart and scribbling notes about the gauges. Years later, *Full Monty* left Bluffers Park in much the same weather, which lasted barely two hours before we were "corkscrewing" due to a peculiar and aggressive following wave pattern. Glancing to port, the Darlington Nuclear plant stood out in odd-looking contrast to the homes and occasional farms bordering the lake. Port Hope, Newcastle, even Oshawa, were ports of refuge, but *Caper* and *The Full Monty* were both focused on reaching Cobourg and we silently passed them by.

Depending on the weather Cobourg is a six-to-seven hour, seven-knot passage from The Bluffs, with several alternate harbours if the lake becomes unmanageable or if you have a mechanical failure. "George" as we called *Caper's* antique autopilot, wheezed on unfazed for the next uneventful six and a half hours, but the sophisticated Robertson autopilot on *Full Monty* tended to wander and veer towards land. I tried to adjust it, even had a couple of scientific types check out my work, but each time I started her up she veered towards land and I wonder if she was sending me a message. Late afternoon we spotted the huge outer marker of Cobourg harbour and from ten miles away had an entry chat on the VHF with the staff in the Marina. When the yacht club is full (as it was on this occasion) you park along the inner basin wall and pay the same marina fees–so rounding the harbour wall we were fortunate to locate a quiet berth along just aft of the Coast Guard rescue boat where we tied up, leaving some slack in our lines for the night. I welcomed the quietness of Cobourg and was able to carry our portable generator ashore behind the nearby wall, thus providing my own power. However, during the night some poor soul on the lake needed emergency help and the unmuffled roar of the Coast Guard MTUs took me several inches off my berth as they fired up their diesels for a quick rescue.

As *Caper* entered Cobourg marina looking for the wall, we saw a couple on the motor cruiser Wig-Wam frantically waving to us. Peter and Sean from Bluffers Park Yacht Club were the former owners of *Caper* and they instantly recognized the distinctive lines of their old boat, so not long after they were cycling around the wall to see what we had done to spruce her up. Next day we were expecting crew members Carol and Cliff Atkin, former neighbours and all around good sports to join *Caper*, so we borrowed complementary Schwins from the marina and set off to explore the town. Cobourg has invested in restoration and has some lovely classic homes and public structures representing their built heritage. Victoria Hall was a former private school and is now a retirement home for Cobourg's senior citizens and that night the crew ate dinner at the Cactus Restaurant where we have enjoyed many entertaining meals.

The outer harbour in Cobourg also has a large mooring field which is a semi-protected anchorage with quite good holding, so if you elect to drop the hook, just make sure that you don't drift too far to the east, as it shallows quite rapidly. From Cobourg heading east, it's either Brighton, which we don't enjoy, or through the Murray Canal and onward to Belleville. Brighton is at the northwest end of Brighton Bay and boaters will be advised by the duty officer to carefully line up for the narrow channel, as it shallows quickly and can easily get quite messy. Our preference has been to push onto Belleville to stay at the Municipal Marina or the yacht club alongside. Also there is excellent anchoring a few leagues west inside Big Bay, and the last time we cruised there, we saw an interesting boating oddity.

Hard to believe it floats

We were motoring through Big Bay coming around the island opposite Napanee and saw the profile of a large tug, not often seen in these waters. We drew closer in increments of our 1.5 knot speed differential and saw there were actually two tugs in line–a bit like

World War II destroyers steaming in each other's wake. What really caught our attention was the kilometer-long pipeline, sealed at each end, with marker lights along the top like a shimmering dorsal. This entire section of an apparent cooling system was being float-towed from Napanee, where it was welded together, along Lake Ontario to the Toronto Islands and I could only imagine how these two experienced skippers were coordinating the 90 degree turn around the Adolphustown ferry with that pipe between them. Toronto has been developing an innovative system to cool its downtown buildings by using ultra-cool water from the depths of Lake Ontario as nature's heat exchanger. To bring this water downtown, a system of pipes many kilometers long are extended into the lake and connected to the cooling system in the office towers. Once the cool water is piped into the offices, it will be recirculated back into the lake for re-cooling. This was what they were towing.

The Bay of Quinte

One of our favorite cruising regions is the Bay of Quinte, with relatively long stretches of uninterrupted scenery and a couple of interesting anchorages in Hay Bay behind Ram Island close to Picton. We have often stayed at the Prince Edward Cruising Club in Picton and loved demonstrating her maneuverability by spinning *Full Monty* on her axis inside the narrow fingers to nestle gently against another cruiser. From Picton it's a relatively easy run into Kingston, and we love the scale of this day which allows us to daydream while coasting Long Reach, before being rudely awakened by the lake swell snorting between Amherst Island and the mainland. The Brothers Islands and shoals can be tricky, with a shelf protruding into the main channel, so under no circumstances try passing between these scraggy islands–just enjoy the cormorants through your binoculars.

Nineteenth Century Kingston (my future home)

In Kingston you have a choice of Collins Bay, Confederation Basin, Kingston Marina, or the Kingston Yacht Club. We have tried each location in this pretty city and were most comfortable at Kingston Marina, which has no frills but an outstanding location. If you are piloting a two deck-trawler into this marina and eventually up the

Rideau, you will need to wait for the La Salle Causeway Bridge to lift, but the schedule is in the Ports Guide and it's no hardship. If you are in a single deck powerboat, you can slip under the fixed road-bridge at the east end of the causeway. By the way, there is excellent anchoring just off the outer docks of Kingston Marina, with lots of water and it is usually quiet. From here the buoyed channel running east is the Cataraqui River, and about a mile upstream is the first lock station on the historic nineteenth-century Rideau Canal at Kingston Mills.

Some years later we move to Kingston, Canada's first capital and one of the underappreciated gems of Eastern Ontario. It is blessed with a marvelous (in the past, strategic) location bordering Lake Ontario with lovely limestone architecture and a tangible sense of community. Kingston's extraordinary heritage is wrapped up with the British colonial design for North America and after the War of 1812, the British feared an attack from the young American republic and a US military victory would have been easy to achieve by blockading the Thousand Island region. This would have caused a huge headache for the Brits, whose supply ships were using the St Lawrence River to seed their colonies around the Great Lakes. To increase their options, the Brits decided to build an alternate supply route, giving them of a defensible inland waterway, on which goods and munitions could flow–which was the Rideau Canal.

Side trip up the Rideau Canal on *Full Monty* I & II

Colonel By of the Royal Engineers was chosen to execute this project and the Rideau Canal emerged out of the bush, linking swampland, rivers, lakes, and tiny communities, often using revolutionary engineering and canalling techniques. Colonel By effectively linked Ottawa to Kingston by constructing the highest dams of the time, engineering canals and defensive lock stations with blockhouses to ward off an enemy attack. That attack never came, and we were left with the oldest continuously operating canal in North America, where the locks are still hand cranked using original machinery.

Full Monty II the Albin 27

On moving to Kingston we decided to downsize from our Taiwan-built *Full Monty* to a smaller boat. My work was becoming complicated, and we felt it was better to own a less complex boat and one that I could single-hand if necessary. After scoping the field, looking at other displacement boats, and going through the wonderful process of admiring other people's marine babies, we decided there was no doubt about the value and capability of the Albins. The challenge was locating a 27 with the right engine, in decent structural condition, and preferably buying from an owner enthusiast–when we heard about an owner in Fort Myers who was keen to demonstrate Blue Crab. The A27s were designed in Sweden as pilot boats, which is obvious looking at one from the side. The pilot house front section is reminiscent of work-boats we see in countless commercial harbours, while underwater the hull resembles a sailboat without the keel. The design was eventually adopted by Albin in Connecticut, which modified the moulds to offer two models, the aft-cabin cruiser and an open-deck sports model. Albins come equipped with a variety of diesel power including the horrible 65 HP Peugeot, an equally horrible 65 HP Nissan, the robust 157 HP Isuzu six cylinder, and a monstrous 350 HP model so called "Harbour Master Special," but an A27 can be operated with a modern 60 HP Yanmar, which is all the power you need to move her at hull speed.

Our newly acquired *Full Monty* II is the tough Albin 27 we saw in Fort Myers, equipped with a single 157 HP Isuzu diesel and two small sleeping cabins. She has a decent compact galley, a sociable centre cockpit, and a well-designed bathroom and head. We have found her to be an exceptional little ship, well mannered and easy to control. After using *Full Monty* II for a season, I looked at her from the water and realized that a careful modification would turn her into an even more usable boat, but I was unsure how to make the alterations without sacrificing aesthetics, so I sketched her profile and inked in what we had in mind. Our A27 came with a hard wheelhouse and like all Albins, she had a canvas back stretched over aluminium frames. The canvas was a tad leaky, and if we invested in new fabric, that could cost 50 percent of my re-design idea–which was to fabricate a seamless aluminium extension of the wheelhouse, far enough back to cover the aft cabin, built strongly enough to handle my Zodiac and for occasional use as an observation platform. I made several small models of the A27, glued on the plastic extension, and was happy to see that it resembled an original factory build. With aesthetics out of the way, I designed the structure, and located a builder to get the job done.

Defending the Rideau Canal

Across the harbour from Kingston was the 19th century dockyard where the British built their Great Lakes ships and today that point of land is occupied by the Royal Military College (RMC), Canada's sole remaining military university. To defend the southern approaches to the canal and the shipyard, the British built an integrated series of defense structures, which today dominate Kingston's waterfront. Magnificent Fort Henry is the main element, along with several well-preserved Martello towers guarding sundry points from attack–all definitely worth visiting.

Technical provisioning

All of our boats were fully equipped for efficient operation and for safety at sea and while taking this seriously, we were mindful of affordability and what makes sense for the water where we are operating. On *Caper* we used paper charts, an early Garmin 45 handheld GPS, a depth sounder and a radar unit. On *The Full Monty* I and II we migrated to a Standard Horizon Chart Plotter, augmented by waterproof charts, a more accurate depth sounder and a more accurate radar. We carry a full set of first class life jackets, man overboard alarms, boarding ladders, flares, smoke bombs and marker dyes. I upgraded the VHF units to the best I could buy and augmented these with two hand-held units for ship to shore communications. I also decided to carry an inflatable to primarily act as a dinghy and a life raft if necessary.

Cruising within the Great Lakes, a life raft is slightly overkill, but I wanted a margin of safety and the 10-foot Zodiac was accommodated on the roof. The ground tackle on all my boats has always included a decent length of chain attached to a robust anchor line, with two anchors to choose from. Our main hook was always heavy and well designed for the job we had in mind while the "lunch-hook" housed on the bow platform was used on most trips. Provisioning for a Great Lakes cruise was relatively easy because of the re-supply potential just about everywhere. Despite that, if your little ship has limited refrigeration it can often be frustrating to extend supplies until the next store cruises over the horizon–and one has to be creative at times. We have read so much in our boating media about how well one can dine onboard in the cockpit even while at sea. My favourite trick was to bring along my bread-maker and set the timer so that it flooded the boat with smells of fresh baking at the time we needed to leave the dock.

Across Lake Ontario–Kingston to Oswego

The east end of the lake tends to be breezy, playing havoc with the best-laid plans of trawlers and their crew and our crossings over the years have been a mixed bag of calms and roller coasters, and just about everything this lake can throw at us. Our preference is for a smooth pleasant crossing watching the twin stacks of Oswego emerge gently over the horizon and with a couple of well-marked shoals to move around, it's a reasonable seven-hour straight shot at about 7.5 knots.

Caper left Kingston for Oswego at 07:00 with clear skies and calm water. The weather gods do not always smile on our little ships but lately we seem to have been blessed and George on *Caper* was singing his tune, turning the wheel as if by magic. On *Full Monty* I remember our trusty Robertson continuing his love affair with the cows by turning us towards land whenever we were in sniffing range. On both trawlers we cruised at 7 knots, which got decent fuel consumption on both the 318 gas Chrysler and the twin diesel Ford Lehman's. Oswego is a sleepy town with quite an extensive port which trans-ships salt from the under-lake mine in Goderich and more recently Aluminium ingots which are pressed into Ford F150 pickup trucks. The USS Bounty was in port while we were there on *Caper*, but I missed this classic ship in Toronto and was unable to visit it in Oswego as we had to complete US entry formalities and plan for the first day in the canal.

The Antique Boat Museum in Clayton New York

It is possible to break this cross lake segment into a few interesting days, and my preference is to visit the Antique Boat Museum in Clayton, New York–Mecca for any boat enthusiast. The collections of wooden craft are superb, housed in a lovely designer home and as well curated as you will find in any world-class museum–and it is clear that these people have a vision. For many of us boating wonks, finding a museum such as this is quite special and tends to make us dream. Apart from mouth-watering wooden boats, there are collections of specialty engines, skiffs, racing sailboats, memorabilia, and a program of summer-long events designed to animate the museum and allow it to breathe. They also have a fine collection of boating industry literature, so if you want to research what a deflector plate looked like for that unique and innovative "Dispro,"[1] this is the place for you. It is just awesome.

Entering the United States at Oswego

Oswego, originally protected by eighteenth-century Fort Ontario, is the northern gateway to the Erie Barge Canal. The canal originates at Lake Erie far to the west, but for Canadian-based boaters, Oswego is the access point. We generally enter the United States using the Video Phone system, which was a droll experience last time we tried it. The phone is attached to the outside of the fuel shack in the Oswego municipal marina, and you need your passport or some authoritative photographic ID. Nowadays one can also use a Nexus card, which may or may not speed this up. The officer on the other end (Atlanta this time) asked me to place my passport face up on the machine, then using remote control he rotated the camera until he could see my passport and mug shot. He then rotated the camera horizontally so he could see me–at which point, if he had a split screen, he would have two matching images. After immigration cleared us into the US, the marina helped fax a request for a cruising permit–which was a bit cumbersome, I thought.

The Erie Canal system

"Clinton's Ditch," aka the Erie Canal, was once a critical component of the long, tenuous freight route moving produce from America's Midwest to Europe and good old Yankee enterprise figured that a waterway linking rivers, lakes, and villages from the south shore of Lake Ontario would be a profitable asset to this trade. After the usual challenges, the inland waterway, eventually called the Erie Barge Canal was established, and the story of the builders' progress is worth reading and we kept a summary of it next to our marine charts.

The Erie Canal Fender system

This canal is quite lovely, full of surprises and interest and over the years we have never lost enthusiasm for this unique inland journey. Oswego is the northern terminus of this system, and once through the first lock, after purchasing a round-trip pass and a set of updated canal charts, we were on our way. Preparing for our first journey, we had read warnings of grimy locks that would stain the sides of transiting boats green and friends had waxed poetic about the scenery, but emphasized the need to hang straw bales to keep green slime off our bright work. In fact by the time we made our first journey the grime has been substantially cleaned up and compared to the invasive zebra mussels, the grime is not much of a menace. But you still need to protect your fenders, because what grime exists really does stain.[2]

Canadian boaters transiting the Erie Canal for the first time will be surprised how the cables which boaters hang on to are unsecured at the lower end whereas in the Canadian canals these are secured at both ends. My first visit on *Caper* to The Erie was a total surprise as I grabbed the line and, along with *Caper*, we floated into the center of the lock. I remember wondering how on earth I would get *Caper* back onto the lock wall, but the trick is to lean outward, apply pressure with your feet and slowly leverage the boat back onto the wall. I have no idea why they don't secure the lower ends of the cables–it works so well on the Rideau. Canadian boaters will also be surprised at the lockmasters, many of them grizzled, tattooed characters looking as though they would be better suited to a rock band or a Harley rider's group. They are just as skilled as their Canadian counterparts and were always helpful, mostly with an excellent sense of humour.

The amazing Bridge House Brats

Despite magnificent scenery and enticing attractions, it is the people you meet who make these trips meaningful, and none more so than the amazing Bridge House Brats. Traveling south on *Full Monty*, we almost missed this experience because yours truly was weary after a long day and happy to tied up at the north end of Phoenix lock #7. The high mooring wall was parallel with my radar and my lines would be chaffing, so I was poking around for an old hose to insulate them when a gruff character asked, "Why in heaven's name are you mooring there"? When we sorted out his logic, I realized that two hundred meters south was a far better mooring location and thirty minutes later I was focused on four nine-year-old children holding out their hands for our lines. Now, I am not accustomed to handing the lines of my trawler to a bunch of nine-year-old strangers, and for a few of seconds I kept my engines in neutral and idled out in the stream trying to figure out what to do. But when my brain fully processed the scene, I spun *Full Monty* inward, crabbed towards the children and seconds later, with a theatrical circular flourish of their hands, they had us beautifully tied to the dock.

Several years ago Cathy Lee noticed local children harassing passing boaters, and word amongst the transient boating community was spreading fast. Boaters are a valuable source of revenue for any community and given the state of the economy, Cathy could see where this was heading–so with her own money she seeded this youth-at-risk project and launched "Bridge House Brats"–which now provide an excellent selection of services to visiting boaters. These nine-to-twelve year olds deliver menus from local restaurants and act as dock waiters, serving breakfast in bed or delivering a full evening meal to your mooring. They will wash your boat, run errands for you or even "babysit" your boat if you need to depart for any reason. Phoenix at Bridge House is now a desirable place to visit and on our return journey, Hélène, ever the French teacher, had their eight-year-old radio operator bidding us *au revoir* as we headed home.

Next day we cruised south from Phoenix and checked into Pirate's Cove which had excellent clean showers for visiting boaters. *Caper* had to make do with a cooler full of ice and the galley was continually trying to avoid spoilage–while *The Full Monty* had an excellent fridge, which made life easier. Early next morning was picture-perfect weather and as *Caper* left port we saw a medium-size beaver gliding past us, her tail leaving a V-shaped wake. Sadly our optimism soon ended when we realized that the head (toilet for you non boaters) was plugged and in need of creative work, but mercifully my friend Cliff was an expert with heads and with creative plumbing, managing to resolve the issue without losing his life. Soon after we were contemplating the crossing of Lake Oneida and rechecked the charts to familiarize ourselves with their far-apart buoys.

Lake Oneida is a rather shallow lake, with a narrow buoyed channel leading from Brewerton to Sylvan Beach on the opposite shore. It is reasonably well marked with far-apart reds and greens, but you need excellent vision to pick them out. We have crossed Oneida ten times and no crossing has been the same because the "Lake Oneida Mirage" comes up with the slightest heat, making the surface shimmer and the markers seemingly move around. I have seen duplicate faux markers appear some distance from the real thing, so I always run a bearing from one side to the other to minimize the risk. On Oneida the wave patterns have varied from dead calm to a short nasty chop or a combination of both, all within the space of two hours. None of this is serious and you just need to keep in the channel until you are back into the canal.

St Johnsville

This is a tiny port, just a few meters off the main canal and a quiet backwater generally with few boats on the wall. Last time through here we called ahead and getting no reply on the VHF or cell phone, I just pulled off the channel and nosed our way in. Unfortunately this was one of the few times we received the "wave off" as they had too many reservations for the night. I can't imagine where those reservations were coming from at that time of the evening, but we nosed away and found another spot to tie up.

By the time we reached St. Johnsville, *Caper's* supplies were running low so using a transient mooring we decided to raid the "Big M" where everyone is boat-friendly and the owner was quite a character. His speciality hobby is building the dreaded "Potato Canon" which he demonstrates by firing a large #1 Grade A spud across the river two hundred and fifty feet into the field beyond. He sells these for $75 each, but a quick calculation estimates that he nets $55 profit on each sale and so far he has sold six this year. We declined to buy this home-made bazooka of culinary mass destruction and have come to realize that the Erie Barge Canal represents different things to different people. For our crew, this was an interesting waterway full of history and intrigue, with Manhattan as the prize. For local residents it was a day out to photograph boats, and for others it was a source of income, as the canal requires a large staff to operate at peak efficiency.

Little Falls was our next planned overnight and the entire town was out celebrating what seemed like "Canal Days," lining the mooring wall and waving madly as we slid by. I was weary and wanted to call it a day, so we settled for a quieter location two miles down the canal. Unfortunately my chosen spot turned out to be close to a noisy highway, so crew member Cliff rendered a wonderful impression of an English Shire horse and with a rope tied around his waist lugged *Caper* three hundred meters to a quieter spot.

Passage-making is one of the best ways I know to meet interesting characters, and Thor and Penny from Canada were cruising *Aquavit* down the canal towards the Caribbean. Penny was a Brit, and Thor, along with two relatives hailed from Sweden and it was at this point in the journey that several people approached us with offers of a ride into town for supplies, but sadly we were not yet acclimatized to these kindnesses and needed prodding. Thor soon straightened me out and we realized that a tradition of helping transient boaters exists along this canal system.

Our call at the Schenectady Yacht Club reminds us of our relaxed and laid back days at Highland Yacht Club in Toronto. Gerry the ever-helpful dock master runs a very informal club/marina and has always found me a spot for the night, often close by the main channel on a finger dock vacated by a member. Few yacht clubs south of Rochester recognize reciprocal privileges, which exists between clubs in the Great Lakes, so Schenectady charges a modest fee which is well worth it considering their swimming pool, lovely surroundings, laundry, showers, and excellent dock master.

The amazing Ron Bloom

Especially notable in this section of the Erie Canal was the amazing and affable Ron Bloom, the mobile marine expert who was constantly assisting boaters with expert repairs. For some time we had experienced charging problems on *Full Monty* and after trying the obvious remedies we needed help. In a couple of hours Ron had quickly established that both of our Motorola alternators were cooked, but fortunately he located a pair of new AC Delcos, which would put out more juice at half the cost of our original units and he suggested we limp into Waterford, where he would be waiting with the replacements. Sadly the devil was in the details and the Delcos, while being just what we needed, required a different mounting bracket and to fabricate another bracket on the spot was not practical. Ron then pointed out the interesting surroundings where we were temporarily marooned and promised that he could have the original Motorolas rebuilt fairly quickly. This seemed like the solution to our technical challenge and a good time to pause our journey. Ron is an absolute gem and for boaters making the grand circle or just local mariners enjoying a day on the water, he is a good person to have around.

We were now approaching a section with elevated land and some of the buildings were starting to look quite handsome as we passed a complex which turned out to be a private residence with no less than fifteen bedrooms. That evening our buddy boat Aquavit was moored stern to stern with *Caper*, so we pooled resources and had an excellent potluck supper with great jokes followed by "Silent Night." Often we don't have electricity, which is not an issue as our lanterns are very effective, but I also carry a small Honda generator with two hundred feet of electrical cable, so hiding it behind a tree or a fence and muffling the sound is easy. Thor on Aquavit lent me his inverter to recharge our cell-phone and asked why the Englishman (Cliff) was not doing any work on the boat while the rest of us were handling lines and attending to chores. The query sent Cliff into a frenzy of activity and thereafter he handled the aft lines where Thor could observe him working. Needless to say, Cliff had been working as hard as any crew member, but his station was up on the bow where Thor could not see him. Not content with moving aft, he insisted on mopping the aft deck whenever Thor was in earshot.

Three Rivers/Waterford New York

At Waterford New York, the Erie Barge Canal meets both the Hudson River and the Champlain Canal and is an important confluence point for boaters. At this point cruising south, you leave the tranquility of the protected Erie Canal and enter the mighty and tidal Hudson River at its northern end. Three Rivers has an excellent mooring wall and courtesy of the community, the town provides free mooring, free electricity, free water, free showers and free Internet access. Like many other communities along the canal, Waterford realizes that offering a welcome to passing boaters generally attracts a pay back in purchases and they are absolutely correct and while on their wall, this crew spent all kinds of money and repaid their kindness.

Hélène's Pipe

Our navigation on *The Full Monty* had been relatively smooth, with Hélène often challenging my assumptions and usually being right. We now had one lock to go before reaching Three Rivers and a well-earned rest before tackling the Hudson. Prior to setting off from Toronto we had checked every section of the charts for low bridges, just in case *The Full Monty* was unable to pass through. Our Bimini[3] was collapsible and the mast would easily come down, but we were unable to disassemble the upper deck and could not afford an impassable object. With the last bridge in sight, I heard Hélène say "There are men working above this bridge"–which could mean that the posted height had been altered and we were in for trouble. So we slowly approached the bridge and discovered a temporary debris-platform underneath the bridge rendered our mast just five inches too tall–which posed an interesting problem. However we eventually backed down the canal, secured *Full Monty* to a farm fence, and lowered the mast onto the aft railing. Next morning I sheepishly took out my hacksaw and lopped fifteen inches off that mast and created "Hélène's pipe."

The Great American Tug Jamboree

Each year a selection of classic working tugs assemble at Waterford for the annual Tugboat Jamboree commemorated by a wonderful tapestry which was available for sale at the center. Many modern tugboats join this party, and there are usually twenty classic working boats berthed along the Waterford wall, which removes space for transient boaters. If you are planning to attend, it might be wise to call ahead and ask about alternative mooring. At this event the famous Erie Barge Canal tug *Urger* is a real showstopper, and one of the most entertaining events is the "Tug Push"–the maritime equivalent of a tractor pull. Matched pairs of tugboats are deftly maneuvered by their experience crews into what can be described as the "tug-boat-head-butt-position." Each vessel gently places its bow firmly against the bow of an opposing tug and when the referee gives the signal, they pour on the power. This spectacle is a well-known event and the banks are lined with enthusiasts from Manhattan, Montreal, and Boston.

Price Chopper

Like many crews traveling this route, we needed groceries from time to time and Price Chopper on the other side of the Hudson had its own dock with sufficient water for either of our trawlers, so we could motor across, tie up, and replenish the commissary. Luckily local knowledge once more intervened and suggested that rowdies had been launching shopping carts off the dock and no one was sure how much water was actually available. Solution–run the dinghy across to do the shopping.

The Federal Lock and the Hudson River

Just south of Three Rivers is the famous Federal Lock, which is as far north as the Atlantic tide can be felt. This combination barrage and lock station is the tidal control point on the Hudson River and after being released through the southbound gates, in theory it could be non-stop to Ireland … but first through Albany and Manhattan. The Hudson River is a never-ending surprise with all manner of nooks and crannies to explore and we particularly love those distinctive Hudson River light houses, strategically placed along the waterway–and we also marvel at how far north commercial shipping comes, often straddling the channel and crowding out our trawler. Several river port towns are well worth visiting, with names out of a nineteenth-century music hall. We particularly liked Saugerties, Kingston on Hudson, Castleton on Hudson, and Catskill Creek.

West Point

Many years ago we read that West Point was impressive from the water and we have never been disappointed. This famous military academy has an awesome tradition and if you look carefully, you can see how this institution has expanded over the years to dominate this entire Hudson River hillside. Our favorite technique is to wait until the academy is coming up ahead (going downstream) and then coast slowly and silently by in neutral in the embrace of the river, savoring the architecture and the sheer presence of this institution's history.

Poughkeepsie Yacht Club

It is not easy to time our crew exchanges, but cell phones make it easier to know where they are, and we have twice used Poughkeepsie Yacht Club for this purpose–because the railway line runs past the club and it's a relatively easy taxi ride to the local station. The downside for transient boaters is the rocking and rolling from commercial traffic four hundred meters off in mid channel and Hélène was rocked clean out of bed one night by a huge bow wave coming off a tanker. This and the constant noise from the groaning docks makes it not such a great place to overnight.

The Catskill Mountains are relatively close to Manhattan, and the architecture now reflects the wealth and style of a former "Great Gatsby" era. This former vacation Mecca for the New York elite was once known as "The Borscht-Belt," using this ethnic culinary term to describe its affiliation with many former immigrant Jewish families from the Eastern Seaboard. Moreover the famous Catskills resorts incubated many well known entertainers such as Danny Kaye, Sid Caesar, Jerry Lewis and the quirky and lovable Woody Allen. Also you know you are in the USA because the sheriff's boat has just passed by full of shotgun-toting officers heading who knows where, but I doubt they were chasing the cowboy who almost capsized us. What also amazed me were the blank stares from boaters as we pass them by and wave our fraternal "hello." I remember putting this down to *Caper* being a working boat design, but in the same area with *Full Monty*, exactly the same thing happened.

On *Caper* we were heading for the friendly Riverside Marina at Catskill Creek, where we used hot showers and the laundromat to catch up on our personal chores–while Cliff was on the pay phone attempting to check the rail service for his rail trip to Manhattan and La Guardia when seemingly out of nowhere, a high school marching band, complete with drums, tuba, and an entire brass section appeared, drowning his conversation with Metro Links. This was the final night for some of our crew, who kindly offered to host dinner in nearby Mike's Restaurant with Cliff insisting on picking up the tab. At the end of our meal the owner declared they didn't take plastic but cash would be acceptable and if you were short of that (and we were) Mike would accept a personal cheque. He says he has never had a bad cheque, which speaks volumes for small-town hospitality and the boating community.

Ignorant boaters

American waters in the New York area have to be the worst when it comes to boating etiquette and although we have woodenheads in Canada, nothing compares to the "me-first" attitude of these fast boat owners. When we hit the Hudson I asked crew members to keep a watch ahead, based on the principle that eight eyes were better than two and sure enough a power boat came blasting by from astern at 25 knots, just fifty feet to starboard of *Caper*. When the wake hit us, one crew member was almost thrown overboard and in the panic, our Boxer, Darwin darted through the open door of our cabin into the wheelhouse. Lunch came cascading down from the plates above and compounded the mess as Darwin was torn between her panic attack and the smell of food. The crew was angry but philosophical, but poor Darwin started shaking with fear and never quite recovered. We scanned every marina as we motored south in the hope of catching that clown for a serious discussion about etiquette, because Darwin's state had left us with a dilemma concerning what to do about the return trip if she would not stop shaking. The poor dog was literally gasping for air which indicated a constant palpitation of her heart and we truly feared for her safety, so we tried the "Gravol hidden in peanut butter" trick but nothing calmed her down, and we eventually went into Manhattan, purchased a dog cage, and shipped her home by air. Sadly the actions of that cowboy imprinted her with a fear of the water and she was unable to go boating again.

Saugerties on Hudson is another of those lovely river towns developed when the economy was more robust and smaller towns more sustainable. We had been passing architectural gems of lighthouses, some perched on rocks in mid-stream and others defining bends in the river and if it was not for the constant wake of commerce and cowboy boats, the Hudson would be almost bucolic.

The Staatsburg Yacht Club in Poughkeepsie was the river port where we'd agreed to pick up our new crew members Boni and Karen and they were unloading their kit as we tied to the outer finger dock and powered down. The heat was fierce accompanied by high humidity, and we were bathing poor Darwin in cool towels to lower her anxiety. We contemplated moving to a permanent mooring, but the docks were being pounded by river traffic so we bid goodbye and rented space from White's Marina in New Hamburg for the night. Cliff and Carol were leaving early next morning, so we had a farewell dinner and went to bed early.

New York New York and New Jersey

I have always loved New York City, from the days when I worked on Bleecker Street in Greenwich Village and inside the Flatiron building in lower Manhattan. It has vitality, culture, fabulous architecture, guts and a selection of amazing characters. More recently it was horribly maimed by the Islamic fundamentalist terrorist attacks of September 11, which killed thousands of people, including many hard working and dedicated American Muslims. To describe the former site of the World Trade towers as a "scar on the landscape" only touches the surface of this dreadful episode in the history of this extraordinary city and its equally extraordinary people. In some respects this surprise attack was an east coast reprise of what happened in Pearl Harbour during WW2.

Visiting New York by boat takes careful planning, and sourcing an affordable marina in Manhattan for *Full Monty* was prohibitive. On the other hand, Liberty Marina across in New Jersey was about US$2.20 per foot and although this was three times what we would pay at home, it was about 25% of a decent hotel in Manhattan, so with that rationalization in mind we reserved a berth in Liberty and resolved to enjoy ourselves.

New York Harbour gets a lump of coal in the proverbial Christmas Stocking when it comes to bizarre boating behaviour. This time we were on *Full Monty*, making for Liberty Marina and we had to cruise the entire length of Manhattan Island to just north of the Statue of Liberty where the marina is located. Unfortunately this coincided with the afternoon commute, when every fast ferry was blasting across to the Jersey side of the river, chock full of worker-bees. *Full Monty* was obliged to pick her way between twenty of these fast ferries which were leaving huge rolling wakes, often crossing fifty feet ahead and leaving no margin for error. There was no consideration for our trawler which was picking her way through the mess–just abusive radio traffic hurled at us by these clowns. A year later we were not surprised to hear about the accident when a ferry hit a pier with loss of life. Our advice is to schedule your transit past Manhattan out of the rush hour, preferably on Sunday.

Manhattan is worth visiting for many more days than we had available and we resolved that our next visit would be for at least five days. Walking is really the only way to get a true feel for this metropolis, and we never tire of it. We were pleasantly surprised at how people were willing to talk with us, given the reputation that New Yorkers have for self-preoccupation. Just about everywhere we paused, someone was happy to chat. As a boater I loved wandering through Liberty Marina, and as a transient visitor I was given an electronic pass to each of their docks. It was here that we met two New York boaters living aboard their fifty four foot sailboat, built in St Thomas, Ontario. The couple had secured build plans that perfectly matched their requirements for a Cruiser-live-aboard lifestyle and had scoured the world looking for a yard where they could get best value for their money. After coming close to building in New Zealand, they decided on Canada, where Kanter Yachts in St Thomas built this handsome sloop equipped with twin diesels, bow thruster, and a magnificent interior where we sat and chatted about their life aboard. They told us the sobering story of a day in September 2001, while they were lazing on their aft deck enjoying the view of the Twin Towers and the Manhattan skyline. As they looked up, those two large commercial aircraft we have seen repeatedly on television flew into the Trade Center right before their eyes. Their story of what happened afterwards–the panic, the tears, the anger and the feeling of helplessness–are still vivid. As we sat with them, they cast an occasional glance over to the empty void where once the Twin Towers had stood.

Journey north

We needed to refuel *Caper*, and in these days of diesel cruisers we always get stares at the amount of gas pouring into our tanks. Patiently we explain how miserly the amazing 318 Chrysler is, using only a gallon each hour to propel the forty footer, but we knew that some of those stares were concern for the amount of gas we were carrying. On the opposing river bank in Manhattan was the *QE2* and, not far away, the *Enterprise* aircraft carrier decked out with every conceivable warplane the US possessed. Motoring north, the current was against us and it was noticeable how much slower we were moving and how much longer it took to reach the George Washington Bridge. This was one of the few days it had rained since leaving Toronto, and the thick drizzle was combined with intermittent banks of fog and as tanker traffic between New York and Albany was at its peak and with such poor visibility we decided to run the shallows, keeping well out of the main shipping channel. We knew the tankers were there from the VHF traffic and the constant wake coming at us, and I was thankful for *Caper*'s shallow draft.

Back in Saugerties we bumped into Kathy and Rick Santor, who have restored a magnificent 1927 Elco complete with porcelain basins and brass rails. This is one of the inshore fast-boats designed by the famous Elco Company of New York, who were responsible for an entire series of navy boats during World War II. We were now heading for Troy, New York, at which point Boni traded her position as chief navigator for bow lookout. The river has an entirely different personality when approached from the south and even the architecture of the homes seems slightly different. Ahead we could just see the federal lock and once more it was time to re-adjust the fenders, ready for the Erie Canal transit. Boni was planning to jump ship the next day in Schenectady, and we reached our mooring just before nightfall. I slept on deck every night while cruising on *Caper*, but the rain now moved me inside. Next morning we easily located a landing place close to the highway, and as Boni deftly jumped ashore, we backed carefully out of the mud and back into the channel. The bus was leaving in 30 minutes and probably made the milk run between here and Toronto.

It is odd what one meets on the river, and the apparition in the distance turned out to be version of a bicycle that floats and we stared in silence as a raft built from 2 x 4s drifted by, complete with a large paddlewheel and four humans pedaling like crazy. We cruised into Amsterdam, New York, to the sound of a reggae band, a Latin band and a rock group all in the space of two miles. This was our designated location for replenishing the commissary, but as we were leaving the mooring it rapidly became entertaining as two A-16 Warthogs from the nearby Air National Guard flew over to take a closer look and then proceeded to make bombing runs down the river heading directly for us. These aircraft are a leftover from the Vietnam War but remain an effective and incredibly tough bombing platform–currently feared by the Taliban. I was unsure if the main attraction was *Caper's* salty lines or the lack of tops on the female crew members.

The locks on the Erie Canal are huge, some with barn-like doors and others with giant guillotines that descend on steel shafts and ram shut with a massive clang. The smell in the locks was musty and primeval, while the groans of expanding metal, wooden doors straining against water and the hissing of release valves made this truly impressive. The prop-shaft on *Caper* was always a worry because the assembly was under-engineered and not well supported on its long run out to the propeller. One rapidly becomes tuned to the ambient noises on one's vessel, and the sound coming from under the floor was not acceptable. I could hardly stop mid-canal as there were boats up my stern, so we lowered the RPMs to 700, thereby taking the strain off the shaft and looked for somewhere to pull over. Luckily *Caper's* three-foot draft allowed me to nose alongside a field, and once we lassoed a fencepost, took up the floorboards and located the issue. Having experienced this before, it was easy to locate a loose hanger bearing and we were soon out of the pasture and once more into the stream.

Passing through Lake Oneida, I remembered Skinner's Marina at Sylvan Beach, and as we didn't want to go searching for lake markers in the falling light, we nosed in and berthed for the night. Happily Skinners had a laundry, which helped with the washing but the showers were bereft of hot water and not that inviting. At Lock 7 we met Mike and Katie Marre and their nasty little hound, a teeth-bared, fangs-showing Schipperke (pronounced Skipper Key). Their steel trawler *Mister Fish* was originally a Louisiana shrimper, which they had converted into a live-aboard. *Mister Fish* was bought at auction and Mike, being a welder, was able to remodel her into a traveling enterprise, adding a lovely wheelhouse and a circular staircase between decks. Aft of the engine room Mike had built a full stand-up weld shop to ply his trade. They are true water wanderers, stopping wherever Mike could find work and moving on when the kitty was replenished. Their horrible little Schipperke was a Dutch Barge guard dog, entirely fearless and highly effective. They are totally territorial and it had saved their lives on two occasions. Minetto, New York, had the cheapest fuel around, so we pulled up to their marine dock whereupon the gas jockey connected a length of hose to the roadside gas pump and from sixty feet away replenished *Caper's* tanks. The local store was selling handmade soap called Sallyeander, which was aromatic and lathered well, but I passed on the chocolate mint soap as I might have eaten it in error. Returning to Oswego, it was time to unship the fenders, lift the radar mast, extend the radio antennae, and generally make ready for the big lake and our run west to Rochester.

Lake Ontario almost home

Darwin would have been unhappy with the movement of *Caper* or *The Full Monty* as we rolled and rocked for the next ninety minutes en-route to the Genesee River. On *Caper* we were using a basic hand-held GPS and wrongly second guessed its bearing for the outer wall of the harbour. Feeling sheepish we exited the wrong bay and were soon struggling against the out-flowing Genesee River as we motored inland to the Rochester Yacht Club. Rochester is an interesting city with outstanding attractions including the George Eastman House showcasing the history of photography and housing the nation's most precious film archives. Arriving in the early evening, the sun setting over the community of Charlotte and a forty boat regatta on the lake, it looked quite inviting. It was relatively easy for *Caper* to be located at the Rochester Yacht Club but on later visits on *The Full Monty*, they were reluctant to take us in. Behind the club is the waterside home of a local resident who showed us their life-size chainsaw carvings in the garden. The carver teaches chainsaw carving and often collaborates with a nearby metal sculptor. We were made very welcome by these gracious people and invited them to breakfast on *Caper* next day.

Leaving Rochester on *Caper*, we were joined by *Wedgewood*, a sailboat from Port Credit, Ontario, and together we battled the short sharp swells coming from behind, slapping the stern as we hand-steered into Point Breeze. Crew were diving for the Gravol, breakfast was rolling around inside, and I needed to steady the motion for the run into Oak Orchard Yacht Club. Next day we were determined to arrive in Wilson, New York in good time to clean up and prepare for the lake crossing back to Highland. The weather was definitely deteriorating but nothing too serious, and I've found it's better to hand steer to soften the motion and reduce the slewing back and forth. I had been watching a water spout for some time in the direction of the Wilson port entrance, but so far there was nothing on either the weather channel or the regular VHF. I took some bearings and it seemed to be sitting right where we wanted to go, so I altered course to the north, thinking it might be drawn onto the land. *Wedgewood* was still with us, experiencing problems with their sails which forced them to motor into Wilson, pitching badly in the confused water.

Our arrival at the Tuscarora Yacht Club was uneventful, but the relentless rain had penetrated the upper seams of *Caper's* wheelhouse and we planned to do some caulking next day. Actually next day was designated as clean-up, as we were making a non-stop run for Highland Yacht Club and wanted to arrive in reasonable time. Being on the water for several weeks makes for an untidy boat, and I wanted to arrive in ship shape.

The Lake Ontario crossing was memorable but not particularly pleasant for the crew, who were flat on their backs with large doses of Gravol in their systems. For me it was quite hard work because for the next ten hours, I was hand steering the boat, coping with pretty aggressive swells and from time to time some badly confused waves. *Caper* was absolutely amazing and I was continually reflecting on the builder Camille d'Eon who designed the hull not for family cruising, but for hardy lobster fishermen working the Atlantic. I was working quite hard to bring *Caper* home without too much stress, but *Caper*, on the other hand was handling this with great aplomb, and if she could talk, she might have said, "That was fun, Stevie, m'bye–now what else can you throw at me"?

The passages on our two trawlers *Caper* and *The Full Monty* to New York City and our experiences along the Erie Canal left us with strong memories of the Hudson River Valley and the uniqueness of recreational cruising. Many years later I find myself traveling the same route by land, visiting daughter Nicole and her family, who live close by the Tappan Zee Bridge across the Hudson.

---

[1] Dispro refers to a wonderful Canadian invention, the name being short for Disappearing propeller. The Dispro was a small, two to three person wooden boat with a small engine connected to a long propeller shaft with a slender plate hinged beneath the shaft. If the boat ventured into the shallows and approach a rock, the plate would hit first and gently ease the propeller shaft upwards into a small box built into the boat–thereby protecting the propeller from being destroyed.

[2] Erie Canal fenders–Take a 2x4 of whatever length you wish to fender, say sixteen feet long, and drill three ¼" holes through the 4" section. Thread strong ¼" rope through each of the holes and tie a large knot on the underside. Now you have a three ropes coming up through your 2x4 which can tie to your cleats and hang OUTSIDE your three fenders. This way the 2x4 takes all the grime, while your fenders hold the 2x4 off the boat, allowing it to slide along the lock wall, protecting the finish. Make one of these magic fenders for each side of your boat.

[3] Bimini is the term for one of those canvass covers one can see over the cockpit of many boats. It is named after the Bahamian island of the same name.

CHAPTER 19

History of Tourism - Last Supper on the Last Cruise

The climate seemed to be deteriorating and most people were hoping for a change–with less rain and more sunshine, but the weather gods were disinclined to cooperate and the rain just kept falling, leaving people wondering if they would ever get a respite from mud lined streets and waterlogged fields. For months on end it had been pouring, causing rivers to overflow their banks, rendering trade routes impassible and leaving residents nervously glancing skywards, wondering if their prayers might be answered. News of entire villages being swept away was filtering through the sodden bush telegraph and generally sanguine community leaders were uncommonly concerned with how to cope. Domestic animals were becoming restless in their pens, especially those unused to wallowing in muddy water and there are sightings of wolves and coyotes skulking around the community, migrating towards higher ground. News in the countryside generally travels slowly and remote villagers hear about opportunities long after their urban counterparts have scooped up the deals–but this morning riders on horseback were plodding down the sodden Main Street shouting something about a ship leaving for a dryer climate and did that ever get people's attention.

Approaching the coast one can hear the hubbub of family groups impatiently lining up to come onboard this ship, with donkeys trumpeting requests for their next bag of feed, territorial geese honking to claim their patch of earth–while ropes were creaking to hold the vessel to the shore. For the last two weeks the inexperienced marine crew had been stocking up with food, along with nourishment for their pets, while the navigation tablets and celestial charts were checked and rechecked to ensure a safe passage...somewhere. For months, envoys had been traveling the length and breadth of the land, broadcasting news to anyone who might be interested in this voyage, but as berths were allocated on a strictly space-available basis, there was only a finite number available and some would be disappointed to discover there was "no-room-in-the-inn." Town Criers were generally used to announcing significant community news and ten men with huge barrel chests leaned over the port-side rail in perfect curved-formation and in unison shouted... "we are your captains speaking–welcome onboard commodore Noah's Ark on your voyage to salvation." In this era of mass tourism one might consider this cruise on the good ship Noah's Ark to be the world's first organized sea voyage. For the participants in this biblical tale-it was a mythical life saver.

The tourism industry has been a huge part of my Noah's Ark of a life and as this book is based on some of my experiences in the field–I am offering an encapsulated history of this fascinating and engaging industry. This is by no means a definitive analysis of the business where I earned my livelihood–my book on that topic will be forthcoming next year, but it did seem appropriate to write a truncated version in an attempt to place some of my experiences in context.

An alien thought–disposable time?

When thinking about the tourism industry one has to accept that disposable time for organized tourism was virtually unheard of prior to the 17th century–when citizens were more focused on the daily necessities of life, such as harvesting, feeding and defending one's flock and family–while living within a boundary in a defined and structured society. In those days disposable time for leisure purposes was only available to those with land, income, power, influence and access to education, and only with the dawn of the 20th century were "Bank

Holidays" introduced, while by the latter part of the century, paid holidays were becoming the norm.

The rulers of the vast empires of Greece, and particularly Rome, literally paved the way for mass movement between cities and countries, with their extensive road-building programs. Driving this activity was the production of regional food which would require efficient transportation to carry it to less fertile markets where better prices were generally available. Thus inter-city commerce and market gardening provided compelling reasons for communities to improve roads–that might have been originally constructed for legions of centurions to stroll down en-route to battle. As commerce expanded so did the need for some of the facilities we now take for granted.

The current accommodation sector was preceded by roadside inns, Taverns–and stagecoaches. The transportation sector was preceded by hand-carried "sedan chairs," horseback and carriages. Our current GPS facilities were preceded by mile marker Inukshucks and hand drawn signposts fixed to trees. Bandits seeking to capitalize on this new mobile society generated safety patrols to dissuade robbery. Foreign currency from other lands would require money exchangers. Speakers of foreign languages would require translators. Thanks to the Romans we now have baths in our homes and spa towns to rejuvenate our weary bones. Thus an entire structure was born, that would eventually facilitate the movement of people for non-commercial and non military purposes, fostering the birth of what we now call VFR… or Visiting Friends and Relatives. During the period when Rome ruled a great deal of Europe, a substantial middle class emerged leaving some evidence of their consumer habits, so one can presume this merchant-class segment did its share of leisure traveling, especially to go bathing–thus spreading their disposable income and unwittingly opening history's first spa industry. In 1763 Grand Tours of Europe were initiated and later in the mid 1800's, Italy was regarded as the intellectual capital of Europe and upper class British society comprised of wealthy land-owners, diplomats and scholars may actually have started the phenomenon of Cultural Tourism–by visiting Italy to seek enlightenment from its art, literature, science and health spas.

Whose history is it anyway?

History is a tainted science, depending heavily on who is writing the script, along with whose perspective they are recording (or whose propaganda they are supporting) so one might consider another type of tourism from those we are familiar with. Perhaps some of the Crusaders heading for Jerusalem in 1095 on horseback thought they were participating on the world's first organized holiday, with, it has to be said, a fairly non-tourist agenda, as they trekked eastward. When Hannibal the Punic Carthaginian commander and his army conducted the famous elephant march over the Pyrenean Alps to attack Rome in 250 BC, local residents might be forgiven for thinking that the circus had come to town–admittedly with slightly different acts in mind. Closer to home, when our neighbours the Vikings paddled their longships across the North Atlantic and visited "Vinland" in year 1000, they were establishing L'Anse aux Meadows in our easternmost province of Newfoundland, where they built a modest community outpost in a most organized and bloodthirsty manner. The voyages of Marco Polo, Sir John Franklin and David Livingstone come to mind along with an entire host of explorers, all with a slightly different perspective might also be described as early tourism. But until evidence emerges to the contrary (as it will) I am happy to accept Mr. Cook's holidays as "first recorded" for pure leisure purposes, as opposed to discovery-with-possession-and-plunder in mind. After all the former British Empire and its Industrial evolution (some might say revolution) provided many of the inventions and the subsequent infrastructure which formed the technology foundation for our current industry.

Thomas Cook the Baptist

Reliable history shows that a Baptist minister named Thomas Cook residing in the UK, was responsible for the world's first organized holiday, when in 1841 he organized a rail trip between Leicester and Loughborough, enabling five hundred and seventy of his fellow believers, paying one shilling each, to attend a temperance meeting with their peers. Buoyed by the success of this non-commercial trip, Mr. Cook then offered an entire series of domestic pay-as-you-travel trips, which inevitably led this nascent organizer-marketer and his faithful flock to venture overseas to the Paris Exposition of 1855. Mr.

Cook was an interesting business planner with a broad vision of the world he was exploring, which led him to issue the world's first hotel voucher in 1867, thereafter planning the first "Around the World" tour in 1872! While Thomas Cook may have been the father of modern group travel, another Englishman Thomas Bennett born in 1841 and secretary to the English consul in Oslo, organized trips for the British aristocracy into Scandinavia and set up an enterprise called "Trip Organizer"–offering virtually the same advisory service that modern travel agents do nowadays. However the tourism industry would not be possible without what we call the supply-chain entrepreneurs, who invested in and sometimes invented the transportation and accommodation sectors which Mr. Cook and Mr. Bennett needed to organize their holiday programs.

Rail travel

I grew up close to York in the UK with tales of George Stephenson's 1829 Rocket firmly planted in my mind as the first operating steam powered engine, which was not entirely true, although the Rocket did feature several innovations (tall smoke stack–central boiler–separate fire box) which determined the design of locomotives for the next 100 years. In 1807 the first recorded rail passenger service using steam power was inaugurated on the wonderfully named Oystermouth Railway operating in Swansea Wales, but any story about rail transportation needs to pay homage to the era when rail carts and carriages were pulled or pushed exclusively by human hands, human legs, or the four hoofed power of the canal horse. Use of rails can actually be identified as early as 600 BC when a series of parallel rails called the Diolkos were used along the route of the modern Corinth Canal to haul ships across this Isthmus of land. In 1550 hand propelled carts called "Hunds" were used in Germany and were later brought to Britain's Lake District by German miners, who were contract workers in the mines of Cumbria. Between 1550 and 1804 every "train" was hauled by horses until steam power was established and later refined for commercial and recreational use.

Accommodation

The latter part of the 19th century was a milestone in the

accommodation sector of the tourism industry when the Savoy, Claridge's and Carlton hotels opened in London and in 1903 the world's first branded hotel chain "Trust House" opened their doors to merge and eventually expand into the brand we knew as "Trusthouse Forte." Hotel development in the US paralleled that of Europe and in 1792 the City Hotel in New York opened its doors, while at the dawn of the 19th century the Tremont Hotel in Boston opened to become the first five star hotel on the continent. The US introduced the concept of the motel or motor hotel, followed by vast hotel chains which built cloned buildings–giving birth to the slogan "once you have stayed in one of our hotels you have experienced them all–with no surprises."

Air Transport

The Dutch airline KLM was created by Albert Plesman in 1920, The Russian Civil air authority in 1921, Finn air opened its door in 1923, while in the United States Tony Jannus operated the first scheduled winged flight in 1914 between St. Petersburg Florida and Tampa–flying a mere 50 feet above Tampa Bay. The 1920s saw the world's first recorded charter flight and by 1950 the growth of air transport was making long distance tourism easier for those with less disposable time to take a more traditional sea voyage. The Second World War created huge technical advances in military aviation which spilled over into the commercial sector and soon found its way into passenger aircraft. As the frequency of services and the capacity of aircraft grew, the fares cascaded downwards, to the point where more people were able to consider short and long distance air travel for their vacation. In the UK entrepreneurs were taking note of these achievements and started a tourism revolution when large travel agencies and tour operators chartered entire aircraft–thus lowering the cost of their overseas holidays. Nowadays the ability to use our local airline much as our grandparents used the bus and train services in their day, is only one advantage of the maturing aviation sector of this industry.

Water transport and the World of Cruising

Tourism facilitated by water transport has been recorded across The Great Lakes and the rivers of North America, with First Nations in Canada paddling significant distances to meet neighboring tribes at well organized Pow Wows. Similarly in Asia, Africa and Europe when road systems were less developed than they are today, there is evidence of indigenous communities using water to move people and goods from one region to another. In 1783 the first recorded steam vessel–the paddle boat Pyroscaphe operated in France, making a heroic fifteen minute journey on the Saône River before the engine failed and in 1790 John Fitch inaugurated the world's first recorded riverboat service on the Delaware River between Philadelphia and Burlington New Jersey.

The world's first recorded commercial shipping service was offered by the famous and wonderfully named "Peninsular and Orient Steam Navigation Company" (P&O) which was inaugurated in 1822 with a Royal Charter inscribed in 1840–to carry mail between Britain and Egypt, via Gibraltar and Malta and the first recorded passenger service was offered in 1844 to these same destinations. Cruising as a tourism option was popularized in 1889 by the German ship Augusta Victoria, but the first vessel built primarily for cruising was the German ship Prinzessin Victoria Luise, which was launched in 1900 and designed by Albert Ballin who later became the General Manager of the renowned Hamburg-America Line. Cruising spawned the wonderful acronym "POSH" which some readers will know represents a cabin one could reserve PORT side OUT and STARBOARD side HOME. This POSH option of cruising with the sun streaming through one's porthole on both legs of the journey, has now embraced an entirely new meaning– as we know too well. Cruising between these early years and the 1960's was a relatively minor part of the tourism industry, generally being the purview of those with the time and money to spend on a rather long sea voyage–but in the late 1960's everything changed, when several brilliant entrepreneurs realized the potential to move cruising from its niche into the mass-market end of the tourism industry.

The growth of modern cruising is a success story worthy of an in-depth study demanding greater time and space that I have within this book and credit is due to the risk takers and the visionaries who were able to look into the crystal ball and see just how far they could take this industry. Nowadays there are upwards of 150 of what I call mainstream large passenger ships cruising the oceans from the Caribbean to Alaska and from the Mediterranean to Asia–including the seemingly inaccessibly water in between. However, the relatively young cruise industry has already segmented itself and while mainstream cruising on huge wedding cake-like vessels carry the vast majority of guests, the emergence of stylized identifiable and focused segments is what makes cruising so interesting for me.

I particularly like the river cruising segment which offers slender, elegant, shallow draft boats on rivers and canals in Europe, North America, Asia, South America and North America. River cruising appeals to the many guests who might be concerned with the rocking and rolling (often erroneous) sometime associated with an ocean voyage, but the most attractive feature is the closeness and accessibility of the river bank and their contiguous communities. In the US there has been a resurgence of the Steamboat Era on the Missippi, Snake and Columbia rivers with replica turn-of-the-century look-alike steamboats complete with staff dolled up in period costume.

However what really excites me about the cruising industry are some of the sub-segments, which from a business perspective I find particularly interesting. The emergence of adventure cruising on shallow draft ocean going small-ships is especially attractive if the ship has guest speakers onboard who can offer nightly enrichment talks about shore excursions in the ports-of-call. Similarly interesting is the emergence of expedition cruising on ice-class ships, which are able to poke their noses into seemingly inaccessible nooks and crannies of the Antarctic extremes, sending their guests ashore in sturdy Zodiacs looking for Penguin Rookeries and the remnants of 19th century whaling fleets.

Exotic Grand Regional Tours

Thomas Cook's concept of the Grand Tour has been embraced and refined by the tourism industry to the point where trips to exotic lands are now relatively commonplace–although it has to be recognized that world unrest and terrorism has rendered many superb destinations off limits. The exotic grand tour now embraces what we call "enrichment tourism," especially as practiced by many US University Alumni organisations on behalf of their members. These often complex and rewarding overseas visits are accompanied by a member of faculty with specialist knowledge in the region they are visiting. Thus a three week tour to Israel, Egypt and Jordan might be led by a scholar in Middle Eastern studies who will enable a greater understanding of the region, the history and its people. An African safari might be led by a member of the World Wildlife Fund who would have insider contacts and in-depth knowledge of the region's animals, people and politics.

Who's on first?

The fascinating confluence of a digitally educated consumer, undaunted by the prospect of doing research to plan their trip and the extraordinary facilities offered by the Internet, is causing a revolution in how consumer tourism is planned, transacted and executed. I grew up in the business when "The Distribution Channel" of the tourism industry was not only well defined–it was intact, efficient and entirely able to serve the needs of yesterday's consumer. Broadly speaking there were Tour Operators who created holiday packages–which were comprised of accommodation, transportation, meals, transfers and even guide services and daily sightseeing. These packages were originally focused on group travel and sold through travel agencies, but by the mid 1970's an increasing number of people were comfortable traveling alone and used the same tour operators to provide holidays they could enjoy as (mostly) couples–as distinct from traveling with a group. Nowadays because of the internet and an increasingly confident and experienced consumer, the distribution channel I grew up with is rapidly eroding, to the point where the "middle-men" of the industry will soon become a relic of the past, and when most of the travel arrangements will be done directly between the consumer and the end suppliers. Of course there will always be room for the innovators and the specialists in difficult to navigate destinations, but the business model of the tourism landscape is rapidly changing.

My role as Gun Dog

In some respects my role in the industry can be likened to the gun dog that accompanies a shooting party out to bag a brace of grouse. The shooters know the grouse are out there and the beaters scare the bejeebers out of the birds, but without the gun dog and his keen nose sniffing out the whereabouts of the birds–the hunters would go home empty handed and the birds would rot in the fields. For many years I have been gun-dogging around the globe, sniffing out the more interesting destinations, but more importantly–figuring out how to make it all work in the interest of the traveler. This collection of recollections brings together some of the experiences I have enjoyed– and it has to be said occasionally endured to make it all work. I hope you enjoy them as much as I did. Now where can I reserve a berth on that Noah's Ark of a ship?

CHAPTER 20

The Battle for Barriefield
(an entirely different experience)

The Kingston City Council chamber was packed with noisy and excited supporters from the opposing sides, the media were broadcasting live and the mayor was braced for what would turn out to be a battle-royal. For months this acrimonious debate had been raging, in newsprint, on local television and occasionally on the radio and passions were running high as we approach the final vote on the issue. This is the story of how a tiny community of less than two hundred residents defended itself against the resources of Kingston's City Council, which thought that being elected to public office gave them a license to run roughshod over a district within the city. It is a warning to other small communities who might face similar high-handed action by their elected representatives and an example of how one modest neighborhood refused to lie down and play dead.

Finding a new home

We were considering relocating to Kingston, and while Hélène was being interviewed as a French Immersion teacher, I had to make myself scarce for a couple of hours, so I took off in the general direction of the Rideau Canal and promptly got lost in a community reminiscent of an English village. Here were mostly smaller homes, many of them constructed out of limestone, some faced in clapboard, many sitting right at the street edge–just as in nineteenth-century Britain. This was unlike much of the Kingston I had seen, which tended to be modern and angular rather than creaky and cranky.

Our new home is in Barriefield Village located across from Fort Henry which dates back to the nineteenth century. There are ninety homes in the village and about 182 villagers of all ages and occupations. In recent years the sound of children playing in gardens and backyards is breathing life into what was overwhelmingly a mature population and these little newcomers are a welcome addition as they discover surrogate uncles, aunts, and grandparents who were celebrating their irrepressible cheerfulness. The village has connections to the War of 1812 when stonemasons building the Rideau Canal needed somewhere to live and Barriefield was far less gentile than it is today. The highway ran through Main Street, Green Bay was home to small boat builders and more than a few raucous taverns, plus a ferry which ran across Anglin Bay into Kingston. In 1820 Commodore Robert Barry, commissioner of the nearby naval dockyard gave his name to the village, which was laid out in the English style of the era with many homes typically built close to the street–a military grid pattern forming the heart of the village with heritage homes built of limestone or wood or delicate calcium-stained red bricks. Entering the village nowadays, life becomes detectably slower, much quieter and even less stressful than small-town Kingston. In 1975 the village was awarded heritage status by the Province of Ontario, making Barriefield the only thus designated village in the province and while some villagers had misgivings and were suspicious about the restrictive nature of this new status, the responsibility of being custodians of Barriefield's provenance was embraced by most residents, some of whom serve on the Heritage Committee of Kingston's City Council.

Our village green space

Many English villages have what we call "green space" or "Cultural heritage landscapes" around their perimeter–while some villages have an actual village-green close to their geographic center. Barriefield's green space surrounds the village, with the added bonus of a lovely sinuously, rugged tree lined rock garden facing adjacent Fort Henry.

Similar to other villages, Barriefield has been exposed to development within its boundaries, whereby empty lots have been purchased and large homes, sometimes out of character with the period nature of the village, have been built. Some villagers are uncomfortable with the new homes which have altered the balance between the original and contemporary dwellings, but for others it is a fact of 21st century life and the available lots have rapidly dwindled to the point where new-builds are becoming increasingly rare.

Barriefield has always been a military community and to this day we are surrounded by contemporary and historic military installations. The contemporary barracks straddle Highway 2, containing residential housing and operational communications–and the world's finest communications museum, which faithfully records the history of "signals" through time. Below the village is Royal Military College (RMC)and on the adjacent hill is historic Fort Henry–so Barriefield has been associated with the military for as long as local history has been recorded, and its War of 1812 roots defines its built heritage. Troops were trained in slit trenches adjacent to the village and saw action in World War I at Passchendaele and it can rightfully be claimed that Barriefield Village is a living custodian of Kingston's military, social and cultural heritage.

Bad news travels slowly

On a bright Sunday in 2009 a passing villager casually mentioned that the City of Kingston was planning to build affordable housing at the edge of our village on the green space adjacent to Highway 15. This came as a surprise, because word of council activity is generally broadcast by bush telegraph and I was alarmed that such a dramatic topic had not reached the village. We called Councilor Leonore Forster who reluctantly confirmed that a discussion was taking place in council and the process was complex with some of it in-camera due to the possibility of a land acquisition. Through a Freedom of Information request we later discovered that secret talks concerning a development in our own backyard had been taking place for no less than nine months!

Much of the green space around Barriefield was owned by the Department of National Defense and had recently been declared surplus for disposal. This was perplexing because the lands are an integral component of the village's Cultural Heritage landscape and the city was now proposing to build an affordable housing project on them–which would effectively double the population of Barriefield Village. Amazingly, a local architect who (hard to believe) was a member of the Municipal Heritage Committee–an organization entrusted with the uniqueness of the village, had been asked to produce a design for the project to be built on this space. No wonder this was being discussed in-camera and when they understood the implications most villagers were simply stunned that we had not been consulted, while others expressed outrage that the city would contemplate building on a Cultural Heritage landscape–but the discussion was soon to become more complicated and controversial.

Affordable housing shortage

Kingston is short of affordable housing and according to the city this is exacerbated by the scarcity of affordable land. The protocol attached to federal land disposal describes a hierarchy whereby the province has first right of refusal, followed by the municipality and as a last resort by a private developer. As the province was not interested, the city was potentially looking at "free land," which they reasoned would reduce the cost of any housing project–and given the dire need for lower-cost housing one can understand the immediate reaction of council and staff; however, as the record shows this was not as straight forward as it seems.

The city is obliged to hold any meetings concerning land acquisition in-camera, and while we accepted that principal, there was uneasiness within the village and suspicion this might be a vehicle for increased secrecy. Suspicions persisted that city staff and some councilors wanted to delay news from reaching Barriefield until it was too late to mount a citizen's objection, therefore a group of villagers immediately convened a meeting to examine the ramifications of the development and to discuss what our response might be. We were astonished the city would consider building adjacent to a provincially recognized village. We were concerned that the 19th century military remains would be desecrated. We were concerned the $1 land cost might lead the city into a vortex of costly approvals, rendering the project financially impractical, saddling the tax base with spiraling costs. Our concern also extended to the fact that an affordable housing project at the intersection of two busy highways was the wrong location for any dwellings–remote from food stores, medical services and the support required by new residents.

City council was split on the issue and while some were playing to the gallery of low-cost housing supporters, others were open to reasoned discussion and two distinct sides were forming with many villagers believing that a reasonable debate was being cast aside by a council faction that demonized Barriefield as an enclave for privileged people. As a researcher, I could hardly believe that council members in full view at a public meeting and with so few empirical facts at their disposal could make that statement. The village does have residents with comfortable incomes, earned from productive lives as business people, educators, professional practitioners and trades people, but the village is also home to single mothers, short-order cooks and retirees living on fixed incomes. Any unbiased observer would soon realize that Barriefield is hardly a self-serving gated community for the rich and famous, but this shoot-from-the-hip council-faction cast the NIMBY ("not in my back yard") card in an effort to brand Barriefield as elitist. Some councilors were quite articulate, reasonable and passionate about the need for affordable housing, but others were merely grandstanding on their soapbox–eventually becoming ranting microphone hogs.

Council acting with Third-World secrecy

I felt we were under attack from our council which was displaying the characteristics of third-world unfairness and secrecy, when on October 20, 2009, a motion to begin the housing development was scheduled for discussion and the city was reported to be "prepared to deal with complaints from Barriefield villagers." Whenever we presented our concerns, always in an articulate and reasonable manner, some councilors gave the impression that we were impinging on their territory when we asked for standing in the debate. Reflecting on decades of apathy towards municipal politics, it was galling to see how some councilors reacted to our engagement in the political process. I can't speak for others but my impression was that some were acting more like third-world politicos displaying arrogance, paternalism, and entitlement than worthy elected representatives in Canada's first capital city. Towards the end of this tale our suspicions about secrecy were validated, when council was reprimanded by the provincial watchdog for misuse of its privileged position.

In Barriefield Village something special was happening and our community was galvanizing into more than the sum of its parts–as neighbours intelligently discussed the issues, dropped into each other's homes to solicit opinions, and offered perspectives on what we were facing. As newcomers to Barriefield we knew few people outside our street, so the opportunity to learn about the village from long-time residents was inspirational and while the village was closing ranks, we were also communicating with the city, attempting to learn more about its plans and participating in discussions about our own back yard. After a few exchanges it became apparent that the only way we could make progress was to present a cohesive community position and discuss this with our co-stakeholders–so we called the first of many village meetings and started the Defense of Barriefield.

It is important to note that villagers truly felt under attack from their own city, but not from all councilors and not from all city staff– as we discovered with palpable relief that some of these people were open to reasonable discussion, while others had a preconceived agenda, and no matter what we presented, no matter how reasonable our argument, no matter how absurd the economics of the proposed build program–their lack of response spoke to their predetermined, entrenched position. In the process of this prolonged debate we noticed certain councilors voting as one block. One councilor, Steve Garrison, who's surname reflected his mentality, led the block in favour of the affordable housing project and spoke passionately, but often sarcastically–which I felt tarnished his standing as an elected officer of the city. His supporters mostly voted alongside him, seemingly lacking a personal voice on the topic, as though the issue was too complex for them to handle and the only reason for their presence was to raise profile for the next election. Meanwhile we were stunned to learn that neither the city's Heritage Planner nor Kingston's Municipal Heritage

Committee had been aware of the building proposal–which was an outrageous omission and when viewed through the period-prism, was at odds with the Heritage District Conservation Plan, that had guided preservation of Barriefield for more than twenty years. The fact that the city chose to keep this from the KMHC and its own Heritage Planner spoke volumes of disrespect and started to explain more about the city's nervousness and use of in-camera sessions.

Galvanizing the community

At our first Barriefield village meeting at J.E. Horton School, the village turned out in force and as newcomers, Hélène and I were happy to meet so many people from our new community and were able to associate names with faces and voices on the phone. Our ad-hoc committee presented the facts as we understood them and it became clear that we had a considerable brains trust at our disposal, who were able to explain why the City's plan was unworkable. We discovered experts on heritage preservation and housing construction, as well as the history of the community from long-time residents born in Barriefield–who grew up here and witnessed all its changes. Most of all we discussed the impractical nature of the plan to build affordable housing on this Cultural Heritage Landscape and how the city was setting itself up for failure. Long before this issue was raised, many villagers held the belief that affordable housing and market price residency were not mutually exclusive and preserving the nature of Barriefield was possible while facilitating affordable housing in the village. To this day the village has single-family homes where families could be accommodated if the city would purchase the homes and apply a rent subsidy. This happens elsewhere where the cost of entry is far higher, so why would it not work in Barriefield Village?

While this debate was progressing, I was compelled to make several overseas trips, and it was highly frustrating to be heading for the airport while a council meeting was taking place. The other element which brings this close to my heart is that I played a role in the competitive bid that Canada made on the world stage, resulting in the Rideau Canal, along with the Kingston defenses, being inscribed by UNESCO as a World Heritage Site. My role was to create what we called a "Cultural Corridor" along the route of the Rideau Canal between Ottawa and Kingston, including some of the contiguous communities that related to the canal's provenance. The heroes of this eastern Ontario success story are the people at Parks Canada and in particular Doug Stewart who was the superintendent of the Rideau Canal at the time this was happening. Doug is descended from a former mayor of Kingston and was appointed to be Director General of this agency. Under his inspirational leadership, the bid for World heritage status was quietly assembled for the day when it would be transported to Paris for adjudication. I remember meeting Doug in the Parks Canada Rideau Canal office in Smiths Falls and the wry smile on his face signaled yet another interesting revelation about the upcoming bid process. Apparently Doug had discovered a firm in Smith Falls that was able to fabricate four handsome wood and aluminum chests that would eventually contain the mass of supporting maps, surveys and historical documents–as well as contemporary photography that showcased this wonderful region. The bid was made, we all held our breath and when the news of the inscription was shared with us you can imagine how happy we were and how ironic that I was now defending the 19th century community adjacent to that site.

Our defense committee comprised of villagers taking time from their busy lives and demanding careers to work on behalf of their neighbours and once formed, the committee immediately started analyzing the issues and examined each facet of the notional city plan. Our steering committee split into sub-groups to examining different facets of the proposed development, reporting back with an opinion based on best-facts available. Some studies dealt with legal matters, some examined council procedure, and others reviewed the financial impact of the project–always with a weather eye on the political activities of Kingston's city council. At all times we made a conscious effort to respect the offices of the councilors we were opposing and while our respect for individuals may have diminished, we felt it was important to respect their office. Mayor Rosen chaired most council discussions with a high degree of personal dignity and a careful hand on the gavel.

Strategy for success

At our initial meeting we agreed on the importance of building a "strategy for success" so visualize fifteen highly motivated villagers meeting in the Schools Museum in the epicenter of Barriefield, working with a defined agenda–topics carefully prioritized and scribes recording every word. Visualize the level of talent which included some pretty accomplished people, and you would be astonished at the lack of egos in the room. In the best community spirit possible our neighbours came home from work, watered the kids, fed the plants, and when babysitters arrived, trekked along icy streets to the village meeting. We also recognized the need to raise funds to cover costs that would invariably arise, and a defense fund was duly established on a pay-what-you-can basis.

Soon, a disturbing quantity of misinformation was being filtered into the media from the "other side" of this debate, most of it unfocused, some bordering on the absurd, but much of it quite personal, targeting the villagers themselves. We needed to counteract the misinformation with well-written, concise, and honest facts, while emphasizing the need to be respectful of council–and taking the high road at all times. On the advice of our media committee we created a basic fact sheet to augment villagers' individual letters to council and to ensure we were all on-topic. We broadened our media outreach to include regional television stations and multiple images of my neighbour Steve, shinnying up his wooden ladder, putting up his hand-built wooden, period correct storm windows for the camera…reside in the village humour archives.

Another committee approached the nearby base commander– after all, the property has been National Defense land since recorded history, and his perspective might be of use when moving forward. Sadly the base-warrior was unable to help and referred us back to the mandarins at "Canada Lands" where the ownership of the Cultural Heritage Landscape temporarily resides. The committee therefore approached the federal agency to better understand their perspective and to confirm that our committee had correctly interpreted the rules.

Mixed media messages

I suspected that our spirited defense of the village was having an effect on the opposing forces, because the attacks in the media became fiercer, more strident and downright nasty, but the rational thinkers on council were now starting to realize that our perspective on due diligence, especially concerning spiraling build-costs could not be ignored, and perhaps with re-election in mind they started to re-examine our concerns. At one public meeting I got my first close-up of the opposing speakers and before it started, I wandered around the room, coffee in hand and in my usual clumsy way tripped over various and sundry people, offering apologies for my outsize feet. These seemed like perfectly reasonable people to me, chatty, good-humoured and out for an interesting evening–in fact quite similar to my village neighbours. We chuckled about this and that, and I returned to my seat thinking these were pleasant and perhaps slightly misguided people. That was–until they approached the microphone and started ranting, whereupon it became obvious they possessed unidirectional hearing, unidirectional thinking and unidirectional optics and were oblivious to any perspective other than their own. They resembled a collective of yesteryear British shop stewards from the mid-1950s.

Those who work in the social housing field recognize there is no single solution which fits every housing requirement, and no single housing requirement suits every neighborhood. In Toronto the social services recognize the value of integrating families within existing communities, where there are established family structures and mature neighborhoods–and we thought that was an excellent strategy. However I freely admit that "NIMBY" describes how I feel about a social housing project being plunked down on the village's Cultural Heritage landscape, in a bargain-basement set of buildings, remote from the services they will need. It is not the right way to resolve the issue of affordable housing, it is setting up the project to fail–and for the record I would feel the same if million-dollar estate homes were planned for the same parcel of land. On the other hand "Yes in my backyard" would be more descriptive of how we felt, because "YIMBY" recognizes the need for low-cost housing and if the city purchased properties in the village, this could be part of the solution. There is no doubt that integrating affordable housing into a market-price neighborhood would raise another set of issues, but with a dose of good-will and old-fashioned help-thy-neighbor, this might stand a better chance of succeeding than a city-designed ghetto on Barriefield's periphery.

The Battle for Barriefield was coming to a close and similar to other highly charged personal and community battles where neighbors united for a common cause, it was a welcome relief. Many of us were gainfully employed in challenging jobs which required our constant attention and the hours required to fight this mess came while the sky was dark and the stars were twinkling. The fractured plan that was hatched in secrecy and incubated by a cabal of polemicists could not stand the test of daylight coupled with full public disclosure, and at the council meeting of October 9, 2010, the requiem for this ill-planned scheme was written–eventually dying the death of a one vote majority.

The street dinner

For a modest neighborhood village to successfully defend itself against the resources of a city the size of Kingston is quite remarkable. At times we were convinced we were not being dealt a fair and honest card, and to this day suspicions remain about the city's long-term plans for the village. Nevertheless, after a long and draining battle the villagers felt that a community celebration was appropriate and as we live in a village that was shaped by history, why not take a traditional approach and celebrate in the built nature of our environment? When the Second World War ended, my family, along with the entire population of Britain, held celebratory community street dinners in every city, town, and village–which is exactly what we did in Barriefield. The talented Barb Carr and David Craig wrote special lyrics to Leonard Cohen's "*Hallelujah*," pickup trucks were placed at each end of Regent Street to secure the dinner venue, and as the warm evening unfolded and the daylight softened-the-scene, neighbours, friends and comrades strolled in with card tables, chairs, lanterns and candelabras and the festivity à la bonne franquette began. The talented Kasaboski family entertained us with their wonderful music and three-year-old Jake Bergeron serenaded us at the mike. Thus closing the saga ... for now.

Cover Photos

1. Polar Bears jousting on Hudson Bay
2. Matamata Tunisia as seen in Star Wars
3. The magnificently restored Leeds City Marketplace
4. Grand Mariner on the beach at Glover Key in Belize
5. Gorgona former Penal colony bathing facilities
6. Loon at Erringtons Lodge Chapleau Canada
7. Vintage De Havilland Beaver Bush Plane at Erringtons Lodge, Chapleau, Canada
8. Cigar Lady in Cuba
9. Kelly O'Hare Kayaking around wreck in Belize
10. Racing in Australia
11. Racing with Stirling Moss

The lost Franklin expedition passed through here

Bathurst Caribou – Resident Caribou herd in the Bathurst area

Grand Mariner on the beach at Glover's Reef *Luther's innovative bow ramp*

Canadian developed orphanage saving hundreds of children's lives

The Beaver, famous of all Canadian Bush Planes

Superb wilderness lodge run by Al and Doris Errington

Goodwood Ecurie Ecosse – Famous Scottish race team transporter

Pre war Maserati at Goodwood

Captain Ulrich's Heinkel bomber

Close encounter on the shore of Hudson Bay

In action with the Holden Race Special in Australia

In action with my Lotus Seven at Mosport

Hélène enjoying one of her superb culinary creations along the Rideau Canal

Albin 27 moored on the Rideau Canal (before we remodelled the roof)

Gorgona Jail looks more like a Nazi concentration camp

Gorgona is a forbidding massive mountainous jungle